EAGLE
HARDWARE
CHINESE HAND
LAUNDRY
PARTY STORE
BEER · WINE
Coca-Cola
Coca-Cola
I &

The Great Rebellion

U.S.ARMY
41212214

The Great Rebellion

Kenneth Stahl

Detroit, Mich 2009

Acknowledgments

Special thanks to my friends at the Detroit Public Library - Mark Bowden, Dave Poremba, Barbara Louie, Ashley Koebel and Romie Minor for putting up with me every Saturday. They were unwavering in their support. Also of great help were Karen Jania and the staff from the Bentley Library in Ann Arbor. Thanks for sticking it out gang. You may rest now; your work is done.

Of course I would be remiss if I didn't mention the most important source of assistance over the years, my parents, who were always there for me through thick and thin.

Let me also offer a hearty thanks and good luck to the kindhearted few who graciously volunteered their advice:

Bill Ferrill
Betty DeRamus
Bob Carroll
Eleanor Josaitis
Tom Armstead
Henry Dudzinski
Russell Stahl
Joey Nimsick
Jennifer James
Prof. Mike Whitty
Prof. Igor Beginin

ISBN number: 978-0-9799157-0-3 0-9799157-0-8

To Our 43...
May they be Teachers

Let there be no strife

Between me and thee

For we be brethren

Genesis 13:8

Prologue

Having previously written papers on the city of Detroit and having lived there, I was always greatly intrigued by the abandoned skyscrapers lining the major thoroughfares. Though battered and beaten over the decades, skillful inspection of these tarnished and venerable edifices still reveals the elegance and splendor of a bygone day. They stand there taciturn; in stubborn defiance to their predicament, having borne witness to Detroit's rapid ascension to world fame and its cataclysmic descent into near insolvency. They know all too well the circumstances and ideologies that have come and gone which brought them to their tragic fate.

Exactly how did this state of decay come about? In suburbanite circles the answer is fast and unequivocal, former Mayor Coleman Young! Since the focus of this book is the 1967 Detroit Riot, which occurred seven years before Young took office, the argument could hardly be made that he inherited a pristine and tranquil city. While Detroit did take a giant step backwards under Young, as did most of America's big cities in the 1970s, he was not the sole, encompassing reason for Detroit's decline and therefore the answers must lie elsewhere.

In the decades following the Civil War, as the South slowly regressed back into a legalized form of slavery, Northerners strongly voiced their objection of how the South seemed utterly incapable of giving the black man his due. When the automotive boom hit the North, blacks left the South by the millions seeking the freedom and prosperity the North offered.

Now the shoe was on the other foot. Northerners now had their chance to show the world how righteous they were now that blacks were their neighbors. But blacks and whites were not ready to live together yet. Not in 1915, not in 1943 and not in 1967. But as the French philosopher Camus once rationalized, "We are all condemned to live together." Only by learning from our mistakes of the past can we possibly hope to build a lasting future.

The Civil Rights Movement created great expectations but its hard-fought gains were too slow in coming and the economic gains were not proportional to the social advancements. As decades of lingering ghetto frustrations mounted, peaceful civil rights demonstrations were replaced by urban riots. As the flame of rebellion spread across the country, the civil unrest could be charted by the path of burned-out cities that dotted the map. One would have reasonably expected the trouble to have come from the Jim Crow South, yet the vast majority of riots were not only in the North but oftentimes in cities where black opportunity was the greatest, like Detroit.

The Great Rebellion was Detroit's defining moment. The Vietnam War, together with the Civil Rights Movement and the urban riots, represented three monstrous rogue social waves which would all meet up in the mid 1960s to form the perfect wave of tumult - a tsunami that covered the country, leaving it submerged in racial and generational hatred.

"Rioting is the voice of the unheard," said Martin Luther King. The ghetto riots that occurred during the 1960s were a unique strain of madness, a blind man's bluff of aimless rage with no discernable goal in mind. Detroit's Great Rebellion exacted a fearful toll on the city and its people. To compensate, the subject was buried for decades as if it were placed in a time capsule for future generations to inspect. That time has arrived.

If viewed in its entirety, the causes of the Great Rebellion would look something like a great layer cake with each layer representing a different time period in Detroit and racism being the all-encompassing frosting. America paid a terrible price for its centuries of racial intolerance. It took a contagion of riots across the country to get that point across. As the specter of the Great Rebellion fades into the shadows of memory, one question continues to haunt us: What have we learned?

Every master of slaves is born a petty tyrant. They bring the judgment of heaven on a country. As nations cannot be rewarded or punished in the next world, they must be in this. By an inevitable chain of causes and effects, providence punishes national sins by national calamities.

- George Mason, 1787

Along
Comes
A
Man

As Antionne de La Mothe Cadillac stepped ashore on that fateful July day in 1701, he threw his arms skyward and claimed this land with all its lakes, rivers, ponds and puddles for His Majesty King Louis XIV. He named it after the narrowness of the river which connected the massive lakes at either end using the French word *Detroit* or "The Straights." Little could Cadillac have imagined that 266 years later the city he founded under the auspices of peace would be embroiled in the worst riot in the nation's history.

The region possessed all the necessary elements to become a thriving industrial power. The world's largest supply of iron ore was at the ready, as was a plentiful supply of coal and limestone and the greatest freshwater highway in the world was there to transport it - the Great Lakes.

The lumbermen had arrived by the time of the Civil War. After having scalped the New England states of its timber, they now set their sights on the virgin forests of Michigan and its specimen white pines. Many a fortune was made beheading this primeval forest. As was the custom of the day, the wealthy lumber barons displayed their wealth by erecting the most majestic dwellings imaginable. The surviving examples are few in number, scattered about the state like seeds in a storm. Nevertheless they are a memorable reminder of those sawdust millionaires who would later help finance the fledgling auto industry.

Motorized Mayhem

The year 1896 proved to be the linchpin of Michigan's modern history. Michigan led the country in lumber production for decades following the Civil War, but by the turn of the century her forests too were gone. As the lumberjacks prepared to move westward again, in a last fleeting act they passed the baton of destiny to the auto barons and there to receive it on their behest was a resolute young Irishman named Henry Ford.

Henry's famous first ride down Detroit's Bagley Avenue in June of 1896, albeit a noisy one, seemed to go relatively unnoticed by his neighbors who were perusing the street. They were quite used to the crazy Irishmen tinkering with his noisy contraptions. This one actually moved without a horse. Unbeknown to them they were witnessing a unique evolution, not only for the country but for society. Ford would put the world on wheels and in that one raucous puff of smoke, life as they knew it had changed forever.

Detroit was a city custom made to support the peculiarities of automobile production. The city was already heavily laced with shops and mills for building horse carriages, gasoline engines were being produced for yachts, and the iron stove industry had for years registered a heavy presence. To now ask a talented pool of machinists to fabricate a transmission or a tiller required only the design.

One of the old "Fore/Aft" Lakers passes the breakwall outside Cleveland. Specially built, these freshwater ships are indigenous only to the Great Lakes. Having plied these waters for over a century, they are a familiar sight to boater and landlubber alike. They played an integral role in supplying area blast furnaces with the minerals required to make the steel to make the cars. They are designed to flex specifically for the mountainous seas found on the Great Lakes which differ in crest-to-crest

The Faces of Detroit

Louis Chevrolet

Ransom Olds

Henry Ford

David Buick

Dodge Brothers

Although the individuals are gone their names and legends linger on through time. These men were the foundation of the automotive industry, and thus Detroit, but it was Henry Ford they were all chasing. Ford's incredible ingenuity and business acumen enabled him to dominate the industry and for decades he and he alone was the emperor of the automotive world. These are the faces that built Detroit and gave it the time-honored moniker "The Motor City."

Another of the odd cast of characters to have their name immortalized on car hoods and trunk lids was the Scotsman David Dunbar Buick. Fate would always play a cruel game with David Buick and in the end it seemed as if he had been born under a dark star. Originally a plumber by trade, Buick invented the process that bonded enamel to cast iron, leading the way for the creation of white bathtubs to our civilized life. Buick possessed brilliant technical ingenuity but always struggled financially to keep his companies afloat.

Like Ford, Buick was a bit of a "mad professor" who was in his element while tinkering away in his shop. When the automotive craze hit around 1900, he caught the bug and began experimenting with gasoline engines. Selling his plumbing company to raise capital, he organized the Buick Manufacturing Company. In tandem with his partners, they invented the famous "valve in head" engine or what is better known today as the "overhead valve" engine. Early Buicks were so dependable they were often referred to as a "doctor's car".

Buick spent all his capital in the process of developing his car and fervently began a search for investors. A banker from Flint approached him with significant capital on the contingency that Buick's car could successfully make the trip from Detroit to Flint, thus proving its mettle. Buick accepted the challenge. The first attempt met with failure as the prototype gave up the ghost near Pontiac and suffered the ultimate humiliation of having to be pulled back to Detroit by a team of horses. On the second attempt, the prototype managed to rattle and wheeze its way to Flint and won the confidence of its backers.

If only David Buick could have matched his business acumen with his technical adroitness and determination he would have become fabulously wealthy. Unable to maintain capital, he was an early casualty of the volatile automotive industry. Taken over by GM founder Billy Durant, the Buick motor car became the cornerstone of the company and had the uncanny knack of always adapting to the times, something its namesake could not.

Perhaps a fitting if undesirable epitaph for Buick, it was once said of him, "David Dunbar Buick made a hundred men millionaires but himself died in poverty." The doors of success were never open wide enough to let Scotland's forgotten son through. He slowly faded away into obscurity, dying virtually penniless in Detroit's Harper Hospital in 1929.

David Buick

Louis Chevrolet

If ever there was a character that had racing seared into his soul and high octane coursing through his veins, it was Louis Chevrolet. Like his peers, he had phenomenal mechanical ability but was always more enamored with racing automobiles than manufacturing them.

The Swiss-born Chevrolet seemed destined to share a fate similar to his peer David Buick in that despite his enormous talents and considerable successes, it seemed as if a dark cloud of misfortune hung relentlessly over his head.

The brothers Chevrolet (Louis, Arthur and Gaston) were all world class racers who cheated death many times over with their hell-bent-for-leather racing demeanor. At one point Louis held the world land speed record of 111 mph set in 1905 and succeeded in breaking his own record the following year at 119 mph.

Louis drove in several Indianapolis 500s. Younger brother Gaston won the race in 1920 driving a car Louis built. Louis' Indy exploits would be the high-water mark of his career. The tide began to turn when Louis teamed up with GM's Billy Durant. It was to be a stormy relationship between two very headstrong men.

Using Chevrolet's famous name, Durant contracted Louis to design a car to compete with the Model T. Philosophically the two were totally out of phase. Louis built a large and expensive six cylinder. Durant had the car scaled down drastically, much to the chagrin of Louis, and the two parted company forever.

Fittingly enough, the brothers Chevrolet are all buried in Indianapolis. At the Indianapolis Hall of Fame Museum is a bronze bust of Louis followed by his lifelong creed, "Never give up."

Although Ransom Olds often found himself playing second fiddle to his rival Henry Ford, in many respects Olds was ahead of him.

Like the other pioneers, Ransom made his own footprints. Almost ten years before Henry's famous ride down Bagley in a gasoline-powered automobile, Olds had engineered a three-wheeled steam car. For decades, steam engines for ships and trains had proven not only dependable but remarkably powerful. There were drawbacks for automotive use, however. Boilers had to be lit and often took some time to develop the steam necessary to propel the vehicle, an expenditure of time restive customers were not willing to incur. Also, steam was brutally harsh on equipment which led to frequent and extensive maintenance.

With the sweeping advancements on gasoline engines being engineered by the Germans Daimler and Benz, the point was soon driven home to Olds that steam propulsion was inadequate for automotive use. While the steam powered automobiles like Stanley and White would remain on the scene for some time, their fate was inevitable.

Like Henry Ford, Olds was born amidst the tumult of the Civil War in 1864. Perhaps it was the equally tragic Reconstruction Period that followed which galvanized his generation to heartache, making them impervious to failure.

Olds dabbled with electric cars for a while but batteries of the day proved too unreliable. By 1900, Olds had completed the gas-powered car for which he would be remembered, the famous Curved Dash Olds.

Olds's stay in Detroit would be brief however. A scant two years into production, a fire tragically destroyed the massive complex off Jefferson Avenue. Olds was quickly enticed by Lansing officials to return to the city in which he grew up. For a variety of reasons Olds accepted the offer and the Olds Motor Works quickly entrenched itself in the state capital.

John Francis Dodge

Horace Elgin Dodge

John Dodge

Horace Dodge

Despite the tremendous accomplishments the two brothers packed into their all-too-short lives, perhaps what will always be remembered most about them is that they were brothers, in every sense of the word, as close as two brothers could be. Although not twins, John being the older by four years, they were as inseparable as twins generally are. This was symbolized in their company emblem of interlocking triangles.

Perhaps it was their impoverished upbringing that bonded them together. Too poor to own shoes, they walked to school in the winter snow with makeshift rags wrapped around their feet. Maybe it was the humiliating sting that poverty imbues which fueled their unquenchable thirst for success.

John was the hard-nosed, tough-talking business part of the duo. He was also a notorious drinker who, with brother Horace in tow, left many a Detroit bar in shambles only to return the next day to make amends with the owner. Horace was the engineering genius who could have a set of designs placed in front of him and at a mere glance suggest valuable improvements.

Dodge vehicles were some of the first to incorporate an all-steel body, making them extremely rugged and endowing them with the title of "Ram Tough". Sales were brisk and success liberal as the Dodge brothers took the automotive world by storm.

But the tide of good fortune would ebb for the Dodge boys just as quickly as it had peaked. They found themselves at the New York Auto Show in January of 1920 just as the Spanish influenza epidemic was ragging across the east coast. Both wound up contracting the disease. At first it appeared Horace would succumb while John looked on in utter horror. But just as Horace made a recovery John took a dramatic turn for the worse and died on January 14th. A grief-stricken Horace managed to hang on for another eleven months before succumbing to either disease or, as many suspected, grief.

As a youngster, Henry Ford was fanatical about mechanical processes. There was a standing rule among his family: don't leave any mechanical devices lying around or Henry will take it apart and analyze it. One day while accompanying his father on the buckboard to Detroit, they came across a steam-powered thresher lumbering down the road toward them. This was the first self-propelled device Henry had ever seen. He was mesmerized by the giant beast, a cacophony of steam and noise pulsating from its apertures like a great, mechanical dragon. "I remember that engine as though I had seen it only yesterday," Ford recalled decades later, "I was off the wagon and talking to the engineer before my father knew what I was up to." It was a defining moment for young Henry. His perpetual thirst for knowledge would guide him toward the world of mechanization and a place in history.

Young Henry would soon put the world on wheels and coax the old agrarian society onto the new high ground of automobiles. But the early going was tough. The demand on workers was overwhelming. Resembling mindless automatons, workers were driven relentlessly by the foremen and subsequently spent most of their lives in a near state of exhaustion. As a result the turnover rate was upwards of 60 percent a month. Workers would quit simply to get a dime more an hour somewhere else. New employees had to be trained and many mistakes ensued. Henry's announcement of a five dollar day shook the world. Instead of running away from Ford, mobs of workers now stampeded toward him.

Henry Ford and George Washington Carver were two pioneers cut from the same cloth. Tireless in their pursuits, they saw past color and had mutual respect for one another. Henry was the first to employ thousands of blacks when everyone else was reluctant to hire even one. His $5 day would also be the catalyst for the largest demographic change in American history.

Ford taught successive generations the time-honored American principles of perseverance and sacrifice. The road to success meant outworking the other fellow and paying your dues. Henry reveled in sending shock waves through the corporate world. Endowed with only a fourth grade education, Henry felt ill at ease around the Ivy League blue bloods of industry and no doubt took great satisfaction in showing them up, a feat which he accomplished with regularity.

As an innovator Henry stood alone amidst the world's best. Ford's perfection of the assembly line would revolutionize the industry. His five dollar day, double the industry rate, was scoffed at by the titans of industry who viewed him as unwittingly reckless. On the contrary, Henry Ford knew people. Unlike the entrenched aristocracy whose riches blinded them to the true pulse of America, Ford came up from the bottom and thus was afforded the unique opportunity of witnessing all the layers of society along the way. By 1915 Henry was the most famous man in the world. Henry Ford, more than any other man, shaped the face of Detroit for generations to come.

Eatless Days in Black Bottom

Reconstruction & the Jim Crow South

Lincoln
The Great Emancipator

President Lincoln's Emancipation Proclamation of 1863 officially freed all slaves but was only a token to those trapped in the Deep South. The North's victory two years later gave the illusion of permanent freedom. Union troops occupied the South to implement and enforce the post-war policy called Reconstruction. With the assassination of Lincoln, however, went any hope of a true and just future for Southern blacks. He had been the guiding light and enforcer of Reconstruction. Without him Reconstruction was like a rudderless sailing ship which went wherever the current took it. Had The Great Emancipator lived, it is highly likely the indignities free blacks endured in the century after the Civil War would have been sharply curtailed. After his death, social conditions relapsed right back to the abominable prewar standards.

Lincoln's successor was Andrew Johnson, a former Tennessee senator with blatant Southern sympathies. The Southern states, one by one, met the necessary, yet superficial, conditions to be readmitted to the Union. Congressional legislation was enacted to help empower former slaves toward equality, including voting rights. But Johnson's version was a glaring departure from Lincoln's. As the Southern states drew up their new constitutions, they themselves would decide the role of the newly freed slaves. This was somewhat analogous to putting the fox in charge of the hen house, with similar results.

With much of the South in ruin and communities still mourning their considerable losses, there was little if any concern for the rights of blacks. Congressional Republicans, honoring pledges made by Lincoln, fought hard to give Southern blacks the new rights included in the 14th and 15th Amendments. But the recalcitrant Johnson, heavily influenced by Southern Democrats, fought the Republicans at every turn. The 15th Amendment, which prevented both state and federal governments from prohibiting blacks from voting, left too many loopholes for cagy Southern leaders. Blacks attempting to register were told they had to pass literacy tests, pay a poll tax or satisfy an educational requirement. Few who had the moxie to attempt registering could meet these challenges. Whites, on the other hand, were immune to these voting requirements.

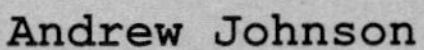

Andrew Johnson

U. S. Grant

Rutherford Hayes

The Reconstruction presidents, Johnson, Grant and Hayes, would play an intricate role in the postwar world of newly freed blacks. Johnson had only one thing in common with Lincoln. He did not believe in succession. Outside of that he had the plantation boss mentality and blatantly betrayed the wishes of his predecessor. He was rewarded for his actions with near impeachment and subsequently was voted out of office, but the damage had been done.

Johnson's successor, the war hero Ulysses S. Grant, inherited a plethora of problems. Johnson had systematically replaced conscientious Union generals leading the Reconstruction effort with generals openly hostile to black sympathies. The result was a slow, agonizing degeneration right back to antebellum ideologies and plantation dictums.

As blacks began to gain a toehold in local politics, the white backlash took form as a group of Confederate veterans, seeking to foment their anger, formed the Ku Klux Klan in 1866. The Klan was often made up of top community leaders including sheriffs, judges and politicians, making it nearly impossible for blacks to get a fair shake.

The Klan quickly struck fear into the black community. Blacks attempting to shape their own destiny often met with a violent death, which commonly included lynching. Newly elected black politicians were routinely murdered by the Klan while law enforcement looked the other way. Naturally, blacks who strongly desired to vote quickly lost their enthusiasm.

Grant led a crackdown on the KKK, in some cases going so far as to declare martial law. After ten long years of Reconstruction, however, the country began to turn a deaf ear on the calamities in the South. Many of the Radical Republicans who had steadfastly supported black rights had retired or been voted out of office. Grant's successor, Rutherford B. Hayes, in one of the most controversial elections to date, all but sold out black rights in a deal that would nudge him into the White House. It seemed as if history was bent on repeating itself.

Jim Crow

The term Jim Crow originally referred to a character from an old minstrel show dating back to pre Civil War days. It was a white man dressed in blackface performing a mocking rendition about black life. It proved immensely popular with whites.

In post Civil War days Jim Crow came to refer to local laws and customs designed to enforce segregation and prevent blacks from gaining any political, social or economic power. While the North made some inroads towards desegregation, the Jim Crow mentality persevered throughout the country. Its hotbed of course, was the South. This concept was further buttressed by the 1896 Supreme Court decision of *Plessy v Ferguson* which declared that separate but equal facilities were constitutional. Referred to as Jim Crow laws, they were enforced until President Lyndon Johnson ended the indignity by signing the Civil Rights Acts of 1964 and 1965.

With the final withdrawal of Union troops in 1877, Reconstruction had come to an abrupt end, as did the hopes and aspirations of free Southern blacks. The Democratic Party, in those days referred to as the party of white supremacy, slowly returned to power throughout the South. The ghostly apparition of the Old Confederacy had re-appeared and with it the continuation of the black agony.

The Old South had changed little since the Civil War. Reconstruction, despite some noble efforts to rectify inequities, proved to be a myth. Even well into the 1960s blacks were terrified of white reprisal if they tried to register to vote. But it was more the everyday affronts of being treated like a second class citizen that inflicted the most egregious of injuries.

By the early 1900s, Jim Crow had grown to monstrous proportions. The dehumanizing "Colored Only" and "Whites Only" signs began to appear on the scene. With each passing generation the indignities built up until a cement-like hatred permeated society. Because Reconstruction was such an abysmal failure, we would have to do it all over again in the 1950s and '60s.

Library of Congress

Dark Days in Dixie

Cotton Fields

Prison

Blacks who migrated north during the 1900s wished to leave the misery they experienced in the South behind for good. It was this same misery that brought about the formation of the blues which became the subject of many of their songs. The blues were a combination of dreams unfulfilled, biblical belief, spiritual ebullition and present/past agonies and aspirations.

(Above, left) This young man sang about the endless toil of working in the cotton fields for "the man" and the newfound hopes of the post Civil War days.

(Above, right) Blacks were sometimes imprisoned on trumped-up charges if for no other reason than because their labor was needed. Here a prisoner of the notorious Angola State Prison sings about suffering and hard luck, both of which he was well acquainted. Black prisoners were given the worst details such as draining swamps honeycombed with snakes and gators, or digging in coal mines under perilous conditions. Whether it be prisoners on the chain gang or sharecroppers in the cotton field, the blues helped express pent-up feelings and vent a multitude of hostile frustrations to help discouraged blacks make it through yet another day.

As the postwar dreams of prosperity withered away for Southern blacks, one former slave lamented, "We have very dark days here. The rebels boast that the Negroes shall not have as much liberty now as they had under slavery. If things go on thus, our doom is sealed. God knows it is worse than slavery."

After General Sherman's March to the Sea was concluded, he solicited the advice of former slaves on how best to facilitate them in the postwar South. A black preacher advised him to give each free slave "40 acres and a mule." Acting upon this, Sherman began granting ex-slaves abandoned plantation lands. President Andrew Johnson later nullified this and ordered the lands returned to their former owners. Johnson's version of Reconstruction was much different than Lincoln's. He saw it strictly as a reunification of North and South, not helping ex-slaves get started on a new life.

As time went on it became more and more apparent that there was little opportunity to be found in the South for blacks and that their newfound freedom was mostly illusionary. Older blacks tended to take it in stride; the agricultural life was all they knew. Young blacks, however, yearned for something better and believed the seeds of opportunity would germinate for them in the North.

The mechanical cotton picker, which made its debut in 1937, would quickly put many a sharecropper out of work. Prior to WWI, 90 percent of blacks lived in the South, in very rural, isolated surroundings where they worked as sharecroppers or field hands. They had little contact with whites. The massive southern black immigrations northward during WWI and WWII now put large masses of blacks in an unfamiliar urban surrounding in close proximity to the white population. The transition did not go smoothly and the fallout put both blacks and whites on edge indefinitely.

Reasons for migrating north

Known lynchings of Blacks
1890-1951

1890-99	1,111
1900-09	791
1910-19	568
1920-29	281
1930-39	119
1940-49	31
1950-51	2

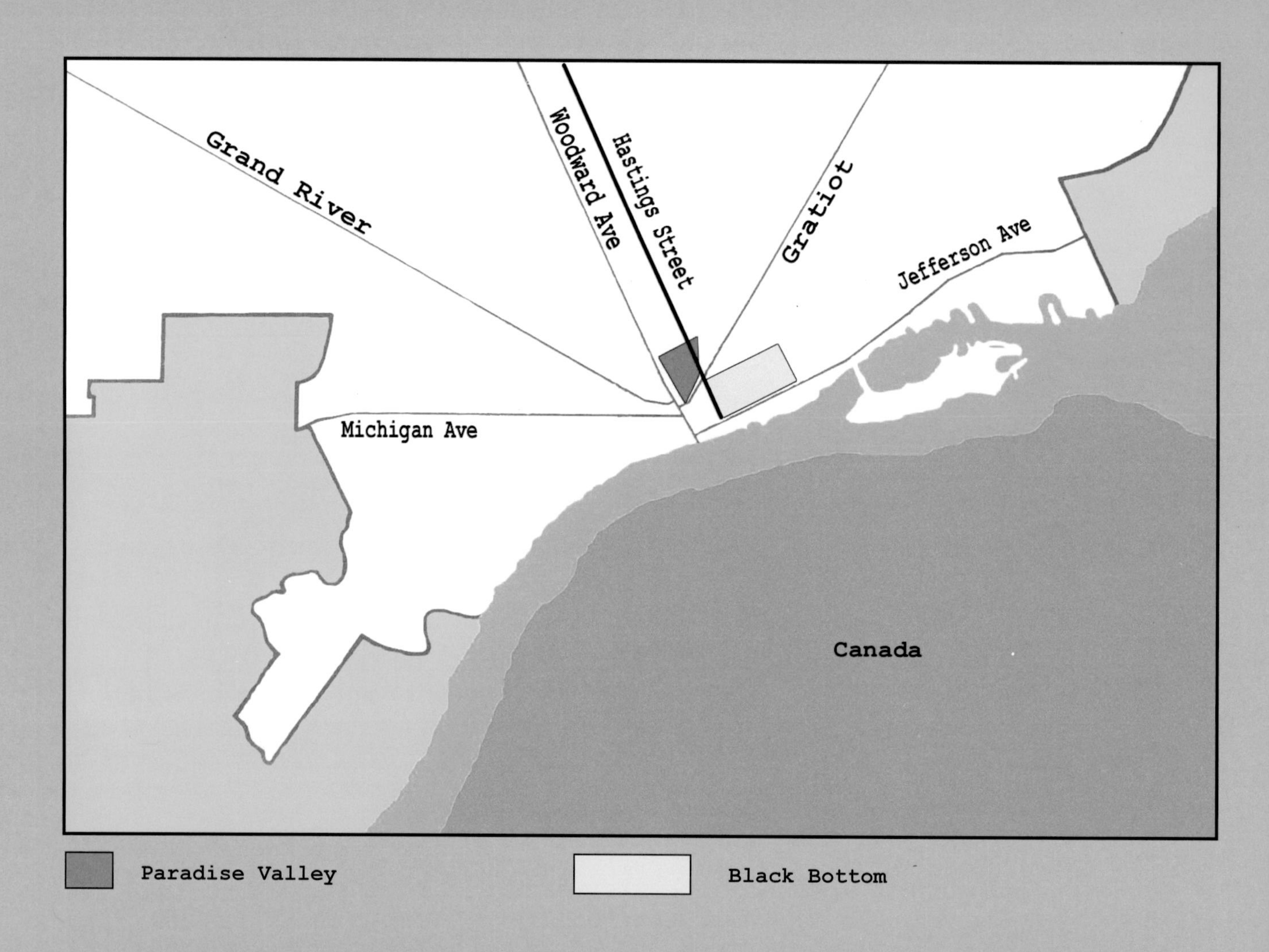

♬ ***"I'm goin to get me a job, up there in Mr. Ford's place,***

Stop these eatless days from starin me in the face."

The automotive boom that hit northern cities in the early 1900s would change the face of America. Southern blacks had thrown caution to the wind and uprooted by the millions for a chance at the high paying industrial jobs and freedom. Detroit's east side neighborhood of Black Bottom was a port of entry for Southern blacks. The term "Black Bottom" was not a racial connotation. Rather it emanates from the days of Cadillac when the black top soil made excellent farming.

Originally Black Bottom was composed of Jewish and European immigrants who flooded across the big pond to stoke America's furnaces. World War I slowed European immigration to a trickle, so industrialists sent labor recruiters south to tap the large and quite eager pool of black labor. They didn't have a very tough sell.

By 1915 social conditions in the South for blacks were as degrading as ever. Their right to vote had been blocked. The law that was supposed to protect them instead was used to keep them in their place and the educational/work opportunities that began to materialize for a fleeting moment after the Civil War disappeared.

Rumors began to circulate in the cotton fields about a city up north called Detroit, "the wonder city of the magic motor," which offered jobs at an unbelievable five dollars a day. That was more money than some made in a month doing the most grueling of field labor from sunup till sundown. Their ship of dreams had run hard aground on the shoals of prejudice. It was time to abandon ship. This they did, en masse.

The severe erosion of manpower was so great in the South that numerous road construction projects had to be abandoned and entire crops were left to rot in the field because the black labor that was counted on to harvest it had left. In a flash white southerners realized their predicament: "There has been lots of darkies left here, and nearly all the good ones is gone."

The black population in Detroit skyrocketed during the automobile boom of the 1910s by 611 percent. During the peak years of 1924-25, forty thousand entered the city, eager to reclaim their dreams. If forty acres and a mule was a lost cause then perhaps forty dollars and a house of their own would suffice. The great migrant melting pot flowed in from Alabama, Tennessee, Georgia, Mississippi and parts unknown. They brought with them a unique Southern culture and would finally be allowed to do what they had been unable to do before - build a community. This they would do in Black Bottom.

The First Great Black Migration 1910-1930

	Black Population		
City	1910	1920	1930
New York City	91,709	152,467	327,706
Chicago	44,103	109,458	233,903
Philadelphia	84,459	134,229	219,599
Detroit	5,741	40,838	120,066
Cleveland	8,448	34,451	71,899

Southern blacks entering Detroit found a city totally unprepared to accommodate them. The most immediate problem, one that would haunt the city indefinitely, was housing. The housing shortage was acute before the Great Migration and would get worse for decades thereafter. Blacks were caught in the crosshairs of redlining, a practice of bankers and real estate agencies who would draw a red line around areas on the local map where they refused to allow blacks in. This left Black Bottom, an enclave of dilapidated wooden houses that should have been torn down before they fell down. Unable to buy, blacks were forced to rent from slum lords. Because the rent was two or three times higher than normal they were forced to take on borders to make ends meet, creating terrible overcrowding.

Detroit Public Library

Hastings Street, the fabled main artery which ran through Black Bottom, was Jewish at the turn of the century. Merchants plying their trade on push carts soon gave way to black, Southern bluesmen, like the venerable John Lee Hooker, who brought their unique brand of blues music with them and cut their teeth playing in the numerous Hastings Street clubs.

There were some niceties associated with working in the auto factories. There was little wage discrimination between blacks and whites. The difference came in job stature and promotion. Blacks were given the most dangerous and health hazardous jobs such as iron pouring, furnace tending or spraying paint. While it is true whites often did the same work, they were frequently promoted despite having considerably less time in. This mentality was confirmed by a plant manager, "Negroes can't work on the presses. We brought the Negro to this plant to do the dirty, hard unskilled work. If we let him rise, all of them will want better jobs." To his credit the manager admitted this was unfair, "But we can't try any experiments here. We are competing with other automobile firms and we've got to keep our men satisfied to keep up the competitive pace. Personally I'd like to help them, but what can I do?"

Detroit Public Library

Blacks earned more money than they had ever dreamed of in Detroit's auto industry, but was it worth the price? Young men grew old long before their time because of the physical toll and hazards they encountered at work.

Joe Louis - Pride of Black Bottom

The most legendary athlete to come from Black Bottom, one that epitomized the community by never giving up, was heavyweight boxing champ Joe Louis. Louis, who was born in Alabama, enjoyed recounting his long journey which centered on Detroit. "I was twelve years old when Pat Brooks (stepbrother) heard about the money Ford was paying. He went up first and then brought us up to Detroit. We moved in with some of our kin on MacComb Street. It was kind of crowded there, but the house had toilets indoors and electric light. Down in Alabama we had outhouses and kerosene lamps."

Joe readily admits he was not a natural fighter as a youth. "Around November 1932 or early 1933 I got my first amateur bout. It was a stag in the Edison Athletic Club. I weighed around 168 then, and they stacked me against Johnny Miller, a white boy. He was a fighter for years and I was new at it. He held a couple of amateur titles and he had fought in the Olympics out in Los Angeles. He was clever with his fists and with his footwork. I never got a solid punch against him. He knocked me down seven times in two rounds. He mussed me up pretty bad. Going home that night I was sore all over and low. I got a merchandise check for $7 out of the fight. I gave it to my mother. She stuck up for me. She told me, 'Joe, if you want to keep on with boxing, you keep on with it. If that's what you want to work at, I'll work for you to get it.'"

Joe remembered that growing up life was tough in Black Bottom even when the economy was jumping. When the Great Depression came it was hard times in Black Bottom because blacks were often the last hired and the first fired, "My stepfather was let out at Ford's because the depression had come. My mother had gone down to the relief place and waited in line to get us a few bucks a week. We kept track of what we got and I paid it all back--$270."

People would ask me, "Joe, when you were a kid in Alabama, living sharecrop in a cotton patch, did you dream to be a millionaire and have rich things like cars, and pockets stuffed with money and fine clothes and all that? I say to them, "I couldn't dream that big."

Joe Louis
Heavyweight Champ
1937-1948

Black Bottom was a tight-knit community. When a family fell on hard times, people didn't sit idly by as their neighbors' furniture was placed on the curb. They had rent parties and block parties where everyone brought food to sell to keep their neighbors from being evicted. There was no such thing as class distinction in Black Bottom. Doctors lived next to janitors, lawyers lived next to mechanics. It was this same esprit de corps that helped Black Bottom survive during the all too frequent bad times.

During good times or bad, there was always one escape, the entertainment district of Paradise Valley and its legendary thoroughfare of Hasting Street. Hastings Street was the Detroit version of Bourbon Street only with a Motown twist. Migrant Southern bluesmen brought a unique style of blues which had never been heard at these latitudes. Chief among them was a twenty-three year old Mississippian named John Lee Hooker. Hooker arrived in Detroit in 1943 and quickly made a name for himself. His eerie Mississippi moans and throaty wails simply couldn't be duplicated. Hooker was at the head of a long procession of bluesmen that made Hastings Street synonymous with blues music. "The street was known more than any other in the U.S.," recalled Hooker. "Anywhere you'd go, you could hear people talking about Hastings Street." Like Harlem, whites also flocked to Hastings Street for the unequaled sounds and high times. Even celebrities like Jackie Gleason made it a point to stop by when he was in town. Hastings Street lit up like a Christmas tree at night, adorned with soulful music and exciting women.

But Hastings Street had a dark side to it. Blind pigs, the legacy of Prohibition, were too numerous to count and with them came the poisonous swills that were brewed in sinks and bathtubs and served to unsuspecting patrons. Prostitutes advertised under the corner street lights and muggers laid in wait amongst the alley shadows.

Detroit Public Library

Victim of Urban Renewal - An old bluesman who played throughout Paradise Valley, brought his daughter for one last fleeting glimpse, telling her, "This is where Hastings Street used to be."

When urban renewal began in 1951, some 140,000 blacks lived in Black Bottom. As the masses began fleeing the wrecking ball, many made their way over to 12th Street on Detroit's west side. Hastings Street was the last to go. As the bulldozers worked their way west, Hastings Street slowly became an urban ghost town of abandoned bars and derelict buildings. Alas, in 1959, the menacing bulldozers stood at the foot of Hastings. History could wait no longer. It was the end of an era.

High Tide on Hastings Street

The federal bulldozer of urban renewal would eventually destroy Black Bottom, Paradise Valley & the legendary Hastings Street, taking with it the unique rite of passage southern blacks experienced in their new northern existence.

like it is now. After the riots, it wasn't the same.
But back then, Detroit, Michigan was the place!
I think about those times a lot.

John Lee Hooker
1917-2001

Farewell
to
John Lee Hooker,
Black
Bottom
&
Paradise
Valley.

Their
memories live
on
in the blues
which,
like John Lee
himself,
are
timeless.

1943:
A Race Riot There Will Be

Pieces of a Puzzle

The summer of 1943 found the United States embroiled in the worst war in world history and industrial might of Detroit was playing an integral part in winning it. Common during times of war, domestic hatreds and tensions grip entire communities, bringing out the best and worst even amongst allies. At a time when Americans were pulling together to defeat its enemies, societal problems of long standing chose a bad time to rear its ugly head in Detroit. In June of 1943 Detroit suffered one of the worst race riots in the country's history, forcing America to take a long, hard introspective look at itself. Analysts concluded there was no one specific cause to the disorder but rather a multitude of causes that had been a long time in the making. It was, if viewed on the whole, just pieces of a puzzle.

With the country at war, the industrial output necessary to win quickly fell upon the large urban areas of the North, cities like Chicago, Cleveland, New York and in particular Detroit. Again, as in 1915, there were more good paying jobs available in Detroit than could be filled.

But blacks were not the only entity envious of a high paying blue-collar job. A veritable tidal wave of white Southerners also flooded into Detroit. Over 500,000 migrants arrived between June of 1940 and June of 1943 alone. Approximately 50,000 were black. The rest were a hodgepodge of poor white Appalachians, unsuccessful farmers, Baptists, Methodists and others. It was Detroit's version of *The Grapes of Wrath.*

Detroit had run the economic gamut over the decades. From a buzzing metropolis of the WWI era flaunting its automotive prominence, to an anemic invalid of the Great Depression in the 1930s, and then back again to a bee hive of activity which WWII dictated.

With well-paying jobs in excess, the Motor City offered unheard of opportunities. This point resonated throughout the South where poor sharecropping blacks were becoming expendable due to modern advances in farm machinery and the ravages of the boil weevil. As for the oppression they incurred from whites, little had changed since the Civil War. Reconstruction was an unmitigated failure. While the physical act of slavery was outlawed the mentality of slavery could not be. For most the risk of moving north was academic, there was nothing left to lose.

When the initial wave of black pilgrims sent word back home that they were making as much as $60-$70 a week, the flood gates were open, leading to the second Great Black Migration from the South to the North. The backbreaking toil under miserable conditions for pennies a day seemed over. To the poor, southern black, the Motor City was an icon for prosperity. Detroit would be the agent of change that would allow their dreams to materialize, a change the South wholly deficient in.

By 1943 Detroit was bristling with black migrants, much to the consternation of the Southern white who also migrated. The rigid racial codes whites had grown up with in the South that kept blacks "in their place" were not as customary in Detroit and the Southern whites often found themselves on a roughly equal social standing with their old foe.

Northern whites also grew indignant about their new neighbors. They did not want to live near blacks nor did they want the labor competition which would certainly appear after WWII ended and the multitude of military production jobs began to dry up.

Even before the arrival of the southern migrants, Detroit was a checkerboard of ethnicities which included Germans, Irish, Italians, Maltese and various Slavs (a very large Polish contingent), all of whom gravitated toward their own sections of the city. Few people really considered themselves Detroiters; ethnicity dictated who you were and where you lived. Detroit had not yet learned how to be a city. Add to the influx of Southerners a few demagogic and communist agitators and you have the most heterogeneous cast of characters in the country.

Detroit had indeed become the industrial benchmark of the world but such rapid progress came at a price. Detroit, in the space of twenty years, had completely outgrown itself. People were forced to live in tents, lean-tos and condemned buildings. After closing for the night, some bars rented their pool tables to sleep on. The housing situation was stretched way past capacity, yet even more workers were needed if Detroit was to keep up with the massive industrial wartime demands that had been placed upon it.

Even as Detroit basked in the light of prosperity and national adulation for leading the way in beating fascism, sinister forces were at work which would bring the city down. Detroit was awash with characters that had an axe to grind. This volatile mix would put Detroit on a war footing of its own.

There was a special effrontery exhibited by the large local Polish population toward incoming blacks. Polish youths, no doubt coerced by adults, frequently conducted lawless raids into black neighborhoods during the summer of '41. Blacks in turn resorted to a tactic called "bumping" where they intentionally bumped into whites on the sidewalk, infuriating them.

Detroit had rightfully been dubbed as the "Arsenal of Democracy" for its capacity to make war. The city was cranking out one-third of the country's war material, much more than any other city. It was an incredible burden to shoulder and the stress began to show through.

Detroit's racial situation had become so precarious and so pronounced that in August of 1942, ten months before the notorious riot, *LIFE* magazine wrote a caustic article entitled "Detroit is Dynamite" admonishing the city at length for its poisonous racial atmosphere and predicting the city would riot:

> **Few people doubt Detroit can do this colossal job. It has the machines, the factories, the know-how as no other city in the world has them. If machines could win the war, Detroit would have nothing to worry about. But it takes people to run machines and too many of the people of Detroit are confused, embittered and distracted by factional groups that are fighting each other harder that they are willing to fight Hitler. Detroit can either blow up Hitler or it can blow up the U.S.**

Walter Reuther Library

Belle Isle, Detroit's largest park, was exclusively white in the early 1900s. With the Great Black Migration north in the teens and 20s, blacks came to frequent the island in greater numbers because of its proximity to Black Bottom. As competition for jobs, housing and recreation space increased, so did the animosity between the two groups and thus the potential for violence. The island was a perfect catalyst for the city's explosive climate.

Ku Klux Klan

From the ashes of the Confederate army came this social club that began terrorizing blacks to keep them from exercising their new constitutional rights. Their overwhelming success caught the eye of the federal government which repeatedly attempted to squash them, thus causing a cyclical existence. By the turn of the century the KKK virtually ceased to exist, only to rekindle in the 1920s to the tune of four million members. It was at this time that they added to their list of adversaries Jews, Catholics, foreigners and organized labor. By the time of the Great Depression they faded away again, only to reemerge one last time during the civil rights heyday of the 1960s.

Born out of the decomposition of the KKK, Detroit had become the stronghold for a shadowy fascist group of night riders known as the Black Legion. Originally formed to procure jobs for southern whites during the chaotic years of the Depression, their hit list included but was not limited to Blacks, Jews, Catholics and unions.

Although somewhat comical in appearance, the Black Legion was every bit as vicious as the KKK and even more feared. It was publicly known they had penetrated the ranks of big business and government. As a result few people dared testify against the Legion for fear of their transparent agents.
Their secretive nature was reinforced by a code, "to be torn limb from limb and scattered to the carrion" if they betrayed any secrets. This is the group that brutally murdered Baptist minister Earl Little, the father of Malcolm X, in East Lansing in 1931.

The Black Legion

Sojourner Truth - A Portent of things to come

The second "Great Migration" of Southern blacks which occurred during WWII caught Detroit badly off guard. Suddenly the city that could bury Hitler found it couldn't adequately house its own people.

The federal government, determined to keep Detroit's indispensable industrial juggernaut rolling, came to the realization that additional black housing was badly needed. But where would the new black housing be accepted? The sight eventually chosen was located at Nevada & Fenelon, right next to a white neighborhood.

There was only one black housing project in the city, the Brewster housing project and it was full. Southern whites were also vying for living space. Locals were under the impression the new housing project was intended for whites until it was given the name Sojourner Truth (after a Civil War slave and poet). Their protestations came swiftly. Strategies were initiated and congressmen were incited, successfully reversing Washington's decision.

Detroit Mayor Edward Jeffries was fully aware of not only the acute housing problem in his city but of the highly combustible atmosphere between the races. Siding with the blacks, Jeffries reeled off a scathing series of telegrams to Washington demanding they rescind their decision. Much to the vexation of the white community, Washington flip-flopped again and the housing project again was set for black occupancy. The move in date was to be February 27th.

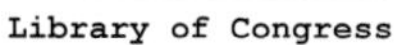

Library of Congress

Walter Reuther Library

Round one went to the whites as over 1,200 well armed protestors showed up on moving day, too much for the Detroit Police Department to control. The first black families who showed up at 9 a.m. thought the crowd too volatile and turned back. Later that day two black tenants ran their car through the picket line, starting off a melee. Detroit police used tear gas and shotguns to disperse the crowd but moving day had to be postponed indefinitely. (Above, left) Locals made their intentions eminently clear. (Above, right) Protestors pose with their "trophy."

**April 28, 1942 - White protestors line up at the entrance to Sojourner Truth as round two prepares to get under way.
Note the protestor with the oversized chunk of wood in his hand and his completely unabashed demeanor as he stands in front of the police car.**

Photos courtesy Walter Reuther Library

This time Mayor Jeffries was better prepared. In tandem with 1,100 Detroit police officers, Jeffries requested and was granted 1,600 National Guardsmen to secure the route and site. Round two went to the black tenants. The inconclusive showdown that was Sojourner Truth simply escalated raw feelings between the races to a near riot status. Everyone seemed to know that somewhere in the future there would be a rematch to settle old scores once and for all. Sojourner Truth was a portent of things to come.

Despite the massive show of force by authorities, the white protestors showed an iron resolve. Again the two sides went at it and had to be forcefully broken up, but the black tenants were finally moved in. With forty people injured and over one hundred arrested, sentiments still ran high. One black tenant exclaimed, "The Army is going to take me to 'fight for democracy,' but I would just as soon fight for democracy right here. Here we are fighting for ourselves."

Walter Reuther Library

(Above - April 1941) Thousands of southern blacks were employed at Ford's River Rouge Complex. In 1941 the UAW waged a strike at the Rouge. Whites walked off the job but blacks stayed behind. Many blacks felt a loyalty to "Uncle Henry." The two groups clashed on numerous occasions in barbaric fashion, ratcheting up the racial tension throughout the area.
(Below) Yet another subtle but telling reason leading to the riot was Detroit's antiquated transportation system, once quantitatively compared to the caliber of a small New England town. Due to severe gas rationing during WWII, many depended on the trolleys to get them to work or recreation. With the arrival of several hundred thousand Southerners into the city in the space of a few years, the trolley system became terribly overburdened. Whites who had stood in shock and revulsion at the mere thought of blacks living near them now found themselves literally elbow to elbow with them on the cramped trolleys. Many fisticuffs resulted.

Bentley Library

Problems at Packard

One step closer to judgment day - Thousands of white employees at Packard walk off the job to protest having to work with blacks.

After the U.S. entry into WWII, the federal government took over all private industries capable of producing war material. This meant for the duration of the war no more cars would be produced. The world famous Packard Motor Car Company was humming 24/7 with the vital production of the giant Rolls-Royce aircraft engines and twelve cylinder Packard marine engines used to power PT boats.

While the UAW hierarchy outwardly supported integration of its work force, its rank and file did not. Whites didn't mind so much that blacks worked in the same plant, but they refused to work side by side with them. Three weeks before the riot, Packard promoted three blacks to work on the assembly line next to whites. The reaction was immediate and swift. A plant-wide hate strike resulted as 25,000 whites walked off the job, bringing critical war production to a screeching halt. A voice with a Southern accent barked over the loudspeaker, "I'd rather see Hitler and Hirohito win than work next to a Nigger."

Although the matter was rectified within a few days by relocating the black workers, the wheels were quickly coming off Mayor Jeffries' wagon. Detroit was spinning out of control and on a collision course with disaster.

You Could Smell it in the Air

For the generations that grew up in the era of air conditioning, relief from the ravages of the sun is only a push button away. Such extravagances were not available during WWII. The most immediate respite in those days was the public beach. If you lived in Black Bottom, this meant Belle Isle.

Sunday June 20, 1941 was a typical day downtown. The sun's lustrous heat felt quite pleasant early in the morning but quickly spiraled to a challenging ninty-one degrees by the afternoon. Some 100,000 Detroiters decided to patronize Belle Isle that day; 75 percent were black.

Sojourner Truth and Packard withstanding, other omens of more recent vintage had laced the air with hatred and impending trouble. Seven days before the riot, a donnybrook broke out in west of Detroit in Inkster between blacks and whites. Two days later the police intervened in yet another melee between blacks and whites at Detroit's predominantly white Eastwood Amusement Park. It was here that the final seeds of that fatal Sunday were sown.

Enter Charles Lyons, aka "Little Willie." Lyons had been a participant in the brawl at Eastwood Amusement Park only five days prior to the riot and was eventually chased from the park by angry white teenagers. Little Willie arrived on Belle Isle that fateful Sunday still seething with animosity and resentment. He met up with seven other black youths, mostly teenagers, and quickly molded them into his own private band of marauding automatons. It didn't take much to imbue them with resolve as they too had had their share of run ins with whites. Little Willie had decided he was going to even the score. It didn't matter that they weren't the same transgressors from Eastwood Park, any white would do.

Charles Lyons
"Little Willie"

The fury of the war had drastically changed Detroit. Because of the dense, interracial crowd that frequented Belle Isle, Detroit police came to believe that if trouble started, it would likely start here.

Belle Isle, the largest city-owned island park in the country, encompasses a spacious 985 acres, but it wasn't big enough to prevent two volatile groups from avenging past grievances on this fateful dav.

Riot Timeline

Sunday - June 20, 1943

3:30 p.m.	- Little Willie and co. begin marauding rampage around island.
4:00	- Patrol Car 1 (Belle Isle) begins busy day investigating reports of black teenagers starting fights. Unable to locate suspects.
11:00	- Tempers flare around island as groups of blacks and whites square off, culminating in a free-for-all at the foot of the bridge, attracting the attention of several hundred white sailors stationed at the naval armory who now eagerly join the fracas.
11:20	- Now some 5,000 (mostly white) at foot of bridge. Riot quickly spreads to nearby streets.
11:30	- Some blacks take their anger out by smashing windows of white owned businesses on Hastings Street, eventually looting them. Whites retaliate by beating blacks on Woodward Avenue. When they ran out of victims they attempted to invade Black Bottom.
(Bloody Monday)	
12:00 a.m.	- Detroit police (almost 200) arrive to break up melee at foot of bridge. Police are unaware of Forest Club incident.
1:00	- Blacks in Paradise Valley, acting on Tipton rumor, begin assaulting white motorists along Warren Ave and Vernor Hwy.
2:00	- Belle Isle brawl disbanded, twenty-eight blacks & nineteen whites arrested. Police believe incident is over.
4:00	- Whites begin stoning black motorists on Woodward and assault black patrons as they leave the Roxy movie theatre.

9:00 a.m. -	Mayor Jeffries and Police Commissioner Witherspoon believe riot is out of control. Governor Kelly telephones to request federal troops. Twelve hour delay before troops arrive. Thousands of whites roam Woodward forcing blacks off streetcars and buses. Rioting continues unabated throughout the day.
11:00 a.m.	White mobs begin reign of terror along Woodward Avenue.
4:00 p.m.	U.S. Army Brigadier General Guthner arrives to meet with governor. Guthner balks at prearranged plan for request of troops. Insists that martial law must first be declared. This would put Detroit under military rule.
6:00 - 9:00	Mayor Jeffries goes on radio appealing for sanity. Governor Kelly declares State of Emergency, still unwilling to declare martial law which would turn Detroit over to the military. The bloodiest stretch of the riot ensues. Sixteen are already dead, ten more will die in these three hours.
9:25 p.m.	Kelly speaks with General Aurand. A "qualified martial law" is imposed. Aurand orders Guthner to send in Rouge Park garrison. Troops from Camp McCoy, Wisconsin are on the way. Colonel Krech's MPs break up mobs at bayonet point. Riot begins to wind down.

Little Willie & company spent the day at Belle Isle beating and robbing unsuspecting whites. The weather was so pleasant, the festive crowds waited until 10:00 p.m. to begin making their way to the mainland, causing a massive traffic jam along the entire Belle Isle Bridge. Most were unaware of the numerous fisticuffs that had taken place on the island that day. Tempers began to fray along the bridge, however, as the sound of horns honking echoed into the hot, sticky night.

The Broadhead Naval Armory, just east of the bridge on the mainland, contained hundreds of U.S. sailors at any one time. For weeks there had been brawls between white sailors and black civilians on or around Belle Isle. Sunday night would be the main event.

Around 10:30 p.m., white pedestrian Joe Joseph, who had been enjoying himself on Belle Isle, began walking across the bridge en route to the mainland. He ran into Little Willie and friends who proceeded to beat him. Startled, Joseph sprinted back towards Belle Isle and ran right into the waiting arms of two white sailors who witnessed the incident, "We saw what happened to you. The Nigger jumped you. Let's go kill that Nigger." The riot, which *LIFE* magazine had so fortuitously predicted, had begun.

Soon isolated brawls broke out up and down the bridge, culminating in a rumble on the mainland. By now the Broadhead Naval Armory had been alerted and hundreds of angry white sailors dressed in their summer whites formed a skirmish line across the foot of the bridge, pummeling blacks attempting to leave the island.

A number of blacks who managed to escape Belle Isle made their way back to Paradise Valley and the giant Forest Club Lounge where hundreds of blacks were enjoying a local band. Rumors began to swirl as a young black named Leo Tipton jumped onstage, and after falsely identifying himself as a Detroit police officer, announced to the crowd, "There's a riot at Belle Isle. The whites have killed a colored lady and her baby. Thrown them over the bridge. Everybody come on. There's free transportation outside."

This, of course, was totally false. Despite the number of beatings no had been killed or even seriously injured thus far. But the frenzied crowd bolted the Forest Club, destined for Belle Isle. When they found no transportation and the roads to the approaches of Belle Isle blocked off by police, they vented their anger instead on the white (Jewish) owned stores along Hastings Street. They began smashing store windows, eventually looting them. Any whites unfortunate enough to be in the area were stoned and beaten.

Mobs of whites retaliated by taking over Woodward Avenue. Unsuspecting black patrons who emerged from the Roxy and Colonial theatres were beaten. The city was awash in hatred the likes of which it had never seen before. By the time it was over, the entire world would be aghast at the violence. Even Nazi Germany's propaganda machine worked overtime informing Europe how the freedom loving Americans couldn't get along with themselves.

State of Michigan Archives

(Above) The white mob catches up with a black man from Paradise Valley whose misfortune it was to be on Woodward, a black No-Mans-Land. Thousands of hysteric whites swarmed Woodward conducting a reign of terror on blacks while thousands more stood by the wayside rooting them on, as if at a ball game. Intoxicated with rage, when no more black pedestrians could be found, the mob began systematically halting the trolleys in search of further sport.
(Below) Rioters help a white women out of harm's way while a frantic search ensues for black passengers whose fate hanged precariously by a thread. When white conductors refused to stop the trolley, the mob cut the cable and the conductor's lot was thrown in with the black passengers he was trying to protect.

AP/Wide World photos

Woodward
No-Man's-Land

Detroit Public Library

Like great, wounded beasts in their death throws, burned-out automobiles clutter Woodward Avenue after their black owners were beaten by marauding white mobs and their vehicles set aflame. Woodward, between the Vernor Highway and Forest Avenue looked like a battlefield. Pools of blood, giant scorch marks branded into the concrete and automotive carcasses betrayed the heinous behavior that defined Bloody Monday. Mayor Jeffries, who later made an inspection tour of the area during the riot, counted no less than seven overturned cars (there were in fact twenty total).

State of Michigan Archives

The U.S. army patrols the ruins of Hastings Street following Bloody Monday.

Riotous blacks quickly found it imprudent for them to leave the safety of Paradise Valley and focused their aggressions instead on the main thoroughfare of Hastings Street. The predominantly white, Jewish-owned shops became the eye of their rage during the early morning hours of Bloody Monday. At first black rioters only seemed to be taking out their frustrations by smashing shop windows, but the temptation became too much and looting began shortly thereafter. Many black-owned shops sported a hastily scrawled "Colored" painted on the window. They were left untouched.

Detroit police showed up in force to make arrests. One looter became irate, grabbed an officer's gun and shot two policemen. He did not live to tell his tale. Detroit police flushed three looters out of a market on Warren Avenue. When they refused to heed the officers' warning to halt, police opened fire killing one of them. A black rioter nearby angrily yelled at police, "We'll even this up later, copper." Also arrested on Hastings was a looter who was making quite a name for himself, Willie Lyons.

In every disaster there seems to emerge some sort of hero. Someone who takes great risk, not for the sake of their own personal aggrandizement but simply to quench a thirst for justice. As is often the case they remain forever anonymous. (Above) A white passenger attempts to sway a blood-thirsty mob that was determined to assault black passengers. Note how a number of rioters closest to the car ignore his plea and continue to search the car for potential victims.

Like a house of horrors, the story of the riot could be told in the carnage that littered the streets of Paradise Valley. A peddler's cart, which once provided an old man with a livelihood, lay overturned, its polished fruits and vegetables still in pristine condition on the street. Its owner was knifed to death after his wobbly legs could no longer stay ahead of the mob that pursued him.

Around the corner could be found an abandoned car that looked like a giant fist had come crashing down upon it, the vehicle's owner clinging to life by a thread at Detroit Receiving Hospital.

Under the glow of a Walk/Don't Walk sign lay two coagulating pools of blood, evidence of an earlier shootout with a sniper who did not live to explain his motivation.

The riot was now completely out of control. The overwhelmed DPD could not cope with the tens of thousands of rioters. Jeffries later commented, "No police department in the nation can successfully alone fight against its civilian population when they decide to take the law into their own hands." This meant that Jeffries would have to enact "Emergency Plan White" and the U.S. Army.

The Delay

Detroit Mayor Edward Jeffries went on the air pleading for sanity "Our enemies could not have accomplished as much by a full-scale bombing raid. I appeal to the good citizens of Detroit to keep off the streets, keep in their homes, or at their jobs."

Michigan Governor Harry Kelly was in Columbus, Ohio on state business when Jeffries called him at 9:40 a.m. Monday informing him of the riot. After much discussion Kelly called the army command in Chicago at 11:00 to request Federal troops. According to the prearranged plan, he now believed the troops were on the way. At this point the army's bureaucratic machine went into overdrive. Colonel Davis, the man who took the call, remembered it as a request for "possible" federal assistance. This alerted his boss, Major General Henry Aurand in Chicago, who now anxiously began thumbing through the army manual to familiarize himself with martial law procedure. This was the beginning of a virtual comedy of errors by the army high command as no one knew what the procedure was to send in federal troops.

Aurand dispatched Brigadier General William Guthner to Detroit to take command when and if it became necessary. In the meantime a flurry of army phone calls ensued attempting to ascertain the legalities of using federal troops to put down a riot. At 4:00 p.m. Guthner, now in Detroit, was told over the phone that martial law must first be declared before federal troops can enter. This was contrary to what Kelly and Jeffries had previously been led to believe.

Bringing in the army was one thing but martial law would mean the abrogation of civilian law and putting the army in charge of the city. This was not what Kelly or Jeffries wanted. Even President Roosevelt was sour on the idea. Known as Emergency Plan White, the army was to enter at the governor's behest and assist the police department. It was that simple. But bureaucracy had thrown Jeffries a curve ball and he knew they must have help by nightfall.

The senior army officer in pre-riot Detroit was Colonel August Krech, the garrison commander at Fort Custer in Battle Creek. Krech had numerous meetings with Jeffries in the months preceding the riot in anticipation of trouble and he too believed that Governor Kelly needed only to "request" troops for him take action. The intrepid Krech had even executed three different mock mobilizations that summer and guaranteed Jeffries he could get his men from the staging area at Rouge Park to the streets of Detroit in less than forty-nine minutes. Krech was good on his word, advancing even further to Fort Wayne, but was forced to hold up because of the political wrangling of his superiors until he could legally enter the besieged city.

Wishing to avert martial law, the federal authorities found a loophole that stated the army could enter a city to protect federal property without declaring martial law. Detroit, they found, was home to a small armory that made rifles and pistols for the federal government. It was flimsy but good enough. The army would enter the city to protect their property and simply restore order in every direction.

Degrees of Insurrection

1) **State of Emergency** - The key to remember is that the elected government is still in charge during a state of emergency. It is a government declaration used by the mayor/governor/president who *may* suspend civil liberties during chaotic times such as natural disasters, riots or declarations of war within their jurisdiction. The Writ of Habeas Corpus (the right to challenge arrest in court) *may* also be suspended. The governor of the state must declare a State of Emergency before state troops (National Guard) can be brought in.
2) **Martial Law** - Military authority takes over administration of justice and order when local authorities can no longer cope with the situation. Civil laws are suspended and military laws are substituted. Curfews are often imposed.
   In Detroit's situation, for example, only the governor or president can declare martial law. When this happens, the commanding general takes charge of the city. This means all city and state laws are suspended, courts are suspended, the police department ceases operation as do state authorities in the area. Civil rights are also suspended until the army restores order and relinquishes command back to civilian authorities.

Detroit Public Library

With the familiar balustrade of the Detroit Public Library in the foreground, the U.S. Army heads for Woodward Avenue to break up the riotous mobs that seemed to be growing not only in size but in intensity. There they encountered between 10-15,000 whites, the "great mob" that Jeffries had seen roaming Woodward unabated and administering justice as they pleased. The sight of well-armed soldiers brandishing bayonets quickly brought them to their senses and caused them to scatter pell-mell. Krech ordered his men, "Fix your bayonets, load your guns and don't take anything from anybody."

The military police then marched down Vernor Highway and into the rebellious ghetto of Paradise Valley. This proved more challenging. It was here they found the feistiest part of the white mob trying to enter the ghetto to rumble with blacks and burn down their houses. The DPD was keeping them at bay temporarily but was badly in need reinforcements. The army MPs were greeted with curses, stones and an occasional gunshot to which they answered with bayonets and tear gas.

The riot climaxed at the Frazer Hotel in Black Bottom after a white police officer was shot by a black hotel patron. As dozens of Detroit and state police converged on the scene, more shots rang out. Police poured some 1,000 rounds into the building, along with tear gas canisters, until the rickety old hotel was as pockmarked as the moon. By 11:00 p.m. Bloody Monday had drawn to a deadly close. The army had restored order but not peace.

he went about doing good

Acts 10:38

Dr. De Horatiis' bier
Blessed Sacrament Cathedral
Detroit

Dr. Joseph De Horatiis came to America with the fervent belief that all men are created equal and even the meekest of immigrants could excel.

Amidst the chaos and tumult of the riot, Dr. De Horatiis received an emergency call which would take him through Paradise Valley. Stopped at a roadblock by a Detroit police officer, he was sternly warned about the potential ramifications. The doctor waved him off; he had a duty to perform.

By the time he got to the intersection of Warren and Beaubien he was stopped by black rioters who beat him to death.

At the funeral, Dr. De Horatiis' lifelong friend, Father Hector Saulino, brought home the gravity of the riot. His emotion-choked eulogy ran on, reminding us that "Many times the good doctor refused to take money and often paid the bills of specialists he called into cases. Many times he loaned great sums of money without taking notes. After thirty-seven years of service he died poor, owed much of that money still. In his death Dr. De Horatiis offers a solution to all wars - Christian charity. When will the world learn that as long as men beat one another and strive greedily and selfishly against each other, peace cannot return to stay?"

A monument for Dr. De Horatiis off Gratiot serves as a poignant reminder of that shameful day long ago.

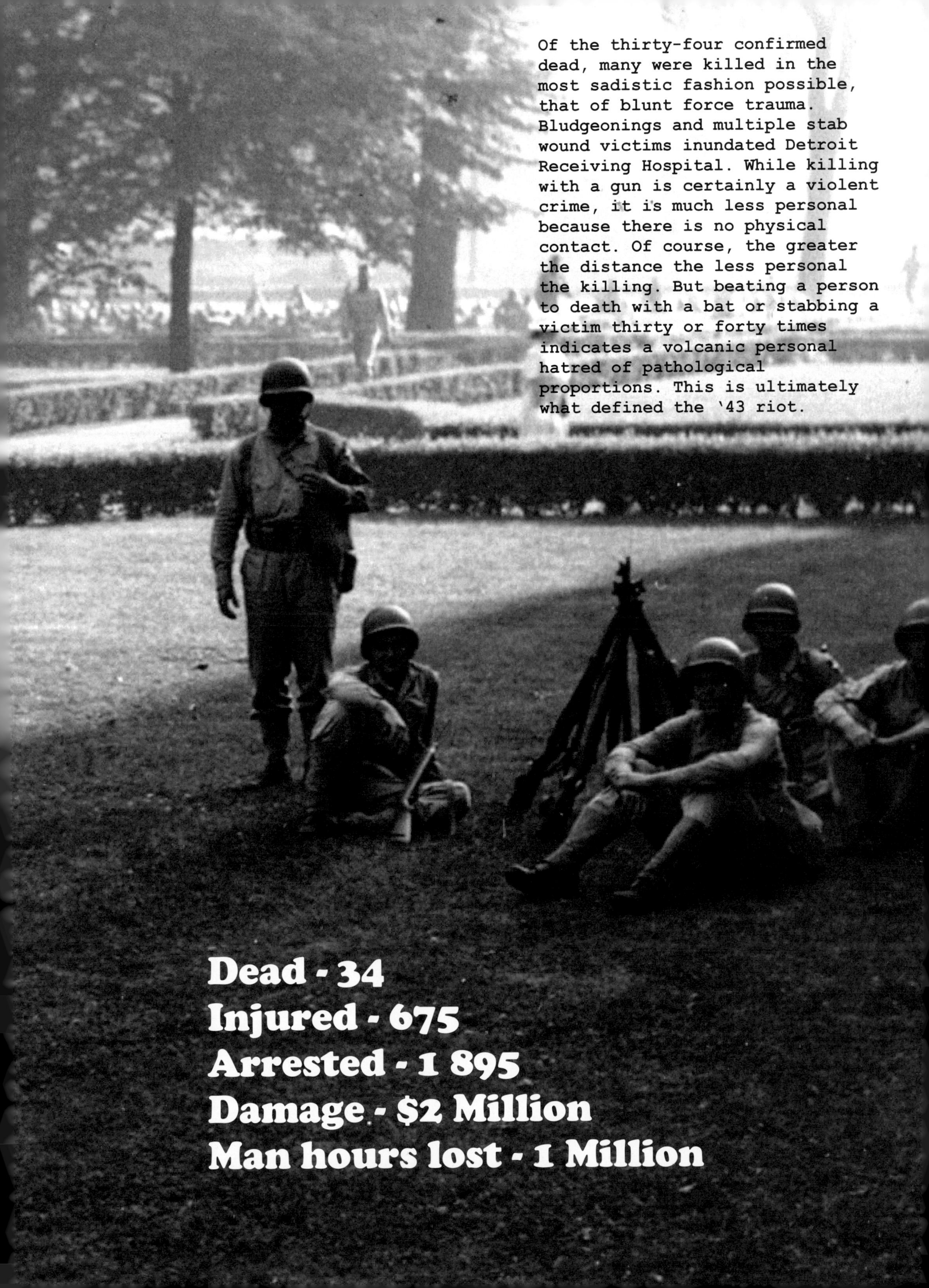

Of the thirty-four confirmed dead, many were killed in the most sadistic fashion possible, that of blunt force trauma. Bludgeonings and multiple stab wound victims inundated Detroit Receiving Hospital. While killing with a gun is certainly a violent crime, it is much less personal because there is no physical contact. Of course, the greater the distance the less personal the killing. But beating a person to death with a bat or stabbing a victim thirty or forty times indicates a volcanic personal hatred of pathological proportions. This is ultimately what defined the '43 riot.

Dead - 34
Injured - 675
Arrested - 1 895
Damage - $2 Million
Man hours lost - 1 Million

"In the democracy of the dead

all men, at last, are equal"

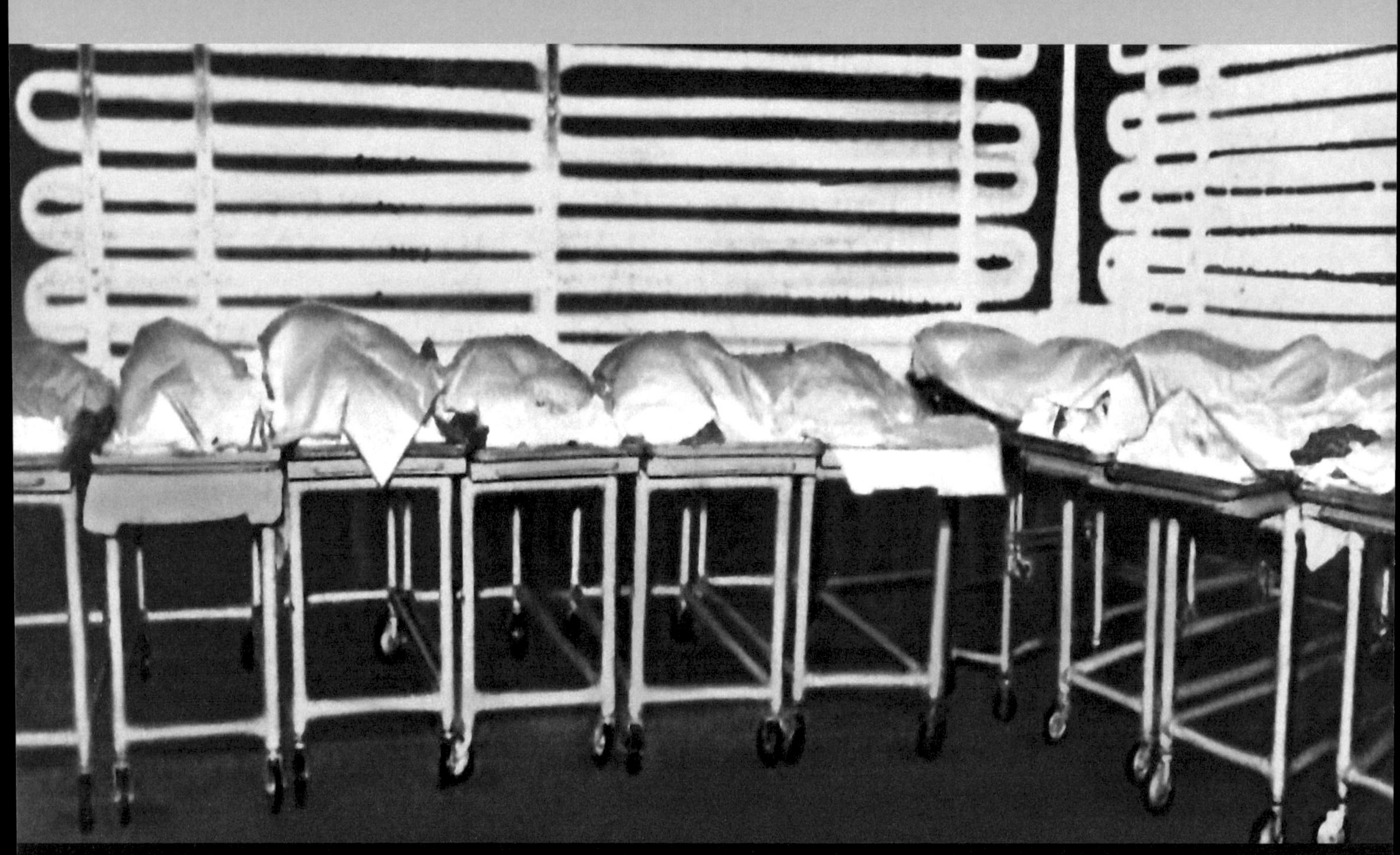

Enemies in life but brothers in death, riot victims, both black and white, lay side by side in the Wayne County morgue.

As a whole it is difficult to critique the performance of the Detroit Police Department because of the wide variety of incidents. Some officers clearly were heroes as they defended badly beaten blacks against mobs of over one hundred while other officers appeared to turn a blind eye to the beatings.

It must be noted that the DPD had lost many of its seasoned officers to the draft and was well under its required head count at the time of the riot. Jeffries had pleaded with the army to stop raiding his police department but in the end there was little if any thing he could do.

Mayor Jeffries post-riot critique on the city's state of preparedness had an ominous ring about it. Decades later his statement would boomerang: "We were greenhorns in this area of race riots, but we are greenhorns no longer. We are veterans now. We will not make the same mistakes again."

July 6th - With peace now restored, the army musters out of Detroit, down Woodward Avenue and past the DIA reviewing stand which held their commanders, General Aurand, General Guthner, Governor Kelly and Mayor Jeffries. It proved to be an uneasy peace, however, and twenty-four years later the army would return, to a city under both different and yet hauntingly familiar circumstances.

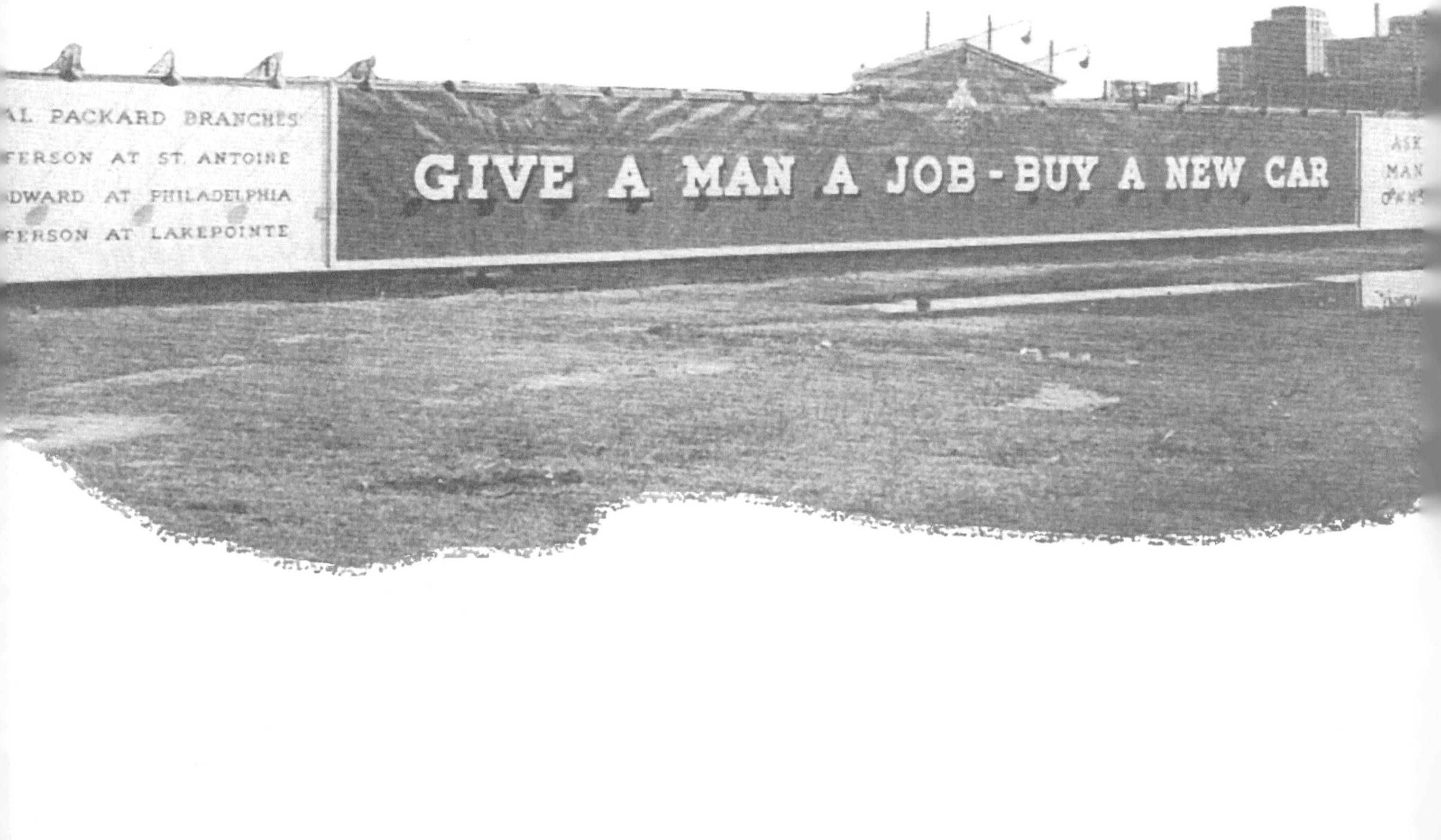

AL. PACKARD BRANCHES
FERSON AT ST. ANTOINE
DWARD AT PHILADELPHIA
FERSON AT LAKEPOINTE
GIVE A MAN A JOB - BUY A NEW CAR

The 1950s: A Most Damning Time

The 1950s: A Most Damning Time

While many may feel that the 1960s were the pivotal decade in Detroit, the 1950s provided many secondary causes which helped grease the skids of anger and give it a final push towards rebellion. The three-headed monster of urban renewal, interstates and economic recession vastly altered the landscape of Detroit in the 1950s and would loom large as a socio-economic minefield that would cause the city to blow up in 1967.

Urban renewal, a term often associated with revitalization of decaying neighborhoods, was employed on a massive scale in Detroit during the 1950s and left a mark of still dubious distinction. **Interstates** carved up the city in the name of progress but its then unforeseen after effects would linger on like a ghostly apparition. Finally there was the **Eisenhower recession** of the late 1950s which shuttered many a Detroit factory, giving additional impetus to those seeking to bolt to the fledgling suburbs or leave the state altogether.

Still bathing in the victory of WWII which made the United States a superpower, American industrial might was unequaled in size or stature. World War II had forced Depression idled factories into a 24/7 frenzy of unprecedented production. Even the despot Stalin tried to model his industry after Detroit. But as the 1950s progressed, American industry once again began a painful throttling back to normalcy.

Detroit, the city that had put the world on wheels, had grown old before the eyes of its shocked citizenry. Time itself had weathered its buildings into tired and shabby shadows of their once youthful selves. The facade of strength and vigor was now a sad mirage. Mayor Edward Jeffries attempted to eradicate the blight by producing a blueprint to reestablish Detroit as a world class city. It was called the Detroit Plan.

The Detroit Plan was hatched in 1946 as a futuristic scheme to accommodate the ever burgeoning traffic load which the automotive boom created and replace the unsightly slums that had been accumulating like the city's industrial pollution. Jeffries began setting aside a paltry half million dollars a year from the budget, somewhat analogous to emptying Lake Huron with a teaspoon. No city had the resources to tackle a job this size. They needed federal muscle. This would come in the form of Harry Truman's Federal Housing Act of 1949 which made available to large urban areas the enormous funding necessary to carry out their projects.

Jeffries left office in 1949 with his dream still in an embryonic stage. His successor, Albert Cobo, would aggressively carry the urban renewal banner forward through the 1950s and drastically change the face of Detroit forever.

Urban Renewal:
One Step Forward, Two Steps Back

Urban renewal, the much vaunted plan for erasing blighted neighborhoods while hiding behind the cloak of helping the poor, in many respects hurt the poor and destroyed once vibrant (albeit decaying) neighborhoods, and replaced them with class-conscious pipe dreams that were socially incongruent to their surroundings. President Johnson, like his predecessors Eisenhower and Truman, echoed the need for rebuilding our cities. "Our society will never be great until our cities are great. In the next forty years, we must rebuild the entire urban U.S."

Urban renewal was the rage across the country in the 1950s but it was virgin territory for city planners. It had never been done on such a colossal scale before. New York City razed large sections of viable neighborhoods, including the venerable Penn Station in 1963, and spent the rest of the twentieth century wondering why. It was the old American adage come home to roost: bigger is better. The more money you throw at a problem the greater your chances for success. Wrong!

On paper urban renewal seemed like a very progressive endeavor - erasing blighted areas and replacing them with modern dwellings brandishing cutting-edge innovations. Below the surface, however, the iceberg of urban renewal reeked of political snake oil. Urban renewal was not used to help the poor. It was used by big cities to fatten their coffers. By razing impoverished slums and replacing them with middle-class high rises, a city's tax revenues would swell significantly. Officials stumbled ignorantly on with their social engineering as entire neighborhoods were leveled under the guise of modernity. The melting-pot poor who were hastily sent packing had to fend for themselves with little or no relocation help from the city. Since it was generally poor blacks who were being displaced, many came to believe the city's hidden agenda of slum removal was really black removal. While the cosmetic appeal of erasing Detroit's most blighted areas would be obvious, city planners failed to take into account the terrible social upheaval they were causing.

The futuristic Gratiot Project would replace densely packed slums with open air parks, playgrounds and sparkling new middle-class high rises. No longer using a conventional grid road system, these projects (called superblocks) were designed with numerous dead end streets to keep through traffic out, creating additional traffic headaches.

Old, ethnic neighborhoods were often segregated for a reason - because the people had so much in common. Subsequently a strong sense of belonging saturated the community. Urban renewal greatly destroyed the homogeneous makeup of the city and often forced the displaced into neighborhoods where they were not welcome.

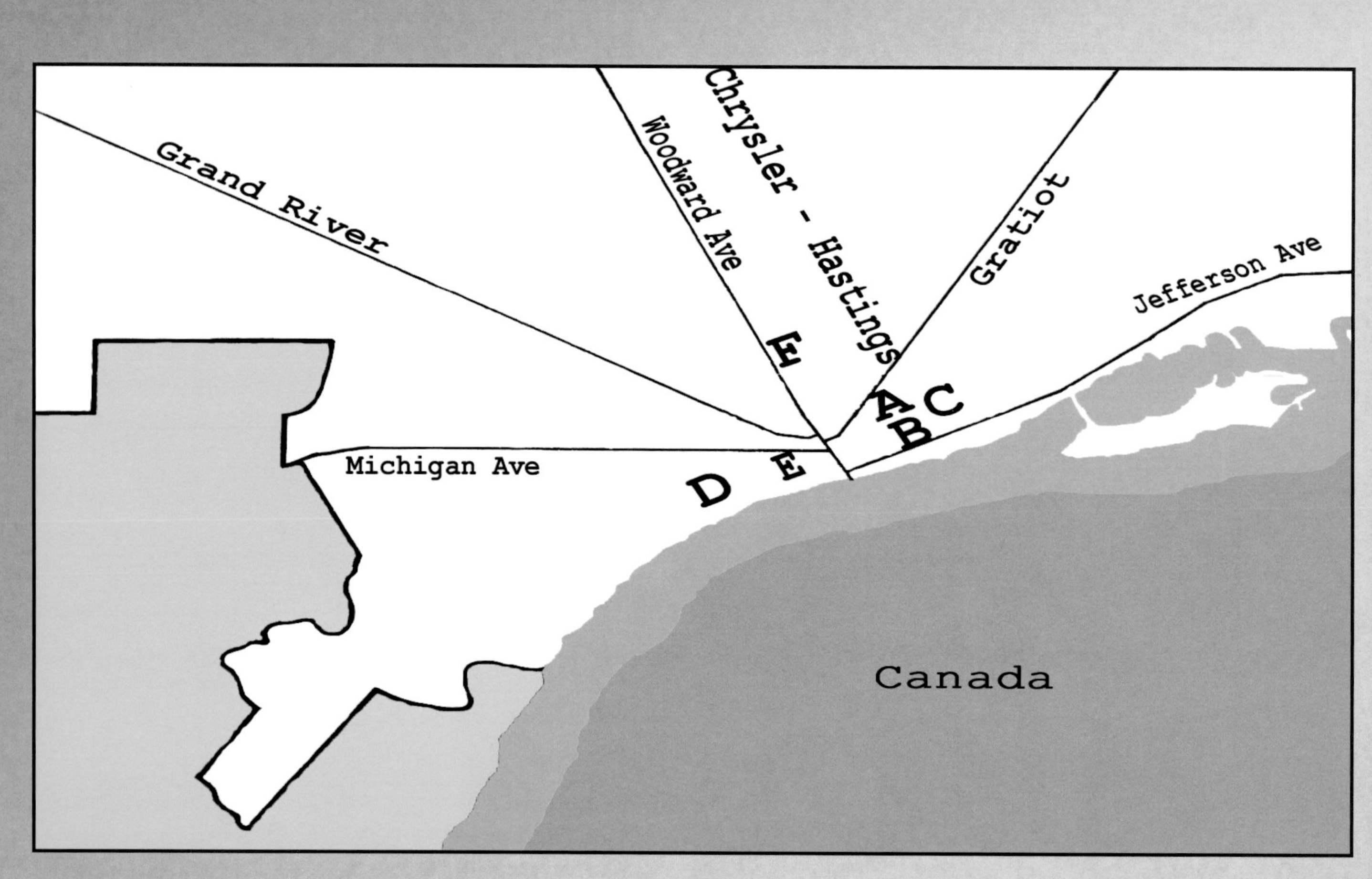

Detroit's massive urban renewal program of the 1950s indelibly altered the face of the city, in particular the near East side. Urban renewal and its aftereffects would play a major social-economic role in setting up the '67 riot.

A) Gratiot (Paradise Valley/Black Bottom)
B) Lafayette (Paradise Valley/Black Bottom)
C) Elmwood Park
D) West Side Industrial (Corktown)
E) Central Business District
F) Medical Center (Wayne State)

Between the three mayors involved in urban renewal (Cobo, Miriani, Cavanagh) they would level thousands of acres of old neighborhoods and in the process create an angry army of displaced blacks who, in the volatile decade of the 1960s, would ultimately unleash their considerable fury against the city itself.

The massive urban renewal projects on Detroit's East side, initially known as the Gratiot Project, offered a solution for stopping the white flight to the suburbs, which by the 1960s was in high gear. Urban renewal attempted to mask its social engineering objective, building neighborhoods according to class and not race. Middle-class whites would not have to worry about the possibility of low income blacks because they couldn't possibly afford the new, upscale housing. Middle-class blacks would probably have the same values so there would be a common ground. The race question, it would seem, was solved.

No one ever doubted that Black Bottom required attention. These wood framed houses were originally built for the influx of German immigrants who arrived in the 1850s. Hastily fabricated, they were way past their life expectancy. Few had running water or bathrooms. The cruder forms of outhouses were simply a seat placed over the sewer. The threat of a major fire was always present. The frequency of rats also made the area unsafe. Despite its cultural history, the blight of Black Bottom had become an embarrassment to city officials who were attempting to reinvent Detroit.

Detroit Public Library

The remnants of Black Bottom, looking inwards towards the city, as the final stages of demolition near completion in 1960. This once vibrant neighborhood, a port of entry for blacks arriving from the South, was systematically leveled for more upscale, middle-class high rises. The poor, mostly black inhabitants were left to fend for themselves. It was an indignity they would not soon forget.

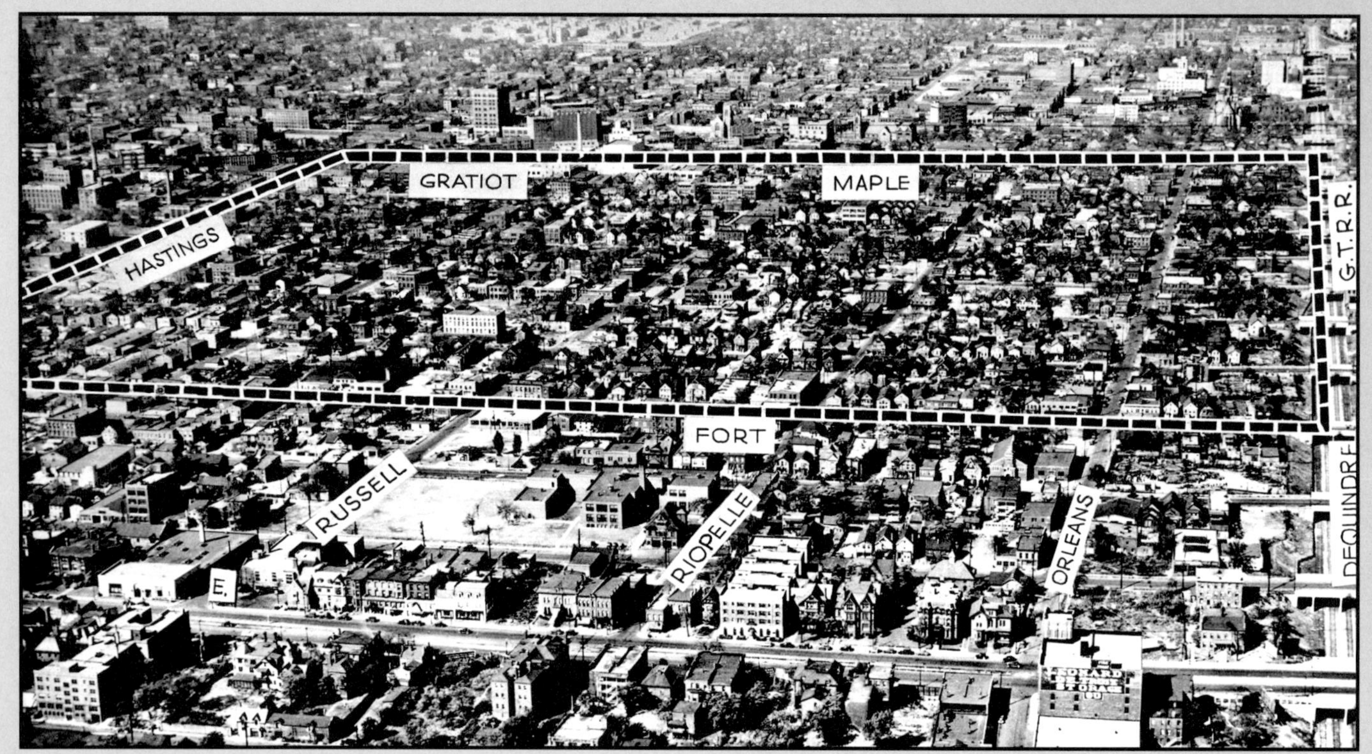

Walter Reuther Library

(Above) The encircled Black Bottom awaits its fate in the early 1950s. The controversy surrounded the fact that Black Bottom contained much of the city's black poor, most of whom were forced to rent because banks would not lend even qualified blacks the money to buy a home. By no stretch of the imagination could they afford the upscale housing that replaced Black Bottom. In the end the city receives vastly increased tax revenues, the middle-class receive new, modern facilities and a clean environment to inhabit but the poor just get displaced. Since urban renewal would take the better part of two decades to complete, where were its former occupants to stay in the meanwhile? (Below) The end of Black Bottom.

Walter Reuther Library

The condemnation of property in Black Bottom began in 1950 and continued for three years. This initial development contained seventy-two acres, fifty-five of which would be residential development and seventeen would be set aside for a park. With great anticipation the city conducted a lottery for the cleared land in July of '52 to determine who the lucky builders would be to transform this former slum into an urban utopia. It was then that something unexpected happened. Much to the city's consternation, no one bid on the land.

The silence at city hall was deafening. An embarrassed Mayor Cobo named a twelve man committee to fabricate solutions. Black Bottom was now only an urban desert. It would lay dormant for six years. The newly plowed up acreage was slowly retaken by nature, causing critics to sardonically refer to it as "Ragweed Acres".

By the time the East side urban renewal projects were done almost two decades later, some 653 acres had been razed for development and over 2,500 families were forced to find somewhere else to live.

Walter Reuther Library

Ragweed Acres

Albert Cobo **Mayor 1950-1957**

While Mayor Jeffries may have initiated the Detroit Plan in the late 1940s, it was his successor Mayor Albert Cobo (above, pointing) who pile-drived the idea into something tangible. Cobo, a Republican, became mayor in 1950 after defeating his Democratic challenger George Edwards (the future Police Commissioner) in a town dominated by Democrats. Many believe it was because Cobo made it eminently clear that if elected he would not support black public housing near white neighborhoods where as the liberal minded Edwards stated he would. The result was a very polarized election and a continuation of racial tensions that would perpetually dominate the city.

As promised, Cobo vetoed eight of the twelve proposed housing projects which were on the table when he entered office. Cobo also seemed to show little regard for the relocation of persons displaced by the massive urban renewal plan. Cobo's explanation was carefree and succinct: "Sure, there have been some inconveniences in building our expressways and in slum clearance programs, but in the long run more people benefit. That's the price of progress." Though regarded as a good mayor by 1950s standards, Cobo definitely set in place a social minefield of problems which would later explode on his successors. Perhaps history has granted him leniency because he died in office. Nevertheless, his failure to address the acute housing problem may have pleased his constituents, but it was to spell doom for the city in the racial upheaval of the 1960s.

Detroit Public Library

The first building to go up and the subsequent linchpin of the East side renewal project was the Pavilion. Designed by famous architect Ludwig Mies van der Rohe, it stressed suburban living in the urban environment. Initial rents went from $85-$211 a month. This was many times more than its previous slum dwelling occupants, who paid more like $5-$20 a month rent, could afford. The Pavilion's accompanying consort was the Lafayette Towers, middle-class high rises built right over the heart of the former Black Bottom.

While the first state-of-the-art buildings did enjoy some early popularity, upon their completion another considerable lag in developer interest caused the land once again to sit idle for years. (Below)

Detroit Public Library

West Side - Chaos in Old Corktown

The urban upheaval that ruled Detroit in the 1950s was not limited to Detroit's East side however. The West side was scalped too, albeit on a smaller scale. Corktown, the West side enclave whose early Irish settlers came from Cork County, Ireland after the potato famine, was also earmarked for urban renewal. Some 169 acres of this historic West side neighborhood were razed during the 1960s and '70s and replaced with light industry and warehouses.

The Irish had built a thriving community along Michigan Avenue in the 1800s. Many of the Irish moved out prior to the disruption of urban renewal. They were replaced by an interesting fusion of Maltese, Mexican and African Americans who also came seeking prosperity.

Walter Reuther Library

As was the case on the East side, old ethnic neighborhoods were leveled for higher tax yielding industry, creating disruption and chaos for those uprooted. The Detroit Plan was one of the earliest and biggest of the urban renewal projects around the country. Administrations were given carte blanche to create what amounted to a social engineering of their cities at the expense of the poor.

Walter Reuther Library

Skid Row, which extended along much of Michigan Avenue westward from downtown into Corktown, was also razed to make room for businesses and the Lodge expressway. Many of its occupants found themselves scrambling for sanctuary. As was the case on the East side, many fled to 12th Street, quickly making it the densest population in the city. Naturally, Skid Row held more than its fair share of nefarious characters who were soon to call 12th Street home, much to the chagrin of its long-time residents. The end result was the highest crime rate in the city and a ticking time bomb awaiting detonation.

Walter Reuther Library

Corktown

The bell of old Trinity,
What a sweet sound to me!
Every time I hear it
There's a bend in my knee.
We didn't have chimes,
For our purses were lean,
But we had faith in God,
And faith in the Dean.
Most all the old timers,
Like myself, moved away,
But we meet, once a year,
On St. Patrick's Day,
And we talk of the changes
That have taken place
Where lived the descendents
Of the great Irish race
In the Dinan boys' store,
Where you drank your "raheen",
A Greek keeps it now,
Selling pop and ice cream.
In Walsh's old home
You'll find Portuguese,
And McCarty's old house
Is filled with Chinese.
Where Mike Rahaley lived
When he drove his hack
There's a family named Dugan,
But their color is black.
You remember old Doody,
That lived all alone?
Well, his place was bought
By a family named Cohen.
In Hickey's old store,
Where they'd trust for your needs
There's a mixture of Danes,
Norwegians and Swedes.
There's even a change
In the night breeze:
Instead of Killkenny cats
You now hear Maltese.
Those foreigners are smart,
About that there's no doubt,
For they didn't move in
'Till the Irish moved out.

Ike has an Idea - Interstates

When General Eisenhower became president in 1953 he brought with him an expansion of a revolutionary idea. While leading the American army through Germany towards the end of WWII, he marveled at how fast and efficiently he could move his troops on the world's first superhighway, the Autobahn. Experiences on the home front during the war also emphasized the point that America's antiquated system of roads was wholly deficient in times of crisis.

Throughout the 1950s the Cold War between America and the Soviet Union raged. In response to this, Ike vowed to create a vast network of roads across the country enabling civilians and the military the capacity of mass transit with great alacrity during times of war or peace. In selling his idea, Ike stated in 1955:

Together, the united forces of our communication and transportation systems are dynamic elements in the very name we bear – United States. Without them, we would be a mere alliance of many separate parts.

Walter Reuther Library

President Eisenhower flashes the victory sign to Detroiters as his motorcade proceeds up Washington Avenue during a stopover. The 1950s were Ike's decade. His highway legislation would have a significant impact on the face of big urban areas like Detroit with the creation of federal interstates. While interstates greatly advanced transportation, it had the double negative effect of carving up viable urban communities and paving the way for "white flight" to the fledgling suburbs, which they helped create.

East Side - The Chrysler Colossus

It was an embarrassing realization that the country which put the world on wheels and developed the atomic bomb had no major system of roads linking one state to another. The concept had been bantered around before Eisenhower but Washington was never serious enough to appropriate the massive funds necessary to carry out this Herculean task. WWII and the Cold War scared them into action.

Ike's Federal Highway Act of 1956 gave him the financial clout to fulfill his super highway fantasy. The federal government would now foot 90 percent of the bill while giving local governments free rein on freeway placement. Like urban renewal, no one really understood the ramifications of carving up large tracts of urban areas and running a maze of expressways through once vibrant neighborhoods. Thus began the catastrophic marriage between urban renewal and interstate highways which would have massive repercussions for big cities in the decades to come.

Walter Reuther Library

Freeway construction wreaked havoc on Detroit. The installation of the Chrysler Freeway carved a jagged swath right through many well established Detroit neighborhoods, essentially taking one large city and splitting it up into many smaller ones, thus destroying much of its ethic congruity. This meager stretch of expressway from East Jefferson to 8 Mile, which cost a hefty $121 million, was completed in 1967.

Walter Reuther Library

Escape of the Middle Class

Symbols of two eras - As one of the last steam trains lumbers over the newly opened Lodge Freeway in 1950 it became a symbolic passing of the transportation torch from trains to automobiles. The freeways did what they were designed to do - move large amounts of people and freight quickly and efficiently, local and long distance.

There were unforeseen aftereffects however. Interstates now provided the apparatus for over crowded urbanites to pursue the "grass and garage" of the suburbs. City officials naively believed the opposite would occur. The dream of living in maiden suburbia and commuting to work in Detroit had arrived, and with it the mad dash of white flight had begun.

White flight was not strictly racially based however. Detroit's ancient housing stock also played a role. Houses built before the automotive era didn't have garages or driveways. Many homes were built almost within arms reach of their neighbors, completely negating the concept of privacy. In conjunction with this, yards were so small they were for all practical purposes nonexistent, which greatly limited the types of recreational activities for the kids.

Packard: Microcosm of Demise

Communities are by definition a group of people living together as a smaller social unit within a larger one having interests, work or kinship in common. Prior to mass transit, people often worked in the same neighborhood in which they lived. As the Eisenhower recession raged across the country, Detroit's factories began to shutter with alarming regularity. This is the problem with basing your economy on just one industry, in this case automobiles. Communities are perpetually stuck in a feast or famine cycle. When times are good, like the 1910s or '20s, everyone gains and the neighborhood prospers. But when the industry hits a downturn everyone suffers. Detroit's most pristine example of this can be found off East Grand Boulevard and the legendary Packard Motor Company.

Detroit Public Library

The Long Arm of Packard - Begun in 1903, the complex would eventually encompass some forty-seven buildings providing over 2.5 million square feet. At its peak during WWII it employed 25,000 people. This aerial photo was taken in 1937. Note that unlike its modern successors there were no parking lots; as few people drove cars to work because they lived near by. Packard was thus the cornerstone of the community and when it closed its doors for good in 1956 the devastating economic domino effect spelled doom for the neighborhood. Examples like Packard could be found throughout Detroit.

(Right) A Packard cornerstone bespeaks of a time when the Motor City lion roared and the world watched in awe. A visitor to Detroit once described the city as the "sound of a hammer against a steel plate." The cacophony of noise and energy was unrivaled by any city in the world. During WWII, Detroit couldn't come close to filling the jobs offered. But as the decades clicked past, the roar of the lion began to fade. By the 1960s the auto industry, which had always been erratic, was no longer a cash cow of employment. The once mighty lion was being transformed into an anemic mouse.

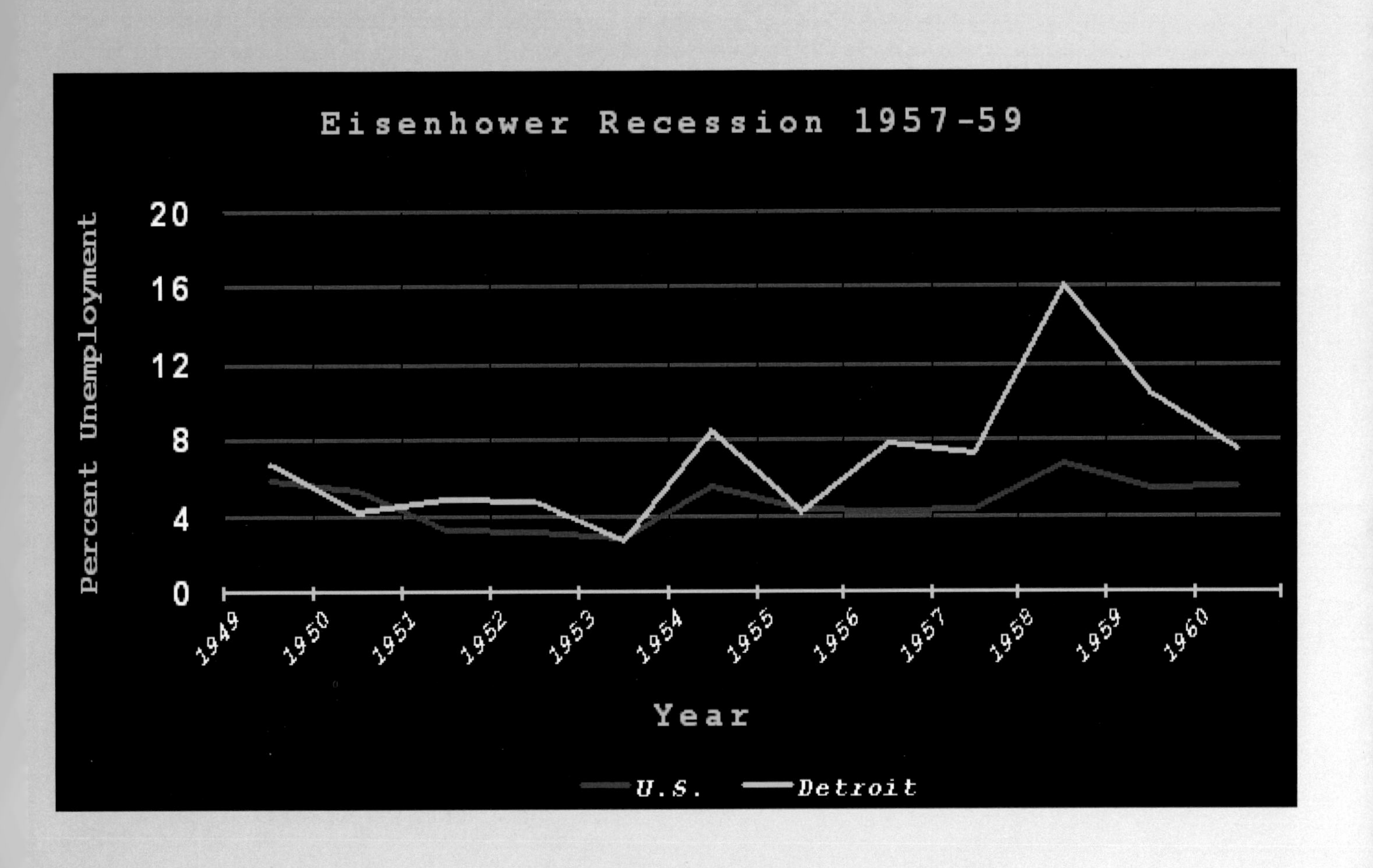

Rows of vacant buildings, which once supported and thrived off Packard, now lie idle or abandoned off East Grand Boulevard.

An abandoned A & P supermarket, which fed the Packard neighborhood, is now only frequented by an occasional transient or aspiring graffiti artist.

There will be no school today or any other day at the Emma Thomas grade school. The weed choked playgrounds, where kids once frolicked, have grown silent, refusing to relinquish the echoes of the baby boomers who quenched their thirst for knowledge in the great shadow of Packard.

Packard

The legendary Packard Motor Company, brought to Detroit by millionaire playboy Henry Joy from Ohio, will forever be remembered for its stunning luxury cars of the 1920s and '30s. Still standing like an urban Titanic, it is both a ghostly reminder of the ruthless competition in the automotive industry and of a time when Detroit had something very special to be proud of.

The crystal blue sky provides a surreal backdrop for Detroit's once premier car company. This legendary plant, more than any other, helped America win World War II. Perhaps symbolic of its tragic plight, the long abandoned hulk of Packard now stands watch over a neighboring graveyard.

On Borrowed Time - The once majestic Packard building, which basked in the glory and panache of the auto industry's Gilded Age, now lies broken and abandoned, quietly awaiting the wrecking ball and an all too ignominious end.

Hudson Motors

Another giant in the auto industry, Hudson Motors was one of the last of the independents squeezed out by the Big Three during the Eisenhower recession in the late 1950s. Hudson Motors employed thousands of Detroiters during its peak. The never-ending consolidation of the auto industry would put Detroit on a one-way street to decline.

Financed by department store magnate J. L. Hudson, the Hudson was a well-engineered and highly respected vehicle that dominated the early Daytona 500s.

1960

Looking more like an obscure Martian chess match, only the stubborn concrete stanchions of the demolished Hudson plant remained.
The final prize for the demolition gods, the powerhouse smokestack prepares to fall, sending yet another piece of Detroit's glorious history into automotive purgatory.

FAMILY MEN Do you want
A GOOD JOB NOW with
GUARANTEED INCOME for Life?
Join
THE DETROIT
POLICE DEPARTMENT
YOU CAN SERVE YOUR COUNTRY AT HOME
RWOVEN SOCKS
ROW SHIRTS
LLORY HATS
Schon's
ADAM HATS
NUNN-BUSH SHOES
COOPERS UNDERWEAR

The Old Guard

Police Departments are always under the public microscope. Their actions must always be correct or they invite public rebuke. According to Arthur Niederhoffer, a twenty-year New York City police officer and a sociology professor at New York's City College:

> **No policeman enforces all the laws of a community. If he did, we would all be in jail before the end of the first day. The laws which are selected for enforcement are those which the power structure of the community wants enforced. The police official's job is dependent upon his having radar-like equipment to sense what is the power structure and what it wants enforced as law.**

The Detroit police department had enforced the laws of the power structure since its creation in 1866. With the rapid social changes of the 20th century, the power structure added halting black encroachment to their list. The DPD could not stem the tide indefinitely, however, and the social bomb that had built up for decades would all catch up to Detroit in 1967.

The long blue line of the Detroit police department. A verse from Shakespeare's *Henry V* accurately defines their ideology:

"We few, We happy few, We band of brothers."

The Old Guard

Louis Berg Jr.
Superintendent DPD
1958-1963

James C. Berg
Deputy Superintendent
1958-1963

Louis Berg Sr.
Superintendent DPD
1940-1944

The Berg brothers represented the Old Guard of the Detroit Police Department. Like their father before them, they were Old School. But the social upheaval of the 1960s was causing all big city police departments to change against their will. Professor Niederhoffer concedes:

> *From within the system, a conflict of values is spreading confusion. The old police code symbolized by the "tough cop" is waning. The new ideology glorifying the "social scientist police officer" is meeting unexpected resistance. The external force of social change has set the police organization adrift in uncharted territory.*

Integrity! That was the common descriptor for Louis Berg Sr., the man who led the Detroit Police Department through it darkest days. "Big Louis" was old school, a policeman's policeman who not only went by the book, over the years he actually wrote the police department manual. The real-time experience that life's hard knocks presented an invaluable lesson to him growing up: "A black eye now and then is an equalizing spice for any education." The Berg family left an indelible mark on the Detroit Police Department, providing over fifty years of distinguished service and molding the department into one of the best crime fighting units in the country.

Big Louis was appointed superintendent after a massive scandal rocked the department. The tentacles of corruption even reached City Hall, sending Detroit Mayor Richard Reading to jail. Police Commissioner Frank Eamon went through the police department with a flame thrower, firing dozens of high-ranking commanders. Berg, who was one of the few found untainted by the graft, was asked to pick up the pieces. He was making swift work of it too until the '43 riot came along, causing yet another of life's black eyes.

Street educations that police absorb offer the highest and lowest of emotional extremes that are difficult to parallel in civilian life. Perhaps that is what attracted Berg's two sons, Louis (Little Louis) and James to the profession. The two boys would often accompany their father on weekends to the old Hunt Street Station where he was the district commander. Here they reveled in the atmosphere of good versus bad and right versus wrong, unleashing a torrent of curiosities against unsuspecting detectives who naively allowed themselves to be cornered. Big Louis, who never wanted his sons to become policemen, would then give his "pesky kids" a quarter and send them to the movies.

After thirty-three years of service, Berg Sr. would himself run philosophically afoul of a strong willed police commissioner. The new commissioner saw the police as a sociological extension of the community and had an extensive collection of graphs, charts and statistics to prove it. The old school Berg viewed the common criminal as a public enemy to society and not as a problem child. His refusal to budge on these principles that had been taught to him over three decades of police work ultimately forced him into retirement. They say lightning never strikes in the same place twice. Or does it?

Despite the elder Berg's protestations, the two boys did join the Detroit Police Department and began a meritorious rise through the ranks that would land them in their father's old office at 1300 Beaubien, the first brother combination to have achieved that distinction. But the "old Detroit" that their father presided over was quickly slipping away. In its place was an ever changing mass of social confusion that constantly took on new dimensions.

Changing of the Guard

George Edwards Jr. had all but given up on the city of Detroit after losing the mayoral election to Albert Cobo in 1949. He was too liberal even by Democratic standards. In 1956, when Governor "Soapy" Williams appointed Edwards to the Michigan Supreme Court, Edwards headed for Lansing and left Detroit behind for good, or so he thought.

Edwards pursued the world of jurisprudence because it afforded him the opportunity to impart his liberal socialist's views. Edwards was born and raised a Texan, where he witnessed more than his share of racist incidents. Now a transplant to Michigan, he understood the southern black frustrations and their perpetual thirst for justice.

Edward's father, George Edwards Sr., was a John Brown type character. A radical lawyer, he was once kidnapped by the KKK at gun point only to be released while his black c clients were beaten. Edwards quickly realized the outcome could easily been gruesomely different. His frequent defense of blacks throughout the Lone Star State continued to draw the ire of the KKK and only swift reflexes kept him one step ahead of their retribution.

The apple doesn't fall too far from the tree, as the saying goes. George Jr. shared his father's socialist views and his thirst for justice. Inculcated at Southern Methodist University and Harvard, he found himself ill-suited for the rigid Ivy League aristocracy which seemed to saturate the Cambridge air.

His meager upbringing had wedded him to a class that was grounded in the stark reality of poverty. His first trip to Harvard took him through New York City for the first time. While fascinated by the versatile uniqueness of New York, it was the bleakness of the garment district and tenements on the Lower East Side that sent a permanent shudder down his virtuous spine.

Edwards was in charge of Detroit's public housing during the Sojourner Truth crisis in 1942. He spearheaded the drive to keep Sojourner Truth a black housing project, a feat which won him much admiration in the black community. He latter became president of the Detroit Common Council, garnering more votes than any of his peers. Believing votes equated to popularity, he decided to run for mayor against Albert Cobo in 1949 and was soundly thrashed. For perhaps the first time in his life, Edwards was forced to question the reality of his convictions and ponder if society was capable of change.

Years later, as the newly elected Jerome Cavanagh began forming his cabinet in 1962, black Detroiters waited with baited breath for his critical choice of police commissioner. The Miriani crackdown had left the city on a jagged edge. Cavanagh would have to choose someone cut from a liberal cloth to demonstrate a different degree of professionalism. Ray Girardin, a Cavanagh confidant and loyal friend, suggested George Edwards, a ghost from Detroit's past who had been pounding a gavel in Lansing as the war drums of Detroit reverberated past his chamber.

With Cavanagh's approval Girardin approached his old friend Edwards with the proposition. Edwards recoiled at the suggestion. "Ray, Supreme Court judges don't resign to become police commissioners." Out of respect for Girardin, however, Edwards agreed to meet with Cavanagh under the proviso that it was merely out of inquisitive curiosity.

Edwards was immediately taken with the brash young mayor. Perhaps it was because in Cavanagh he saw a younger version of himself. Although Edwards was fourteen years his senior, the similarities were uncanny. Both had run for mayor of Detroit while the city was on the cusp of violence. Both fought for the underdog and both ran on a liberal, civil rights oriented platform. Edwards was greatly impressed with the Cavanagh's acute grasp of social and legal issues that still hovered menacingly over Detroit, issues the city had routinely chose to ignore in the past. While Edwards came away from the meeting without a hint of committal, his passion for the Motor City had been rekindled.

Edwards agonized over the decision. In the end it was his spirit of altruism and the flashbacks to 1943 riot which made his decision for him. "If Detroit did blow up in another race riot like the one we had lived through in 1943, I knew I could not live with the knowledge that I had been offered a chance to stop it - and had refused to try."

Word of Edwards's hiring sent a shudder through the Old Guard at 1300 Beaubien. Edwards's long sojourn in Lansing had not dulled his memory of black and white relations. While the black community may have rejoiced at his selection as police commissioner, the white community bristled. His long-standing reputation as a liberal maverick was also sure to meet a cold reception from a police department used to practicing old-fashioned police methods.

Above all, George Edwards was a crusader. He did not resign as a Supreme Court judge to become a token figurehead of a police department, giving rosy idealist speeches to the Rotary Club or presiding over Eagle Scout ceremonies. All his life he had wanted to mold Detroit into his version of a social Arcadia. His stinging mayoral defeat in 1949 left an open wound that had never healed. Now he sought closure. Edwards would go nose to nose with his police department for the next two years. Who would blink first?

Today's policemen are the heirs of that frightful legacy of ill will built up over many years - the man who walks the street bitter at the police may be harboring a grudge of forty years standing.

Detroit Public Library

Jerome Cavanagh and George Edwards

The Old Guard administered the basic cordialities to their new boss but as Edwards began to probe irregularities in police conduct, the resistance tightened. The two sides would be at loggerheads for the duration. Since the Old Guard would not budge, Edwards attempted to break up the senior leadership, but they would not go easily. From the onset, Edwards went into his new job anticipating major changes. Knowing the terrible friction this was bound to cause he vowed he would only head the department for two years so as not to hinder Cavanagh at election time. Edwards would not last two years though. The row he created throughout the department was so intense, he was forced to leave before the police department suffered a total meltdown.

Edwards wanted to take the department to a new level, away from the old-fashioned skull-splitting flatfoot who, while quelling one riot, may have planted the seeds for two more. This type of repressive law enforcement had been sanctioned by public opinion, but not by Edwards. But the public makeup had changed considerably since 1940. Edwards wanted a more progressive law that paralleled the societal changes that were begrudgingly taking hold across the country. He marveled at the British bobbies who didn't carry guns yet managed to keep the peace. As Edwards envisioned it, this was the Rubicon that the DPD had to cross. This transition, however, would come at a price, a price the Old Guard was not willing to pay.

But being a policeman is not easy. Going by the book makes it even harder. No manual can instruct an officer how to win the respect of people who hate you. No amount of schooling can stop the emotional upheaval that police incur on a daily, if not hourly, basis. After seeing legitimate arrests thrown out of court on technicalities, they seek redress by tilting the scales. The line between written rules and practical judgment becomes blurred.

The police feel that they deserve respect from the public. But the upper class looks down on them; the middle class seems to ignore them, as if they were part of the urban scenery; the lower class fears them. Even the courts often appear to be against them, making it more and more difficult to obtain convictions of criminals.

If George Edwards expected a showdown between his liberal ideologies and the Old Guard's dictums, it was not long in coming. In January of 1962, a black Detroiter named Willie Daniels was reported to have threatened a woman with his gun over a $20 debt. When the police arrived at the Daniels home, his wife said he was not there. The police found him hiding in the basement, handcuffed him and, unable to locate the gun, began a physical interrogation.

Two days later Edwards learned of the beating from an informant and recognized an opportunity to turn a negative into a positive. Edwards quite simply was not going to put up with rogue police officers who habitually beat up minorities for the sport of it. While the Berg's frowned on such things, the policeman's code of "We take care of our own" generally took precedent. Until now.

Edwards ordered a police trial board to convene which included himself, Superintendent Louis Berg and Chief of Detectives Walter Wyrod. Edwards' interrogation of the four officers in question revealed a host of contradictions. Even Wyrod was bewildered by the choppy testimonies. The city prosecutor was so ineffective Edwards believed he was in league with the police. The blue curtain of silence could not sufficiently explain away the extent of Daniels injuries, however.

Later that day, Berg and Wyrod tried to cajole Edwards into an acquittal, citing that any contradictions in evidence should be ruled in favor of the police. Edwards in turn demanded a guilty verdict. Wyrod strenuously voiced his objections. "Boss, we can't do that. If I voted these men guilty, my own men would never work for me again."

It was a 2-1 vote for acquittal, Edwards being the lone dissenter. Edwards had lost this battle but the war would rage on. In the months to come the animosity would grow as the Old Guard would do their utmost to push the pesky commissioner out of office. Edwards believed a deliberate slowdown in arrests was enacted to give the public impression his liberal programs were ineffective. Police were hesitant to make arrests because Edwards's liberal policies put them at risk for reprisal or dismissal by using Old Guard methods. Their beliefs were buttressed by the pessimistic views of well known Los Angeles police Chief William Parker, the anti-thesis of Edwards:

> ***I look back over almost thirty-five years in the police service, thirty-five years of dealing with the worst that humanity has to offer. I meet the failures of humanity daily, and I meet them in the worst possible context. It is hard to keep an objective viewpoint. But it is also hard for me to believe that our society can continue to violate all the fundamental rules of human conduct and expect to survive. I think I have to conclude that this civilization will destroy itself, as others have before it. That leaves, then, only one question – When?***

A true test of Edwards's dictum on patience and equality came on June 10, 1962 when the Nation of Islam (NOI) held a protest rally at Olympia Stadium. This was only one month after two NOI members were gunned down in Los Angeles by the police, creating a near riotous situation. Apparently Edwards's altruist reputation had not been lost on Malcolm X who invited Edwards not only to attend but to sit on stage with him and the other speakers. Edwards no doubt swallowed hard when he read the letter. He did not endorse the caustic racial banter of Malcolm X, and his presence on stage could be construed as acceptance of the speaker's message. Edwards tactfully recused himself, electing instead to sit in the audience.

Edwards's commanders counseled him against attending on the grounds they couldn't protect him if something went wrong. Edwards assured them he would be okay, but ordered all units in the area to be on alert just in case.

Malcolm X, to his credit, did not belittle Detroit's top cop but rather acknowledged Edwards's presence and thanked him for his legitimate attempts to provide a uniform type of justice across racial boundaries.

The gathering proved to be uneventful, but Edwards had set a precedent that he was willing to bridge the river of hate for any group desirous of crossing over. This included his own police department.

Walter Reuther Library

Detroit Police Commissioner George Edwards attends a Nation of Islam meeting at the Olympia in 1962 at the behest of Malcolm X. Detroit was not ready for olive branches, however. Animosities between the two races had accumulated again and it appeared that only a bloodletting could start the peace process.

Perhaps the last blizzard in the Cold War between the Old Guard and Edwards occurred in August of 1962 when the Detroit Police Department held its 36th annual Field Day exercises at Tiger Stadium before 35,000 enthusiastic Detroiters. Edwards driver was told the event started at 2:00 when in reality it started at 1:30. Edwards was certain this misinformation was intentional, knowing how foolish he would look showing up late. Edwards showed up unabashed and cheered on the DPD in a tug-of-war against Toronto's finest but this was the final insult.

While the police commissioner was not endowed with the power to hire or fire police personnel, he did have the power to transfer officers. Edwards informed Louis Berg that he was transferring the brothers to the traffic division, a clear demotion. The loss of face was too much for the Bergs and they opted into early retirement. Their surprised resignation shattered department morale and further enhanced the bull's-eye on Edwards. The Bergs were the ideological skeleton which held the Old Guard up and the old school constitution they had written was quickly being torn to shreds. Edwards had won the biggest fight of his life, but at what price?

With the departure of the Berg brothers, the police department began to spin out of control. Edwards became a marked man. His top commanders were against him, Detroiters who voted for Cobo in 1949 still disliked Edwards and there were persistent rumors that Cavanagh himself had had enough of the grumbling.

Word was out on the street that beat cops weren't doing their jobs. Constantly being under Edwards's microscope, many cops were hesitant to make sensitive arrests for fear of reprisal by the commissioner. Morale was at rock bottom. In early 1963 two white Detroit police officers were shot to death in less than a month by black civilians. Edwards "soft stance" on crime was blamed. In July, a well-known black prostitute was shot and killed by a white police officer after she slashed him with a knife. Edwards reviewed the case and announced the officer acted properly. Edwards was being vilified in black and white circles. Rumors swirled that Edwards was secretly seeking an out in the form of a federal judgeship. Whether Edwards felt his mission was accomplished or the walls were closing in on him, we will never know. In December of 1963 George Edwards traded in his shield for a gavel.

Detroit was not ready for George Edwards in 1949. Nor was it ready for him in 1962. He was an idealist whose time had not yet come and when it did he was out of position to guide Detroit. Edwards was great in the short term to tackle difficult social issues and attempt to set things straight, but in the long run he was causing more havoc to the police department than Detroit's criminals. He was simply too much, too soon. If George Edwards could not bring change to society, then society would force change any way it could.

By 1967 there were only a few officers left in the Detroit Police Department who were holdovers from the 1943 riot. One of them was Deputy Superintendent John Nichols, the number two man in the department.

A former army lieutenant colonel in World War II, Nichols was the old sage on the force, the hardnose, go to man who knew how the departmental wheels turned. He had seen it all in his twenty-five years on the force, including the surreal life on the infamous 12th Street:

When you work in a precinct like that (10th) I think you get a different savor than somebody from the outside. I've been down there (12th Street) on Saturday nights when I was working detective at the time and an outside department lieutenant was on a Ride Along Program, and he'd be terrified. And to me it was just an ordinary Saturday night. People lived on the street, people drank on the street, people conducted business on the street because the houses and the apartments were overcrowded and that was where they lived and once you had adapted to that, you didn't see that seething mass of humanity that somebody from the outside did.

Nichols counters accusations regarding the slow, initial response of the DPD at the start of the '67 riot:

Yeah, it was six o'clock on a Sunday morning. But you have to recognize that in running the department you gear the amount of people on the street to the crime picture, a protective crime picture. So six o'clock in the morning, normally in the summer all you see is some fisherman going out and a little old Polish lady going to six o'clock mass. That's about all you see. You don't need 450 or 500 police, and yet that was one of the major criticisms that we got. What do you mean, the city had signs, 144 square miles and only 190 cops but if you'd had 450 out there, people would say, 'What the hell you doing, wasting our money? I've got to have a scout car and two sections of riot unit watching me go to church? Why, what kind of a police department are you running?'

We've got the Commandos!”

The dreaded MTB Commandos, seen here drilling on Belle Isle, were the Detroit Police Departments final answer to riot control. By the time they made an appearance on the scene it could be widely assumed that any hope of a genteel or rational solution to quell the disturbance had long since been exasperated and more provocative methods would now be employed. Girardin was specifically brought in as commissioner to impart his common sense and humanity on what was widely known to be an overly aggressive police department.

A few years into his retirement, Ray Girardin reminisced about his first days as commissioner. “The Commandos were formed after the 1943 race riot, and were similar to the old police flyer, a car that used to be sent out to trouble with six cops who would just break every head in sight, no matter if it was a passerby or old ladies. Well, the Commandos were twelve or fourteen of the biggest men in the stationary traffic division (you had to be very tall for that assignment). But of course when I took over the police department they were all pushing sixty.”

Girardin later inquired, “Where do we keep our weaponry? I was told it was in the municipal garage. I wanted to see it, so we went over. There were heavy clubs - if you hit someone with one, you'd have killed him if you hit him in the ankle.” When Girardin asked to see the department plans to contain a riot he was told, “What riot plans? We've got the Commandos!”

60s Symbols

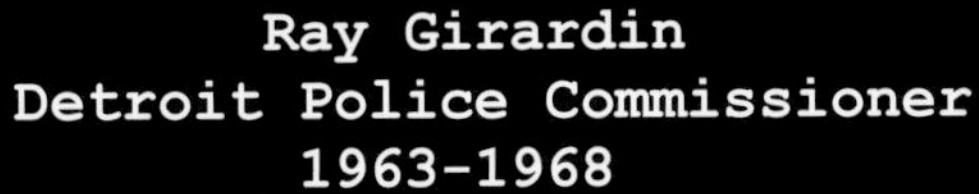
Ray Girardin
Detroit Police Commissioner
1963-1968

Ray Girardin was the personification of old Detroit. Born in the shadow of Most Holy Trinity Church in Corktown, his vast array of personal experiences made him an excellent choice to lead the Detroit Police Department through the turbulence of the 1960s.

Girardin had spent thirty years as a crime reporter for the defunct Detroit Times. As such, he knew the streets, the criminal element and how it functioned. He also understood the trials and tribulations of the average beat cop, often riding around with them in the midnight hours in an attempt to drive that point home.

It has been said that everyone's life revolves around one or two key events. For Girardin, that came his rookie year as a crime reporter when he was sent to cover a prison riot at the old Ohio State Penitentiary in Columbus. A fire of mysterious origin had started and 342 inmates died a gruesome death because the guards either couldn't or wouldn't open the cell doors. A riot ensued and Ray was the only reporter to get in and talk to the inmates who had taken over the prison. Ray built an immediate rapport with the prisoners, many of them hardened lifers, whose street sharp intuition told them Ray would not betray their confidences or skew their story. It was a characteristic that would define his entire life.

Ohio Historical Society

1930 Easter Sunday - The Ohio State Penitentiary goes up in flames costing 342 inmates their lives and a young Ray Girardin his innocence. Girardin was stunned by the macabre scene. Dead prisoners still locked in their cells with their heads buried in toilets in a vain attempt to avoid the deadly heat and smoke that hopelessly engulfed them. It was to emblazon the young reporter with a new perspective on civil rights for all sectors of society.

Prisoners ID the dead

Ohio Historical Society

The Bitter End

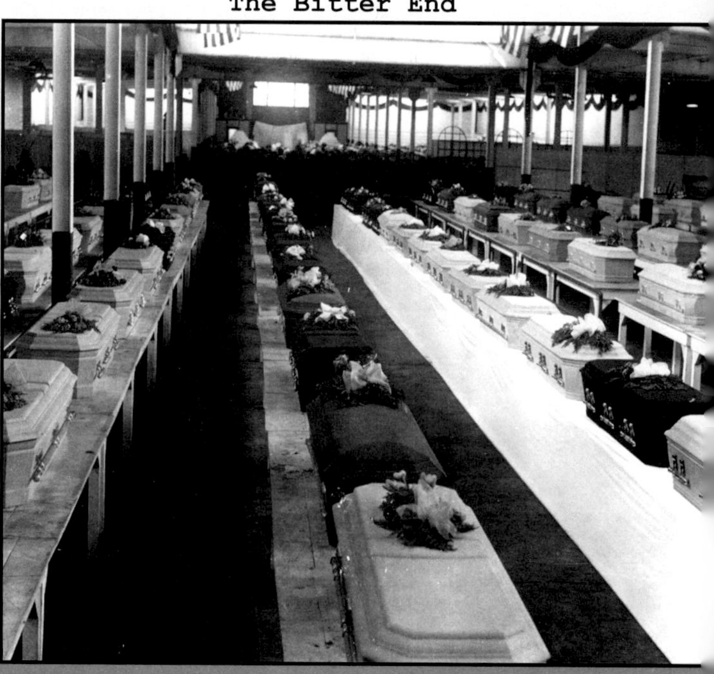

Ohio Historical Society

Girardin knew of the volatile atmosphere that hovered over Detroit and immediately sought to alleviate potential eruptions:

> ***We stopped this business of the police beating up people because they were black, and I say we stopped it because we were firing policemen that did it. And that had a hell of an effect. It was not uncommon, if a person, particularly a black, walked into a police station and complained about a policeman that he'd get the piss kicked out of him and get locked up.***
>
> ***It wasn't a race riot in the sense that blacks and whites were fighting each other, as in 1943. This was a revolution by black people over, I think, the system. I saw the same expressions on the faces of some of the looters hurrying away with an armful of stuff they probably couldn't even use that I had seen on the faces of convicts in prison riots I had covered. It was a wild, glazed look. I suppose it's what is meant by "going berserk". In prison riots they looted and took things they didn't want and burned and destroyed things that were meaningful to them - their gymnasium, the library, the auditorium. And so maybe there's an analogy between prisoners in a prison and prisoners in a ghetto.***

As to why the 'no-shoot' order was given, Girardin responded:

> ***Well, my position very simply was that I didn't want to commit murder. And I don't think if you kill a person, under circumstances like that, because he's stealing a pair of shoes that don't fit him or a television - they can be replaced, but you know, life can't.***

1971 - A lone policeman leaves a final remembrance to his former boss.

RAY GIRARDIN 1902-1971

Jerome Cavanagh:

A Last Flicker of Hope

Louis Miriani **Mayor: 1957-1962**

The sudden death of Mayor Cobo in September of 1957 thrust Common Council President Louis C. Miriani into his office. As is often the case under such circumstances, Miriani received the sympathy vote and was overwhelmingly "reelected" at the end of the year. It must be said of Miriani that he was aware of the smoldering racial problems in the city and like Jeffries, put forth sporadic efforts to set things straight. Also like his predecessors he was put under unyielding pressure by the white majority to tow the segregated line.

Mayor Miriani got caught up in the same predicament that haunted his predecessors: do what was right and create more public housing for the black community or yield to his segregation minded constituents. Initially he tried to please both blacks and whites, an impossibility. Although backed by formidable political machines such as the UAW, the Detroit newspapers and Henry Ford II, he wound up alienating voters in both racial spheres. In the end he followed his constituents and, with the black population now at a viable 30 percent, his decision would cost him the 1962 election.

Walter Reuther Library

Mayor Miriani (above) presides over the Common Council, all except one of which were white despite the city's nearly 30 percent black population. But the winds of change were blowing through every major urban area in the country and Detroit was no exception. While urban renewal of the 1950s may have brought significant physical change to Detroit, the 1960s would usher in the corresponding social upheaval.

Some black families who had moved up from the South had now been here for generations and were beginning to build a power base. Charles Diggs Sr. moved to Detroit from Mississippi in 1913 and became a state congressman in 1938. Following in his footsteps, son Charles Diggs Jr. became the first black U.S. congressman from Michigan in 1954. A Fisk University graduate and former Tuskegee Airman, Diggs paved the way for future black politicians in Detroit.

Charles C. Diggs Jr.

Detroit's Changing Population

Year	Total Population	Black Population	% Black
1910	465 766	5 741	1.2
1920	993 675	40 838	4.1
1930	1 568 662	120 066	7.7
1940	1 623 452	149 119	9.2
1950	1 849 568	300 506	16.2
1960	1 670 144	482 229	28.9
1970	1 511 482	660 428	44.5

The Miriani Crackdown

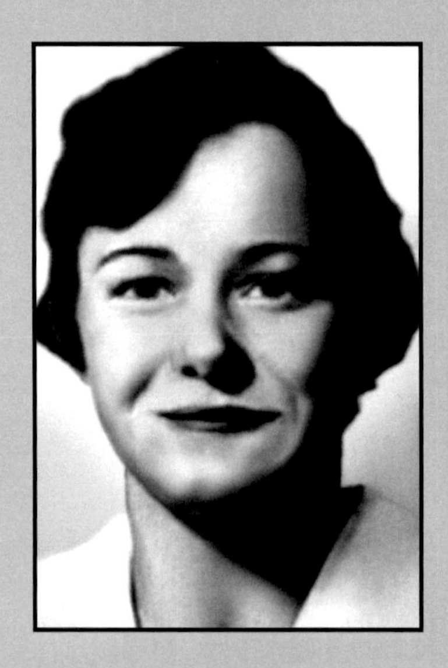

Marilyn Donahue

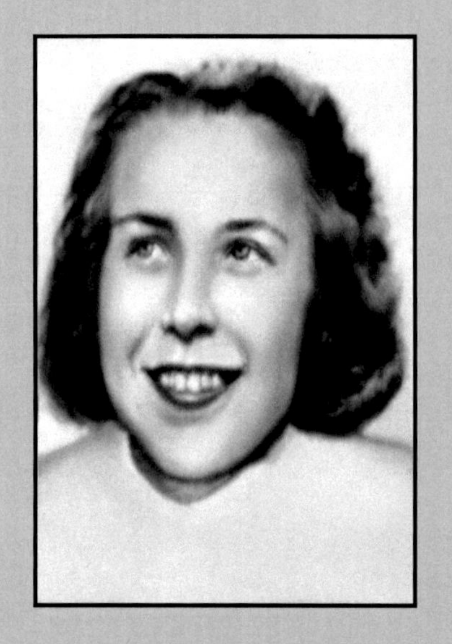

Betty James

Detroiters Marilyn Donahue and Betty James never met each other in their all too brief and tragic lives but their names would be inextricably linked together in getting a young mayor elected and changing Detroit forever.

In the winter of 1960 Detroit witnessed a surge of criminal activity which included the brutal murders of Donahue and James. At 8:00 a.m. on the morning of December 7th, the twenty-three year old Donahue was to unlock her place of employment but instead found the door already unlocked. As she walked in she was startled to see a man at her desk who then lunged at her with a knife, stabbing her numerous times. After stealing her wallet he fled the scene. Donahue's dying description of her attacker revealed he was black, twenty-five to thirty-five years old, 5'5" to 5'8", and he wore dark, shabby clothes. She recalled that he had been in before looking for odd jobs.

The twenty-six year old James, a mother of three, met her fate later in the month when on the 27th of December she attempted to walk the four short blocks from Woodward to Children's Hospital where she worked. She never made it. She was mugged by a man who bludgeoned her with a four pound brass bar and then robbed her, fleeing the scene when witnesses sounded the alarm. They described him as a heavyset black man about thirty-five years old and 180 pounds. Betty James died shortly thereafter from massive head wounds.

It was the deadliest month in Detroit since 1930 and authorities were unable to explain the dramatic increase in violence. White society recoiled in terror at the violent deaths of such promising young lives. The Detroit News, equally appalled, posted a $5,000 reward for information leading to a conviction in either case. Both deaths received daily front page coverage in the Detroit News and crime tips poured in from concerned, outraged citizens.

At Miriani's behest, Detroit Police Commissioner Herbert Hart called for a mandatory six day work week for police and an aggressive dragnet was laid down in an attempt to turn the killers. Over 1,000 suspects were interrogated, periodically netting well-respected black citizens. The black community was outraged by the wanton seizure and arrest of "anyone black who wasn't were they were supposed to be." Betty James's assailant, an ex-convict, was eventually arrested. Marilyn Donahue's murderer was never found. The daggers of 1943 had come unsheathed once again as racial tensions escalated to the point of violence.

Herbert W. Hart
Detroit Police Commissioner
1960-1962

The embattled city now lumbered through the oppressive summer of '61, an election year, and the candidates were now lining up around the corner to take shots at the jowly incumbent. One of them was an unknown lawyer, fiercely proud of his Irish heritage and just brash enough to think he could beat the system. He was Jerome Patrick Cavanagh, a native Detroiter who had never run for anything, but with the cloud of discontent hovering over the city, he believed his lack of a political background would actually work to his advantage. The Miriani Crackdown, as this sordid episode became known as, would be Cavanagh's Excalibur.

While Cavanagh lacked experience, there was no doubt the University of Detroit graduate had a sharp mind. He zeroed in on Miriani's vacillation of the issues, the sorry fiscal state of the city and the racial unrest that kept metastasizing like an unchecked cancer. If elections were decided by endorsements, Miriani would have won in a landslide. He could reel off a host of power brokers who stood behind him. As a result, the phlegmatic Miriani put little effort into campaigning. It was an oversight he would soon come to regret.

As the November election loomed, the black community unified for a solution. Now in search of someone to champion their cause, they began an aggressive campaign to oust the incumbent, sporting buttons with the cynical motto "Phooie on Louis." As luck would have it, a young Irish upstart had entered the race and took his dictums into the black community, espousing long-absent civil liberties and new progressive ideologies. Cavanagh could do no wrong. On election night he was rewarded with a 40,000 vote drubbing of his opponent.

Walter Reuther Library

Election night (November 1961) - The newly elected Jerome Cavanagh addresses both stunned and jubilant supporters after learning of his upset victory. He had done what they said couldn't be done. He had caught lighting in a bottle and swept the endorsement-laden incumbent into the dustbin of history. Like the tragic Shakespearean character Julius Caesar, Cavanagh's zenith would rise to incredible heights and his fall would be just as spectacular.

A Last Flicker of Hope

Walter Reuther Library

1962 - With the highest hopes of the city of Detroit, Jerome Patrick Cavanagh takes the oath of office at the tender age of thirty-three. A little known lawyer, his stunning upset of the incumbent Miriani sent a message to Detroiters that for the first time blacks had power at the voting booth. Detroit staged a remarkable comeback under Cavanagh. Regarded as a Kennedy type figure, his youth and insight represented the new breed of politician emerging across America.

Amidst the tumult of the 1960s America found itself in one of the most difficult transitions in its history. Since the tragic fallout of the Civil War, America wandered aimlessly in search for a more progressive and egalitarian society.

Jerry Cavanagh was reared during the agony of the Great Depression and like so many others the lean times and the charismatic Franklin Roosevelt made a lasting impression on him. Roosevelt was the hero of the Depression era because he cared about the little guy, a lesson the young Cavanagh took to heart.

Detroit's "boy mayor" entered office at the height of the civil rights movement, taking over a city that LOOK magazine once sardonically rasped "was noted for three things: automobiles, bad race relations and civic sloth." Such was Detroit's image in 1961. Cavanagh would thrust Detroit into the national limelight as an exemplar of social progress and tranquility amidst an oasis of public revolt. As one city after another went up in flames during the rebellious 1960s, leaders across the country held Detroit up high as the one city, because of its enterprising young mayor, that would not riot.

Cavanagh made promises to clean up the city, not only in a physical sense but putting to rest the numerous hot political potatoes he inherited. The city was $19 million in the red when Cavanagh took office with the stark reality of a $34 million deficit looming by summertime.

Cavanagh lobbied the state legislature for a state income tax (enacted in 1964) to no avail. With no other recourse he now targeted working Detroiters to make up the difference by enacting a 1 percent city income tax. He especially drew the ire of suburban commuters who were forced to pay the toll but the city's nagging debt was retired

Walter Reuther Library

The new $54 million Cobo Hall was already awash in controversy. Intended to regain Detroit's once vibrant but now flagging convention business, various unions held conventioneers hostage by inflicting their none-too-generous terms upon them. The result, conventioneers took their dollars and went elsewhere. Unlike his predecessor, Cavanagh was free from the foibles of the union because none of them backed him during the election. Henceforth, a system was enacted in which a single union would conjointly assign work with a city administrator present. Union officials were barred from contacting exhibitors. Cobo Hall began to thrive.

The luck of the Irish seemed to beam down on Cavanagh in the early years. The terrible Eisenhower recession, which wreaked havoc on Detroit for several years, seemed to blow itself out by Cavanagh's first year in office. Detroit began displaying record production of cars in 1962. It seemed the Cavanagh Camelot could do nothing wrong. But by 1967, unemployment would revisit Detroit. In the months preceding the riot, 12th Street would see some 15 percent of its inhabitants unemployed, almost 30 percent of those under the age of twenty-five, the very group which led the rioting.

Walter Reuther Library

1962 - Cavanagh had Washington's ear from the onset. President Kennedy, Cavanagh and new Detroit Police Commissioner George Edwards share a lighter moment during a White House visit.

Like many politicians of the 1960s, Kennedy and his successor Johnson could no longer ignore the burgeoning civil rights issues. Kennedy was a politician first and a moralist a distant second. Subsequently he endorsed the civil rights movement with considerable trepidation. Civil rights leaders grew weary of his quick clichés and started to question his resolve. Kennedy sounded off about the indignities blacks had incurred over their history but also knew that American attitudes, while willing to change, must be changed slowly.

The civil rights movement was moving too fast for white America but too slow for black America. It was a tragic double-edged sword. Edwards was the key appointment to the Cavanagh machine. He would attempt to sooth the city's fractured relations with the black community. It was a daunting task for which he would harness little support.

Nationally, for better or for worse, Cavanagh would soon have to deal with a president cut from a completely different cut of cloth than Kennedy. A frequent visitor of Washington, Cavanagh ran into the same problem that Dr. King experienced. With Kennedy, you got to talk for an hour. With Johnson, you got to listen for an hour. Nevertheless, Johnson had a knack for making things happen.

A City Upon a Hill

(Left) In 1630, Puritan leader Jonathon Winthrop sailed for America to become governor of the Massachusetts Bay Colony. He preached to his followers about the high Puritanical standards they must uphold as an example to others: "We shall be like a city upon a hill and all eyes shall be upon us."
Jerry Cavanagh envisioned Detroit as the modern day city upon a hill and President Johnson's Model Cities Program was the mechanism Cavanagh needed to make his vision become a reality.
(Below - May 1964) President Lyndon Johnson unveils his Great Society at the University of Michigan commencement. Two main spokes in the Great Society wheel were the War on Poverty and the Model Cities Program, both of which would figure prominently into Detroit's short but remarkable rebirth.

Walter Reuther Library

"Your imagination, your initiative and your indignation will determine whether we build a society where progress is the servant of our needs, or a society where old values and new visions are buried under unbridled growth. For in your time we have the opportunity to move not only toward the rich society and the powerful society, but upward to the Great Society.

For better or for worse, your generation has been appointed by history to deal with those problems and to lead America toward a new age. You have the chance never before afforded to any age. You can help build a society where the demands of morality, and the needs of the spirit, can be realized in the life of the nation."

- LBJ

Cavanagh's Detroit - The Model City

While the Civil Rights Movement was anchored in the South in an attempt to defeat Jim Crow, there were just as many inequities to be found in the North. Northern prejudice behaved more like a chameleon, having the uncanny ability to blend into the background and not be easily detected. This included job discrimination and redlining practices in real estate.

Franklin Roosevelt was one of the initial trail blazers for civil rights in the 1930s and 40s. Kennedy, Johnson and Cavanagh were the first of his students to come to power and carry his Roosevelt's New Deal banner.

Cavanagh's tenure would be closely linked with President Johnson's Great Society. Johnson's War on Poverty was aimed at assisting urban children to obtain better housing, health care, education and job opportunities. Cavanagh had already launched a similar program called TAP (Total Action against Poverty). Johnson's added federal muscle would give TAP some tiger-like teeth to attack with.

LBJ's Model Cities Program sprouted up from a rather incongruous kernel. It was the Watts Riot during the summer of '65 that shocked Johnson into action. Johnson, like many others, was chagrined by the behavior of black militants. Like no other president before him, he attempted to free the black man from the bondages of poverty and prejudice by passing groundbreaking civil rights legislation, only to see one American city after another ignited by the flame of rebellion. Many whites who were initially sympathetic to the black cause would eventually turn a cold shoulder to civil rights, unable to differentiate between altruist and anarchist.

In September of 1965, Cavanagh, along with UAW president Walter Reuther, prodded President Johnson into selecting a pilot city to shower with federal grants and demonstrate to the nation how a large urban area can be rehabilitated physically and socially when properly equipped. Not coincidently, the two gently cajoled Johnson into believing that Detroit would be a good candidate.

Originally dubbed the "Demonstration Cities Program" (a very poor choice of words in this era of massive counter demonstrations, many people completely misunderstood its intentions), later renamed the Model Cities Program, it was provided with an initial fund of $400 million per year. Its focus was to eradicate slums and replace them with low to moderate cost housing, attack inner-city poverty by bolstering social programs, providing jobs, health care and recreational facilities, all of which would help keep young people off the street and learning instead of rioting. Cities that applied to become a much heralded Model City had to demonstrate their need and have a workable plan to carry out their request.

Walter Reuther Library

Cavanagh presents LBJ with the Spirit of Detroit symbol. It proved to be a relationship of mutual advantage. Cavanagh needed federal money to help solve Detroit's social ills and Johnson needed salesmen for his Great Society. The two got along swimmingly for a while but as the monster of Vietnam continued to rear its ugly head the relationship grew cold. Cavanagh came to oppose the war and by the time of the riot had been openly denouncing it, much to the dismay of his president.

Cavanagh's persuasive powers and determination enabled Detroit to hustle up some $360 million federal dollars to fuel his anti-poverty programs. Only Chicago, with the powerful Mayor Daley and New York with Mayor Lindsey managed to wheedle more out of Washington. Detroit's boy mayor was rapidly making a name for himself.

By 1966, Detroit had become a Model City not only in name but most certainly in stature. Detroit had gained national acclaim as a truly progressive city in a time when many were still regressing. By placing respected liberals in charge of the police department, capturing the lion's share of War on Poverty funds and hosting the highly vaunted March for Freedom, Detroit was enjoying its time on top of the national pedestal. Detroit had become the "city upon a hill, for all eyes to see."

Library of Congress

1965 - With the conflagration of Watts still seared into everyone's mind, big city mayors began preparing for the worst. The Detroit police department's primary riot busting apparatus for decades were the Commandos. Their ferocious reputation, which was well earned, often caused more trouble than it quelled. Cavanagh knew all about the overly aggressive methods of the Commandos and sought to organize a derivative of them that had the same hardened toughness but was not bent on proving it to society.

(Above) Cavanagh watches the newly formed Tactical Mobile Unit of the Detroit Police Department drilling. The special quality differentiating them from the Commandos was that they could absorb physical and verbal abuse (i.e., spitting, rocks, obscenities) without reacting. It was a necessary adjustment in the boiling ghettos across the country that were ignited one after another from routine police incidents that quickly ratcheted out of control. If trouble came to Detroit, Cavanagh believed Detroit would be ready.

The Spirit of '66

Walter Reuther Library

Beginning of the end - The Cavanagh Express came to a screeching halt in 1966.

By 1966 Cavanagh was at his political apex. Accordingly he decided to challenge popular former Governor Soapy Williams for the Democratic nomination of Michigan's U.S. Senate seat in the fall of 1966. Cavanagh's name had been bantered about as a potential gubernatorial candidate or possibly even the Irish Catholic successor to JFK. "On a clear day you could see the White House" was the chatter around City Hall. But in the wink of an eye, the dream was vaporized. Williams won in a landslide. Cavanagh was routed even in the black precincts of Detroit which were responsible for his previous success. It may very well have been that Detroiters did not want to lose the popular mayor or they resented him trying to leave. The fresh young face that took Detroit by storm just five years earlier had aged noticeably. It would get considerably worse. Cavanagh's wife was suing him for separate maintenance, a city council member started a recall petition against him, and in July of '67 his city had a date with destiny. For Detroit's Caesar, the Ides of March had finally come.

Walter Reuther Library

Cavanagh poses in front of the city shield which was enacted after Detroit burned to the ground in 1805. Perhaps the city motto, which was borne of the fire, is an ironic epitaph for his career, a career that seemed inextricably linked to the fate of his city.

Speramus Meliora (We shall rise from the ashes)
Resurcet Cineribus (We hope for better things ahead)

Jerome Patrick Cavanagh 1929-1979

It was the best of times, it was the worst of times, it was the age of wisdom, it was the age of foolishness, it was the epoch of belief, it was the epoch of incredulity, it was a season of light, it was a season of darkness, it was the spring of hope, it was the winter of despair, we had everything before us, we had nothing before us.

A Tale of Two Cities

60s Symbols

George Wilcken Romney
Governor - State of Michigan
1962-1969

George Romney, the 23rd governor of the State of Michigan, always exhibited that special quality that is reserved for but a few, of being larger than life itself. Perhaps it was because he was uniquely honest and refused to compromise his integrity for the sake of his own personal aggrandizement, a rarity in the shabby world of politics. Romney left a rich legacy of leadership, public service and volunteerism while displaying the highest standards of character during a decade when moral debauchery and lax responsibilities were the norm. Romney cast a long shadow over the State of Michigan which can still be seen today.

Walter Reuther library

1927 - Nineteen-year-old George Romney preaching the Mormon gospel in Trafalgar Square, London. Required by his Mormon faith to commit to an overseas mission, Romney was sent to Britain where he preached from city to city, including the notorious slums of Glasgow. Here he witnessed firsthand the unmistakable dearth of poverty which wrenched men's spirits from their souls until only a faithless desperation remained. His missionary service left him with a lifelong concern for the spiritual and physical welfare of the downtrodden in society.

Romney took over the fledgling American Motors Corporation in 1953 when it was hemorrhaging over $5 million a year. His insistence on building a compact car was bold indeed for the '50s when gas was a quarter and guzzlers were in vogue. Within five years AMC was $20 million in the black. The smashing success of the Rambler sent the Big Three reeling and Romney to the Michigan Governor's mansion.

Following his inaugural speech on the steps of the state capital, a surprised Romney accepts congratulations from a rather unlikely source.

Fellow governor and Republican comrade Ronald Reagan demonstrates for Romney the finer points of tossing and catching jellybeans.

1965
Romney greets LBJ, Lady Bird and Hubert Humphrey at the presidential inauguration.

Romney's '68 run for the Republican presidential nomination against Nixon ran aground when both Reagan and Nelson Rockefeller threw their hats in the ring. The combination of the three proved too much to overcome and Romney withdrew his nomination.

Romney, a staunch Mormon his whole life, was highly respected because he lived what he preached. He never smoked, used alcohol or foul language:

Unless God-fearing men and women get into public life to do a job for the people, they will leave the field to the self-servers, the demagogues, the power hungry and the cheap connivers and the people will suffer as a result.

GEORGE ROMNEY 1907-1995

MLK
Pays
a
Visit

Library of Congress

The Supreme Court of 1896 twisted the 14th Amendment into allowing "separate but equal" facilities for blacks and whites. But when viewed in the cold, harsh reality of history, it was anything but equal. Jim Crow segregation laws were more than just separating the races. They were a mort0al blow of indignity that would cascade over the generations until the dam of tolerance could hold no more.

In 1868 the Republican Congress passed the 14th Amendment to the Constitution, which granted former slaves citizenship:

No State shall make or enforce any law which shall abridge the privileges or immunities of citizens of the United States.

The year 1875 would represent the high-water mark of congressional effort to provide an egalitarian society. In this year they passed the Civil Rights Act of 1875:

That all persons shall be entitled to full and equal enjoyment of the accommodations, advantages, facilities, and privileges of inns, public conveyances on land or water, theaters, and other places of public amusement.

By 1883, however, the legal mood had changed as the Radical Republicans were being voted out of office. The Supreme Court of 1883 struck down the Civil Rights Act of 1875, observing that blacks should assume "the rank of mere citizens" and would no longer be the "special favorite of the laws." Justice John Harlan was the lone dissenter:

It is the duty of government in its dealings with the people to mete out equal and exact justice to all.

In 1896 a black man named Homer Plessy intentionally sat in a rail car deemed only for whites to bring attention to this constitutional grievance. He was arrested and his case went before the Supreme Court.

In the landmark case of *Plessy vs. Ferguson*, the Supreme Court had a chance to set things straight once and for all but instead chose to wash their hands of the matter and henceforth it was up to the individual states to legislate segregation.

The majority (8-1) stated that the Constitution

> ***...could not have been intended to abolish distinctions based upon color, or to enforce social, as distinguished from political equality, or a commingling of the two races upon terms unsatisfactory to either.***

Again, as in 1875, Justice John Harlan was the lone voice of reason:

> ***Our Constitution is color-blind, and neither knows nor tolerates classes among citizens. In respect of civil rights, all citizens are equal before the law. The present decision will not only stimulate aggressions, more or less brutal and irritating, upon the admitted rights of colored citizens, but will encourage the belief that it is possible, by means of state enactments, to defeat the beneficent purposes which the people of the United States had in view when they adopted the recent amendments of the Constitution.***

With the *Plessy* decision, the Supreme Court paved the way for a legal segregation of the races and thus Jim Crow. The hard-fought gains blacks and northern Republicans had fought for were gone in an instant. If the highest, most powerful court in the land would not buttress the Constitution, surely no on else would. The Democratic Party, regarded in those days as the party of White Supremacy, had regained control of the South.

With the war drums of Birmingham, Alabama still resonating through the conscience of America, fate would now shift Detroit into the national spotlight. On this one-hundredth anniversary of the Emancipation Proclamation, the country again found itself embroiled in a civil war. For years there had been an undeclared civil war in the Deep South. No, this was not Shiloh or Vicksburg revisited but Albany, Little Rock, Montgomery, Birmingham and scores of other towns where victims of racial prejudice became faceless martyrs of a contrived system of justice.

Now the southern heat would hover over Detroit as the Reverend Martin Luther King Jr. arrived on June 23rd, 1963 to lead a massive protest rally down heralded Woodward Avenue to bring attention to the plight of black southerners and racial injustice everywhere. It would be called the March for Freedom and Detroit's tarnished image would receive a much needed shot of esteem.

There was another anniversary to be observed in Detroit on this hot summer day, albeit a shameful one. It was (not coincidentally) the 20th anniversary of the '43 riot which put Detroit in a spotlight of disgrace around the world. Local Reverend C.L. Franklin, the man who organized the march, felt that the '43 riot was a point of reference: "The same basic, underlying causes for the disturbance are still present. The difference now will be the way our protests and dissatisfaction will be made known."

King, whose base of operations was centered in the South, began testing northern waters for racial intolerance. What better place to start than Detroit, which had a notorious past but, under Cavanagh, an encouraging future.

MLK's Six Principles of Nonviolence

1) **Nonviolence is a way of life for courageous people.**

2) **Nonviolence seeks to win friendship and understanding.**

3) **Nonviolence seeks to defeat injustice not people.**

4) **Nonviolence holds that suffering can educate and transform.**

5) **Nonviolence chooses love instead of hate.**

6) **Nonviolence believes that the universe is on the side of justice.**

Library of Congress

I told my child about the color bar after she begged to be taken to Fun Town, an Atlanta amusement park that she'd seen advertised on television. I knew they did not admit Negroes. But I told her that, even though she could not go, she was as good as anybody else. It isn't easy to explain such things to a seven-year-old.

MLK Pays a Visit

Walter Reuther Library

The 1963 March for Freedom - Detroit

Some 125,000 people participated in this historic demonstration down Woodward Avenue to draw attention to civil rights infractions across the country. It was the largest civil rights march to date.

The march was seen as a standard of civility for civil rights marches. Under the Cavanagh administration Detroit would become known as the Model City because of their commitment to advance civil rights and negate aberrant behavior towards minorities. Detroit would be one of the few northern cities that embraced King: "I've faced so many mobs of hate in the South, this was kind of a relief." Subsequent visits to other northern cities reconfirmed King's suspicions that the hate was nationwide.

It was ironic that in this year of 1963, the 100th anniversary of the Emancipation Proclamation that freed the slaves, blacks were still fighting for fundamental rights such as voting and education.

The March for Freedom was originally intended as a show of support for those in Birmingham where an ominous cloud still hovered over the beleaguered city. But blacks from all walks of life were now for the first time stepping up en masse to voice their disapproval about latent civil rights progress.

Again King would offer a fortuitous hint in regards to the impending race riots: "The shape of the world does not afford us the luxury of an anemic democracy. The price that this nation must pay for the continued oppression and exploitation of the Negro, or any other minority, is the price of its own destruction. The hour is late. The clock of destiny is clicking off and we must act now before it is too late." In a parting shot at the black militant groups who espoused violence and separatism, King sternly warned the crowd, "Black supremacy is as bad as white supremacy."

King, now thirty-four, found himself at the apex of his career. His keen political calculus enabled him to stage the coup of Birmingham that had an unparalleled influence on a previously unsympathetic white community. But King found, much to his dismay, that as he traveled to various northern cities there was often resentment from local civil rights leaders that he was interfering. In actuality, mayors and city council members simply had no confidence in many local leaders and hoped King's great presence could soothe the choppy waves.

On this brilliant 23rd day of June, throngs of people filled Woodward from sidewalk to sidewalk, anxiously awaiting the arrival of their civil rights champion. The King entourage, which had flown in from Washington after a conference with President Kennedy, had arrived late. The parade was delayed, with great difficulty, until King could be transported. As Cavanagh waited at Woodward and Adelaide, a car pulled up. As King got out, the crowd surged towards him: "There he is!" everyone shouted.

As police officials escorted King over to an anxious Mayor Cavanagh to begin the march, Cavanagh at once linked arms with King and yelled as the masses surged towards them, "Hang on!" They tried to talk en route to Cobo Hall but the din of the crowd made it nearly impossible.

Hundreds of curious onlookers lined the sidewalks as the march progressed down Woodward, their idleness singling them out. One marcher waved them over: "Come on, get out here. You ain't in Mississippi. You don't have to be afraid here."

As two of the many fascinated spectators continued to watch the endless sea of marchers pass by, one said in bewilderment, "You know, Detroit will never be the same after this day."

Photos courtesy Walter Reuther Library

Some of the dignitaries leading the march included former Governor John Swainson, Walter Reuther, Reverend C.L. Franklin (hat), Mayor Jerome Cavanagh (2nd row) and in the middle waving, the Reverend Martin Luther King Jr.

There were no incidents during the march. Detroit Police Commissioner George Edwards, in reference to King's traumatic civil rights marches in Birmingham only a month previous, promised King, "You'll see no dogs and fire hoses here."

Walter Reuther Library

At the conclusion of the march, Martin Luther King addresses the capacity crowd of 16,000 at Cobo Hall in a rousing forty-eight minute speech. Two months later King would give his famous "I Have a Dream" speech on the mall in Washington D.C., yet his Detroit speech was really a sounding board for that event. Many of the phrases he used in Washington were initially used on his Detroit audience, which as can be seen above, hung on his every word:

I have a dream this afternoon, that there will be a day we will no longer face the atrocities that Emmitt Till and Medgar Evers had to face. That all men can live in dignity.

I have a dream this afternoon that my four little children will not come up in the same young days that I had to come up in. They will be judged on the content of their character and not the color of their skin.

I have a dream this afternoon that one day right here in Detroit a Negro will be able to buy a house or rent a house anywhere that their money will carry them.

I have a dream this evening that one day we will recognize the words of Jefferson that all men are created equal, that they are endowed by their Creator with certain inalienable rights that among these are life, liberty and the pursuit of happiness.
Yes, I have a dream this afternoon.

Library of Congress

The peak of the Civil Rights Movement occurred in 1963 when King achieved a hat trick of victories. In the spring he won over many with his leadership in Birmingham. In June he soothed the Motor City by seemingly banishing the ghosts of the '43 riot and paving the way for Cavanagh's Model City. (Above) His reached his apex in August with the march on the mall in Washington D.C. By the summer of 1964, however, the mood of the country would change drastically. Riots would plague the East Coast and continue unabated across the country for five more years. Any hard fought gains King had made would be nullified by the riotous destruction of America's big cities.

The Civil Rights Kaleidoscope

The generations that grew up with computers and cappuccino machines are only vaguely aware of the name Martin Luther King. Many are totally oblivious to the kaleidoscope of characters who also endeavored to advance civil rights. Some were direct disciples of King's who echoed and supported his nonviolent philosophy. Others, often referred to as militants, were quite the antithesis. Their accumulation of negative experiences vectored them away from King and into the dark, violent, world which they erroneously believed was the only way to make progress. It was a monumental task for King just to win over the white factions, but with so many black militants pulling in the opposite direction, it was virtually impossible.

As the 1960s progressed, the concept of Black Power became a rallying cry for those who sought to split the civil rights movement between those who trumpeted the courts and ballot boxes as a means for advancement and those who that violence was the only way. On the shoulders of Dr. King fell the task of bringing together racist blacks and whites, moderate blacks and whites, political leaders at all levels and religious leaders who controlled the communities. It was a near impossible assignment, but if anyone could pull it off it was Martin Luther King.

The Civil Rights Movement was like a great recipe with so many different ingredients. While the objective of civil rights was the same--achieving equality--the conflicting philosophies on how to best advance the cause grew more and more divergent as the '60s progressed. As the riots continued to grow in number and intensity, the withdrawal of white financial and moral support for civil rights groups became increasingly significant.

Most black militants scoffed at the concept of integration and instead preached separatism. They were King's Achilles' heel and proved tougher to deal with than the radical whites he was trying to win over.

One of the more outspoken black militants, H. Rap Brown, had a real faculty for fomenting anger amongst frustrated ghetto youth: "The rebellions will continue and escalate. Violence is necessary. It is as American as cherry pie. We will take an eye for an eye and a life for a life." Brown reveled at crossing the line: "If you give me a gun and tell me to shoot my enemy, I might just shoot Lady Bird."

It was impossible for King to distance himself from the rhetoric or actions of the militants. For King it was a battle he would never win. All he could do was rationalize and pray the seeds of logic might take root: "They have a strange kind of dream of a black nation within the larger nation. At times the public expressions of this group have bordered on a new kind of race hatred and an unconscious advocacy of violence."

Detroit Reverend C.L. Franklin – A King Disciple

Born in Sunflower County, Mississippi in 1915, Clarence Laverne Franklin grew up experiencing firsthand the hatred of the Jim Crow South. But the lessons of hatred were not to embitter him: rather than hate back he sought to extinguish these flames by preaching the gospel. It turned out to be an incredible journey for him and for all those who met up with him along the way. Finally settling on Detroit's West Side, he became a legendary preacher who for decades lectured his congregation on the necessities of fortitude and forgiveness.

He knew at the age of fourteen that he wanted to be a preacher and make a difference. The sharecropping life, with its endless weary hours of backbreaking work, was not for him. Franklin knew well the bitter hand of discrimination. Mississippi was the bastion of Jim Crow, removed from slavery in name only. "I knew segregation in the raw," Franklin recalled. "I vividly remember walking to school and being passed by a bus full of white kids, who shouted such abuses as "nigger" and "coon" at me from the windows. I feel very fortunate in having those experiences because I learned a great deal." Instead of reciprocating this hatred, he channeled his energy into learning and preaching the gospel, a skill at which he soon became formidable.

He was a circuit preacher in Mississippi, meaning he preached at a different church each Sunday. Owing to the ruralness of the area, Franklin found himself the pastor of four churches at the same time. He would travel by Model T or horse-drawn wagon, whatever it took to get the Word out.

Franklin came to Detroit in 1946 to become pastor of the New Bethel Baptist Church which in those days was on the corner of Hastings and Willis in Black Bottom. When the city took over the property under eminent domain for urban renewal in 1961, it gave the parish $211,000 for the building even though the church had invested $250,000.

Reverend Franklin moved his church to the West Side After a brief stint on 12th Street, his New Bethel Church wound up on Linwood Avenue.

In an effort to reach greater audiences, Reverend Franklin began recording his sermons on albums which sold in the millions. As a result he was known as "The Pastor of Millions." For some thirty years, his familiar voice could be heard Sunday evenings preaching the gospel on radio.

An outspoken advocate of civil rights, he eventually crossed paths with Martin Luther King and the two hit it off fabulously, becoming close friends. It was the Reverend Franklin who proposed and organized the famous March for Freedom down Woodward Avenue which helped solidify Detroit's image as a Model city.

There was an old man in Mississippi who pastored in a rural community. This minister passed on a few years ago. In his Sunday night services he used to say:

> ***Children, we are going to have a big time tonight; we are going to aim at the moon, but if we fall among the stars, we will still be on high ground.***

- C.L. Franklin

The Reverend Albert Cleage Jr. represented the more militant side of the pulpit in pre riot Detroit. A very polarized figure, whites viewed his sermons as being laced with racial invective while his black congregation roared with approval.

Cleage grew up in Detroit, completing an undergraduate degree from Wayne State University and his theology degree from Oberlin College. A highly skilled orator, Cleage was renowned for his bluntness and the desire to create what he coined a "Black Nation."

He openly espoused a transfer of power from white to black in Detroit, a point of contention which rankled many of the city's leaders who were desperately attempting to mend racial fences.

Outside his United Church of Christ (later renamed Shrine of the Black Madonna) on Linwood, his fiery Sunday sermons resonated down the avenue, probing many of the very souls that would later witness the Great Rebellion of 1967.

Reverend Albert B. Cleage Jr.

We have become a Black Nation. You can see it everywhere. The white press doesn't know what to make of it. White journalists are the most confused people in the world. Sometimes when you read the things they write you think you are reading a fairy tale. Hans Christian Anderson is much closer to reality than they are because they don't have any key to understand what's happening. This is because in their minds we are inferior. We can't hate like they hate. We can't believe like they believe. We can't fight like they fight. So they have to make up some kind of story to explain why we do the things we do. Yet the answer is so simple. All they have to accept is the simple fact black people are black but in every other way there is no difference. If they could just accept this simple fact, they would realize why we cannot accept any more than they could the brutalization, the degradation, the indignities, and the criminalities to which we have been subjected. But they can't see that, and so they can't understand our Black Revolution.

- Albert Cleage Jr.

H. Rap Brown

Born Hubert Gerold Brown in 1943 out of Baton Rouge, he became a potent militant voice and professional agitator throughout the 1960s. Once a member of the FBI's Ten Most Wanted list, Brown had very violent tendencies and was easily the most extremist of all the black militant leaders of the 1960s.

Later changing his name to H. Rap Brown, he regaled in whipping up ghetto audiences into inflamed frenzies, then encouraged them to wreak havoc against the white man. This he succeeded in doing to his black audience in Cambridge, Maryland in 1967. They burned two blocks of Cambridge which included some black-owned businesses. During the melee someone shot at him with a shotgun, one of the pellets striking him in the head (see photo). He was arrested for inciting a riot and sentenced to five years. Less than a month before the Detroit riot, Brown told a Detroit audience, "Motown, if you don't come around, were going to burn you down."

A sociology major from Southern University, Brown was never one to see the world in shades of gray. "I lived near Louisiana State University, and I could see this big fine school with modern buildings and it was for whites. Then there was Southern University, which was about to fall in and that was for the niggers."

After visiting his brother at Howard University in Washington, D.C., he caught the civil rights bug and joined SNCC (Student Nonviolent Cooridating Committee). SNCC was originally a nonviolent student organization which specialized in marches and sit-ins to bring attention to civil rights infractions. After the Watts Riot, however, SNCC began to distance itself from its nonviolent theme under the direction of Stokley Carmichael. Brown was a lieutenant of Carmichael's so when Carmichael left SNCC Brown was named chairman, further earmarking SNCC as an extremist group.

It wasn't extremist enough for Brown, however, so he became a member of the Black Panthers, shortly thereafter writing a book entitled "Die, Nigger, Die."

Brown did a five-year stretch in Attica where he converted to Islam and changed his name to Jamil Abdullah Al-Amin. After his release from prison he moved to Atlanta's impoverished West End where he led the crusade to rid the neighborhood of its drug pushers. In 2002 he was convicted of killing a Fulton County sheriff's deputy and is currently serving a life sentence at the state penitentiary in Reidsville, Georgia.

Stokely Carmichael

A native of Trinidad, Carmichael was a radical cog in the civil rights machine throughout the 1960s. A graduate of Howard University, Carmichael initially took on a nonviolent attitude, involving himself with numerous peaceful demonstrations throughout the Deep South while a member of SNCC. Carmichael was heavily involved in registering black voters in Lowndes County Alabama where blacks were the majority but held no political power because they were bullied into not voting. Carmichael set out to form a party so they could field black candidates. Required by Alabama law to have a symbol for his party, he chose the black panther because of its color, its reputation as a tenacious fighter and its intimidating capacity.

The sight of peaceful demonstrators being beaten and cattle prodded caused his attitude to change. He began to gravitate towards Malcolm X and his philosophy "by any means necessary." Having been arrested over thirty times on superfluous charges while conducting nonviolent demonstrations, his rage began to surface.

He is credited with coining the phrase (and attitude) "Black Power" which became a rallying cry across the nation for militant-minded blacks. King believed this was an unwise choice of words because of its violent overtones. Black Power also implied black unity and black separatism. Philosophically the two were drifting apart as the '60s progressed. Carmichael also coined the maxim "Black is Beautiful" which advocated racial pride, African dress and a rejection of the conked hairstyle. He, too, felt helpless in attempting to stave off the riots:

> ***There has been only a "civil rights" movement, whose tone of voice was adapted to an audience of middle class whites. It served as a sort of buffer zone between that audience and angry young blacks. None of its so-called leaders could go into a rioting community and be listened to.***
>
> ***In a sense, the blame must be shared, along with the mass media, by those leaders for what happened in Watts, Harlem, Chicago, Cleveland, and other places. Each time the black people in those cities saw Dr. Martin Luther King get slapped they became angry. When they saw little black girls bombed to death in a church and civil rights workers ambushed and murdered, they were angrier; and when nothing happened, they were steaming mad. We had nothing to offer that they could see, except to go out and be beaten again

James Meredith

A Mississippi native, Meredith spent nine years serving his country in the U.S. Air Force only to come home in 1962 and be told he could not enroll at the University of Mississippi because he was black. Mississippi governor Ross Barnett publicly vowed to keep Meredith out. Seeking help from Washington, President Kennedy sent federal troops and U.S. Marshals to escort Meredith to and from class. Trouble came anyway. A riot left two people dead, twenty-eight federal marshals had been shot and one hundred & sixty people injured. Meredith held fast and graduated from Mississippi, later getting his LL.B from Columbia University. Meredith's perseverance helped smash the color bar and pave a road of opportunity for his successors.

Library of Congress

"The saddest day of the week for me is Thursday, because that's ROTC day. When I go to class that morning, the Reserve Officer Candidates have on their uniforms. In the afternoon, I often go out to watch them drill up and down the streets near my dormitory. I know that not one Negro in Mississippi has the privilege of taking part in the ROTC program. Surely, there's one Negro in our state who would make officer material."

The Black Panthers

Formed in Oakland in 1966 by locals Bobby Seale and Huey Newton, their original purpose was to protect local blacks from police brutality and stop racism in their community. Their militant theme was greatly inspired by the late Malcolm X and their ire directed at the Oakland Police Department, with which they were at war over too many suspicious shootings. Malcolm X taught them to stick up for themselves "by any means necessary." They adopted Stokely Carmichael's symbol of a charging black panther as their icon to illustrate what happens when you give a dangerous cat no way out.

Some of their immediate goals beyond ridding the community of police brutality were 1) removal of all white businesses from the ghetto 2) exemption of all blacks from military service 3) the release of all blacks currently in jail.

In those days it was legal in California to carry guns as long as they weren't concealed. In an effort to halt police brutality the Black Panthers often rode around armed to the teeth. They patrolled their own neighborhoods armed not only with guns but cameras to tape police brutality. This, however, didn't enamor them with the police department and an ugly power struggle ensued.

In 1967 Huey Newton was charged with shooting and killing an Oakland policeman. Convicted and sentenced to fifteen years in prison, a spirited "Free Huey" movement sprang up around the country as Newton whiled away his time. After three years in stir, Newton was released on a technicality.

Huey Newton was proof of the old adage that you cannot save a person from themselves. He had enough intellect and fortitude to earn a PhD in social philosophy but not the common sense to distance himself from the world of drugs which would eventually kill him.

The Black Panther's trademark, a black beret and bandolier, struck fear into the white community, eventually causing FBI Director J. Edger Hoover to declare that the Panthers were the "greatest threat to the internal security of the country." During a six year period some twenty-four Black Panthers were killed in shoot outs with the police. Other prominent Black Panthers included Eldridge Cleaver, Fred Hampton, Angela Davis and Bobby Hutton to name a few.

AP/Wide World Photos

Black Panther founding members Bobby Seale and Huey Newton

The Black Panthers set about doing charitable works in their neighborhood such as setting up kitchens to feed underprivileged school children and free medical clinics. As Black Panther chapters spread across the country, they were eventually feeding some 10,000 children.

Bobby Seale, an Air Force veteran, was charged with conspiring to incite riots at the 1968 Democratic National Convention, a feat which cost him four years in prison. He renounced political violence upon his release, ran unsuccessfully for mayor of Oakland and wrote numerous books.

Malcolm X and MLK, the two civil rights heavyweights, were philosophically 180 degrees out. During Malcolm's earlier days at the Nation of Islam he was King's most unyielding critic, unleashing poisonous diatribes at the civil rights leader and at times referring to King as a fool, a clown, a traitor, and of course an Uncle Tom.

The only known meeting of MLK and Malcolm X.

Despite Malcolm's sincerity, perhaps even at that volatile point of his life there was a hint of jealousy towards King. King had dominated the media for years, had a world-wide following and garnered the lion's share of the accolades, including the Nobel Peace Prize.

Both were consumed with helping blacks achieve equality but in a fashion paralleling their upbringing. King was baptized in peace while Malcolm, who was exposed to extreme racism growing up, was baptized in anger. At the time this photo was taken a disgruntled Malcolm had already left the NOI for good and in the process was taking a giant ideological leap to the right. Dr. King was in Washington advising Congress about the upcoming Civil Rights Bill. Later at a press conference Malcolm X, to everyone's surprise, appeared at the door to greet Dr. King. While the meeting was amicable it was also awkward. Although still against nonviolence and integration, Malcolm had softened his stance in regards to Dr. King and was now openly showing admiration and respect for him. King was grateful but hesitant. Malcolm had a long way to go before they could work together. Had the two giants been able to link up philosophically the 1960s may have changed drastically, but it was not to be. Two days before they were scheduled to sit down and talk Malcolm X was assassinated and his space was backfilled by violent extremists like H. Rap Brown. Oh, what might have been!

Martin Luther King, in his last appearance in Michigan, greets a student at Grosse Point High School on March 14, 1968. In three weeks he would be dead of an assassin's bullet and the Civil Rights Movement, long since sputtering because of the riots that plagued the country, came to a grinding halt. His legacy, however, lived on. It was the legacy of a rare peacemaker during a time when internal hatreds saturated the country and brought out the worst in humanity. King had parted the Red Sea of rage and to the end he refused to succumb to the notion that blacks and whites could not work things out.

Grosse Point Historical Society

"Say that I was a drum major for justice."

The Great Society

In the 1940s FDR's presidential theme was the "New Deal." His successors, all of them his protégés, would offer similar themes with their own unique twist. Harry Truman had the "Fair Deal." John Kennedy, seeking a more cutting edge theme for a new generation, chose the "New Frontier." Lyndon Baines Johnson, the man of a thousand personalities and a mountainous ego to fuel them all, chose "The Great Society" as the cornerstone to his presidency. Like a giant, Texas-sized umbrella, the Great Society would provide sanctuary for even the most meager of Americans.

LBJ was a heavyweight amongst heavyweights in the political arena. He could use honey-coated flattery or chest-slapping intimidation to get his point across to friend or foe. Former Texas governor and longtime LBJ confidant John Connally described the Johnson he knew:

> ***There is no adjective in the dictionary to describe him. He was cruel and kind, generous and greedy, sensitive and insensitive, crafty and naïve, ruthless and thoughtful, simple in many ways yet extremely complex, caring and totally not caring...he knew how to use people in politics in the way nobody else could that I know of.***

A young LBJ in his teaching days surrounded by his students. His experience of teaching underprivileged minorities endowed him with a lifelong desire to raise the destitute out of the yoke of poverty. "I could never forget seeing the disappointment in their eyes and seeing the quizzical expression on their faces when they had to come to school, most of them without breakfast, most of them hungry. You never forget what poverty and hatred can do when you see its scars on the face of a young child."

July 2, 1964 - Johnson congratulates Dr. King after signing the Civil Rights Act. Two weeks later Harlem rioted. In August of 1965 Johnson signed the Voting Rights Act. Three days later the Watts section of Los Angeles erupted in anger. The flame of rebellion was sweeping the country and not even Johnson's incredible political skills could put it out.

Johnson, like King, tried to stave off the approaching riots by passing civil rights legislation as the racial tensions across the country were simmering just below the flash point. This placed Johnson in a precarious position. The political right cautioned him to slow down his pace on civil rights as the country wasn't quite ready for mass change. King demanded he speed up as blacks had been told for decades to wait, be patient, and he feared they would listen no more.

The Watts Riot of 1965 brought the civil rights movement to a screeching halt. Televised across the country, America was shown hordes of blacks looting stores and a pall of black smoke from arsonists' fires hovering menacingly over Los Angeles. Whites who were previously sympathetic towards civil rights after Birmingham quickly changed their tune and the country became as polarized as ever. Johnson was stunned. He had tried hard to set things right and was at a total loss to explain why the riots were occurring just as headway was finally being made on civil rights.

BACK LBJ
IN VIET NAM
POSTAL
CLERKS
AUXILIARY
THANK
VANCE
OUR
THANKS
VANCE
POSTAL
CLERKS

(Above) We will never know all the murky reasons why we got involved in Vietnam but one thing is for certain: the Vietnam War had a stranglehold on the Great Society that it would never relinquish. At one point we were spending $2 billion a month in Vietnam and, as the riots began sweeping the country, a hawkish Congress viewed pouring more money into the rebellious cities as a reward for rioting. By 1966 Congress began to put the brakes on the Great Society programs and funneled its considerable resources into Vietnam.

(Below) The End - Seven months after the Detroit Riot, Johnson announces to a national TV audience that he will not seek another term as president. Despite his critics, no president since Lincoln had done more to help blacks improve their lot, yet all the riots happened on his watch. Had previous presidents pushed civil rights legislation as hard as Johnson, the catastrophic chapter of the 1960s might have been rewritten. The Great Rebellion in Detroit, LBJ's Model City, was perhaps he last straw.

The Road to Detroit

The end of innocence - Clearly the turning point of the 1960s was the Kennedy assassination. Coming out of WWII America was innocent and bold, confident and naïve, powerful and distant. (Above) As the Kennedy cortege leaves the White House, there was a multiple air of finality about. America had no way of knowing it had lost its innocence for good. The confidence and pride Kennedy exuded was replaced with denial and disbelief, a common reaction following a tragic and unexpected death. America's entry into Vietnam would follow soon after but the war at home was in many respects more frustrating because we learned too late that there was one enemy we could never defeat: ourselves.

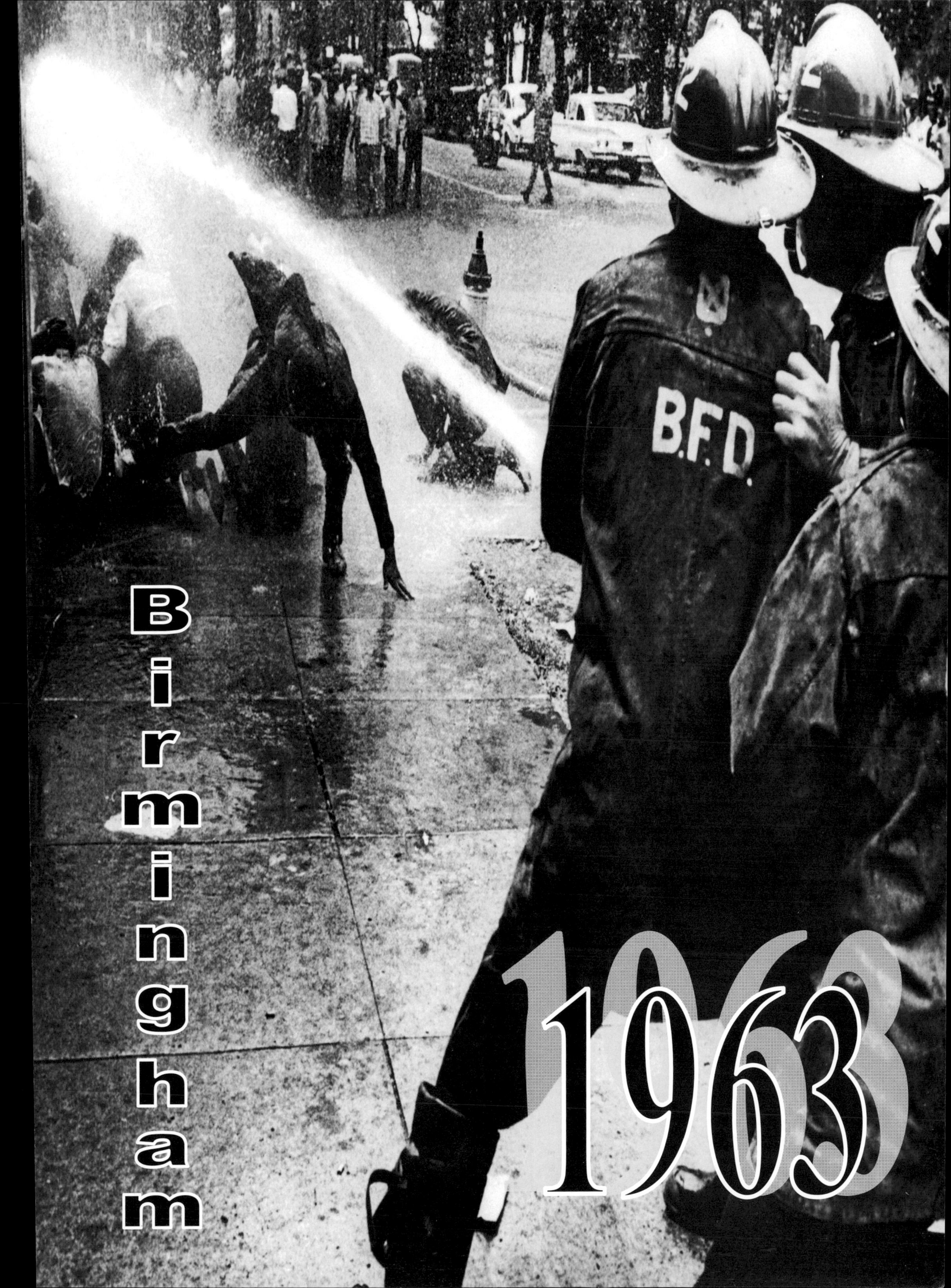
Birmingham
1963
B.F.D.

Birmingham - A Line in the Sand

Perched high atop Red Mountain overlooking the city of Birmingham, Alabama can be found the fifty-five-foot-high cast iron statue of Vulcan, the Roman god of forge and guardian of the metropolis.

Under the steely gaze of Vulcan, the city grew at an incredible rate due to its ability to produce steel. Subsequently dubbed the Magic City, Birmingham's success was forged in steel while its attitudes were galvanized in segregation. In 1963, Vulcan would bare witness to the forging of a different kind, the civil rights movement.

For the Reverend Martin Luther King, Birmingham would be his own personal conversion from iron to steel. While Dr. King and his Southern Christian Leadership Conference (SCLC) had made significant civil rights progress (in the South) since its inception in the 1950s, by 1963 momentum was lagging.

King accurately sensed the terrific unrest in the big urban areas he visited. Everywhere were signs that society was on the brink of racial violence. Time was running out for the nonviolent movement. In order to sell his pacifistic schema, he desperately needed a knockout civil rights victory to prove his peaceful methods worked and to diffuse looming riots. Birmingham would be that genesis.

Birmingham Public Libra

Vulcan - Roman god of forge

Birmingham was named after the principle industrial town in England. It is one of the few locations on earth that possesses vast quantities of iron ore, coal and limestone, i.e. the ingredients for steel. It would seem Birmingham's destiny had been chosen for it.

The steel and mining industry which dominated the landscape readily defined the people. The citizens were mentally and physically a very tough group who toiled a dangerous trade for near subsistence wages. The sting of the Civil War still hovered over the South like an ominous shadow, always there, always reminding. Southerners take great pride in the fact that relatives fought with great distinction and bravery during the Civil War. They were sensitive about the federal government dictating policy in the 1800s and the feeling intensified with age. With the arrival of the Civil Rights Movement, old wounds which had never healed properly to begin with, were once again ripped open.

Library of Congress

Homes of Birmingham steel workers overlooking the giant Sloss furnaces. With the magic growth of the city came an influx of black immigrants seeking jobs. Between 1910 and 1930 Birmingham gained some 46,000 black residents. The rapid change and competition for jobs brought immense hostility to the region. With the onset of the Great Depression in the 1930s and subsequent layoffs of the steel industry, that animosity grew. It would reach a peak during the 1960s.

The Citadel of Segregation

Martin Luther King arrived in Birmingham in April of 1963 still stinging from the debacle of Albany, Georgia, less than a year previous. Initially King had only planned to make a speech there but a full-fledged demonstration ensued. He attempted to fill the Albany jails with protestors to bring media attention to this racially divided town. Albany Sheriff Laurie Pritchett had other ideas. He had studied King's methods and refused to be goaded into any violent spectacles. To keep the situation out of the spotlight he had all arrestees shipped to neighboring towns to prevent negative press. To make matters worse, Albany officials agreed to meet with local civil rights leaders on the premise that King left town first. This created some dissension in the ranks. When King finally left town, Albany officials reneged on their promise. King had been duped and his credibility damaged. Another defeat of this magnitude could not be allowed to happen.

Birmingham's segregated reputation was Albany times ten and Birmingham Sheriff Thaddeus "Bull" Connor was certainly no Laurie Pritchett. Connor was known to have a hair-trigger temper that King calculated could be tripped with the appropriate prodding.

Civil rights activist protesting the segregated hiring practices of Loveman's, a Birmingham department store. Her sign reads:

"Loveman's Respects Money

But Not Negroes!!"

Birmingham was considered by many as the citadel of segregation. The city seemed to be locked in the grips of a Rip Van Winkle slumber since the conclusion of the Civil War. This did not escape the attention of Martin Luther King who, at the behest of a local reverend, was asked to come join the battle against this keystone of injustice. If the keystone falls, all the other stones fall with it. Birmingham was that keystone and Bull Connor represented the mortar.

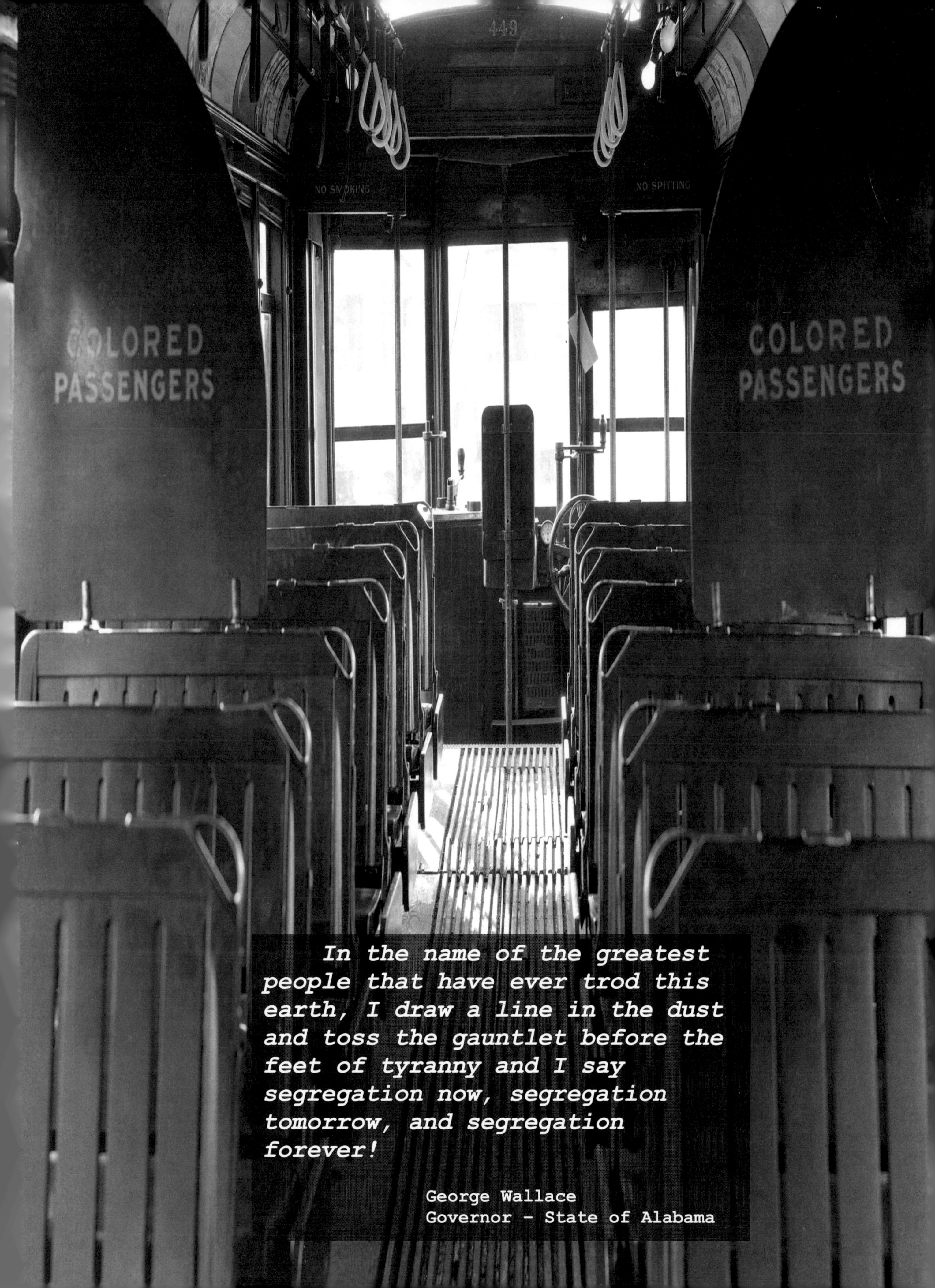
449
NO SMOKING
NO SPITTING
COLORED PASSENGERS
COLORED PASSENGERS
In the name of the greatest people that have ever trod this earth, I draw a line in the dust and toss the gauntlet before the feet of tyranny and I say segregation now, segregation tomorrow, and segregation forever!
George Wallace
Governor - State of Alabama

Between 1957 and January of 1963, Birmingham had some seventeen unsolved bombings. The targets were black homes, black churches and black civil rights leaders. The city eventually earned the cynical nickname of "Bombingham" thanks to the volatile antics of some of its more unstable personalities. Birmingham miners, of which there were many, were well acquainted with the use of dynamite and often very outspoken in their views.

Library of Congress

Birmingham minors - No strangers to dynamite

The Birmingham of 1963 was a city saturated with fear. Blacks feared attempting to vote, blacks feared mixing with whites, blacks feared the KKK and most certainly, blacks feared their own government. For Birmingham blacks the discrimination was across the board, including segregated city parks. When a federal court ordered Birmingham to desegregate the parks, Bull Connor closed the parks to everyone and saw its minor league baseball team leave town rather than integrate.

Birmingham had become a segregational maze. Robotic-like blacks simply followed the Jim Crow signs, "Colored Hotel," "Colored bathroom," "Colored section," "Whites Only." Moderate whites in sympathy with blacks were also kept "in their place" and forced to tow the segregated line. The civil rights bill that Kennedy had supported died amidst a still unresponsive Congress. Blind to the upheaval segregationists had produced, it would take the ugly revolt of Birmingham to jog their conscience into action. By then it would be too late, for once the avalanche of hatred got rolling in the North, there would be no stopping it.

Project "C"

Dr. King and his lieutenants had devised a grand scheme to "attack" Birmingham. To drive the point home it was dubbed Project "C" for confrontation. The confrontation, it was hoped, was to come from the authorities.

Alabama Governor George Wallace, seen blocking the door to the University of Alabama registrar office to prevent blacks from enrolling, did not represent the conscious of all southern whites. He was, however, elected four times and enjoyed considerable backing.

As King prepared to march, yet another chapter in the Birmingham saga was unfolding. The city had voted to replace its city-commission type of government with a strong-mayoral form. The two leading candidates, as luck would have it, were Albert Boutwell and Bull Connor. The civil rights marches and sit-ins were begrudging postponed, lest King give Connor any fodder for his political canon. Although Boutwell won the election, Connor filed suit that under the previous form of government he was still the sheriff, so for the interim Connor not only kept his job but essentially had no boss to dictate policy. He was, in effect, a lame duck dictator and subsequently had little reason to show restraint.

King well knew the volcanic atmosphere amassing in ghettos across the country. If he could win a peaceful victory in Birmingham he stood a chance not only of providing a much needed hope to the underclass but of staving off future riots.

You don't win against a political power structure where you don't have enough votes. But you can win against an economic power structure when you have the economic power to make the difference between a merchant's profit and loss.

- MLK

Birmingham Sheriff Thaddeus Eugene "Bull" Connor was an anachronism in a waning age of segregational chivalry. Elected sheriff in 1957, he vowed to maintain segregation to the best of his ability and within the letter of the law. Now one hundred years after the Emancipation Proclamation, the black man was still oppressed, still in fear and still waiting for the leaders of the country to uphold the Constitution they themselves had sworn to enforce. But Jim Crow would not go easy and many a complicit American city would fall hard with it.

Starting April 6th with a march on City Hall, the demonstrations and sit-ins grew in intensity. In the meanwhile, the Birmingham city jail slowly filled. Initially Sheriff Connor maintained a policy of civility towards the marchers hoping the problem would go away. To thwart them, the city obtained a court injunction on April 10th preventing further marches. King, normally compliant with such orders, now chose to disobey and was summarily thrown into solitary confinement for eight days. The fact that it was Good Friday added a spiritual significance. Birmingham was unwittingly becoming the center stage for this drama that was rapidly unfolding before a national television audience.

Local reverend Fred Shuttlesworth was considered the soul of the Birmingham civil rights movement. He had battled Birmingham segregationists for years and as a result was beaten, stabbed, jailed repeatedly and had his church and home dynamited. Shuttlesworth had been jailed so many times for civil rights demonstrations he considered it a badge of honor. His fearless perseverance and conviction was a light in the dark days of Birmingham.

"I wasn't saved to run."

On April 20th King's exile finally ended with much fanfare. From President Kennedy on down, all eyes were now thrust on Birmingham. Anxious to restart the marches, King was crestfallen to find that his army of protestors had dwindled to a solitary platoon. Adults were being pressured with dismissal from their jobs, the lone contingency they had stated ahead of time they could not sacrifice. King suddenly had no finale to produce.

Over at the high schools, however, King's inflamed rhetoric of the previous weeks had not fallen on deaf ears. Teenage students by the hundreds leaped at the chance to make history. King agonized over the decision but history had taught him that "freedom is never voluntarily given by the oppressor; it must be demanded by the oppressed." King understood the terrific risk involved if any of the kids got hurt, but he had manufactured a great hope and expectation for Birmingham, and with the specter of another Albany looming he dared not disappoint. Blacks had been told since the end of the Civil War to wait, be patient, only to realize that "wait" had become the replacement word for "never". By the 1960s they could wait no more.

Birmingham Public Library

On Bull Connor's orders, the Birmingham Fire Department set up their water canons for the final showdown outside Kelly Ingram Park.

Library of Congress

Birmingham's Sixteenth Street Baptist Church, as seen from Kelly Ingram Park, was the marshalling center where King would unleash his insurgent legions.

As May 2nd dawned on Birmingham, the aroma of the freshly bloomed magnolias, a local favorite, drenched the air with the arrival of spring. It would be the last familiar glimpse of normalcy for some time.

King now had an adolescent army of one thousand strong. As they enthusiastically marched down Birmingham's turbulent streets, an enraged Bull Connor ordered them all jailed. All in all, nine hundred were incarcerated.

On May 3rd, much to Connor's indignation, some 2,500 teenagers showed up. Connor was livid. He ordered the water canons turned on and the raging police dogs brought in. The crowd scattered with the canines in hot pursuit. Back in Washington, President Kennedy, who was watching the spectacle unfold on television, was appalled. He dispatched assistant Attorney General Burke Marshal to Birmingham in hopes of bartering a peaceful solution.

For the next week King was relentless with his marches. As a thousand protestors were sequestered in jail, another two thousand replaced them. Connor was stymied by the turn of events.

By May 10th even the Birmingham fireman were questioning the validity of their actions. Local business leaders, many of whom were avowed segregationists, were mortified at the media circus that had unfolded before the nation. Their beloved Birmingham was caught in the naked spotlight for all to see the dirty little secret of Jim Crow. Both sides finally agreed to meet and an accord was reached phasing out Jim Crow lunch counters and restrooms and to begin hiring blacks in local stores. For the time being King had won the historic civil rights victory he set out to gain, but was it a hollow victory?

AP/Wide World Photos

A civil rights demonstrator comes into contact with a police dog during the Birmingham marches. News crews from across the country came and filmed the spectacle which was unveiled before a horrified national audience. King had exposed the iceberg of racism, not the smaller part protruding above the surface but the giant mass below that much of America wished to continue hiding.

Birmingham Public Library

The dynamite bombing of the Sixteenth Street Baptist Church in Birmingham, only months after King's momentous civil rights victory, further enforced the mentality of "an eye for an eye." Four innocent black girls attending Sunday school were killed by the blast and in an instant the country teetered on the brink of a race war. Perhaps an epiphany, all of the stained glass windows were blown out except the one of Jesus leading young children. Martin Luther King summed up the Birmingham episode succinctly:

> ***We proved to them that we needed no weapons - not so much as a toothpick. We proved that we possessed the most formidable weapon of all - the conviction that we were right.***

Birmingham served to draw a line in the sand to every big city in the country that action against oppressors was necessary if civil rights were to be obtained. But what type of action against what type of entity? The stage had been set in this war without boundaries. Now it would be the North's turn to deal with the "black problem."

July 18-23	Harlem
July 18-21	Brooklyn (Bedford-Stuyvesant)
July 24-25	Rochester
Aug 2-4	Jersey City
Aug 11-13	Paterson
Aug 11-13	Elizabeth
Aug 15-17	Chicago (Dixmoor)
Aug 28-30	Philadelphia

1964

Harlem - The Backlash Begins

The year 1964 saw the World's Fair come to New York City. Its theme, oddly enough, was "peace through understanding." It was an ambitious goal to aim for. Ten years earlier that concept would have been realistic but times had changed. New York was the first city in the world to have a black population of over one million. Only a year after the Birmingham demonstrations and Martin Luther King's historic speech on the Washington Mall, Harlem was more interested in settling old scores than seeking World's Fair frivolity.

The observation towers from New York's 1964 World's Fair still hover high above the borough of Queens. They are a reminder of the last fleeting days of peace before the riotous havoc descended upon New York and the nation. If Birmingham was the line in the sand for civil rights it was Harlem that would cross it. The nation's largest city, which always seemed on a higher pedestal than others, confirmed suspicions that America was on the cusp of something much larger than just a lone police incident gone awry. This was the country's second Civil War. This one would be fought in different places but for the same principal reason: civil rights. It would be a war in which there would be no definite winner.

The Harlem Riot in July of 1964 paled in comparison to riots that would follow but just as every seed needs water to grow, the urban insurrections that plagued the country in the hellish 1960s got their inspiration, directly or indirectly, from Harlem. Harlem was the black Mecca that cultivated and enlightened black minds across the country. It was also the one place the "blue eyed devil" could not dictate terms.

The Harlem Riot was the match to the tinder that had lay dormant for decades. Year after precarious year had rolled by as racial sparks inundated northern ghettos until finally, on a hot summer day in July, one caught, and it would be years before the fires of hatred would burn themselves out. In Harlem's rich history and subsequent slow, agonizing tailspin towards failure can be found the riddle of rebellion.

"Let Me Off, Uptown!"

The Harlem of 1964 had changed considerably from its once vibrant predecessor. The gaunt, drab grayness which now permeates this community belies the fact that at one time Harlem was a quilt work of black cultures that merged to form a colorful dichotomy unique only to New York.

The Italians moved to Harlem in the 1870s when it was little more than a stockyard. When the "El" train came to Harlem, so did the eastern European immigrants. Just before the turn of the century Harlem was Jewish. Land speculators gambled that Harlem would be the new crown jewel of New York and invested heavily. But the market collapsed and row upon row of elegant Harlem brownstones lay empty.

Desperate to pay off their notes, Jewish businessmen subleased to blacks who were more than anxious to leave the nightmarish slums of San Juan Hill and the Tenderloin on Manhattan's Lower West Side. Harlem peaked during the 1920s, the fabled Harlem Renaissance, when it became the capital for black entertainers and literary artists. Throughout the 1930s, Harlem abounded with legendary performers like Cab Calloway, Duke Ellington and Lena Horne. The streets seethed with life 24/7. Whites flocked uptown for food and entertainment at renowned venues like the Cotton Club, the Savoy and the Apollo. Anita O'Day's smash hit "Let me off Uptown" seemed an eloquent descriptor of Harlem's magnetic drawing power.

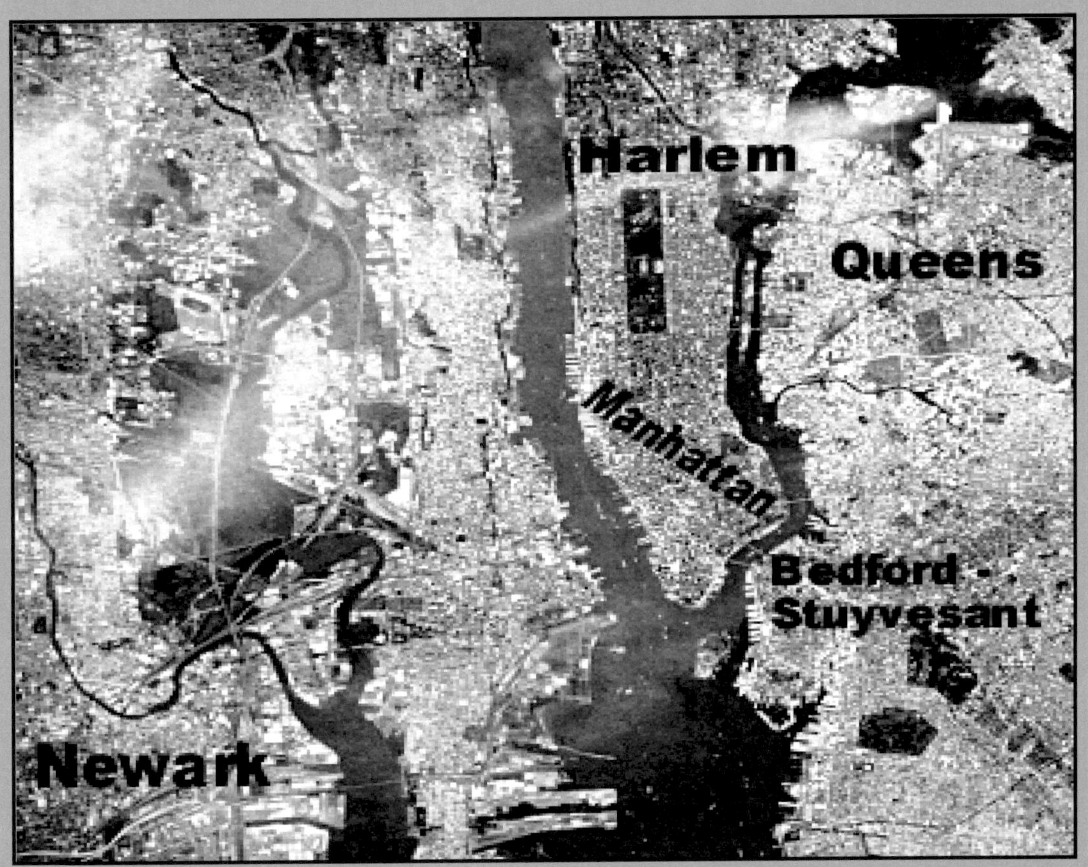

Johnson Space Center

The Slow, Agonizing Spiral of Failure

By the 1940's Harlem had begun to change. The Great Depression had not only forced thriving businesses to take flight but its artistic cream as well. With the great black migration north during WWII, Harlem became the black capital of the world. In another historic first, New York elected its first black U.S. Representative in Adam Clayton Powell who would quickly make a name for himself.

By the 1950s the frivolity of the Renaissance had long since been silenced. Having experienced race riots in 1935 and 1943, fewer and fewer whites dared venture uptown. Those who did were given a very cool reception.

By the 1960s Harlem was reeling towards decay. The big money had left and the luster was replaced by crime and poverty. Harlem was a place where "Mr. Charlie" no longer entered, except in the form of the NYPD. Whites had fled in terror at the impending warning signs of a black revolution. Senseless racial muggings were way up. The tension at 125th Street and Lenox Avenue, Harlem's Time Square, was several atmospheres heavier than anywhere else. The frenzied ravings of street corner man, cataloguing the indignities inflicted by "whitey" and the agonies of the ghetto, found no shortage of sidewalk shufflers to cheer him on. Harlem was caught in the gravitational pull of rebellion and there was no veering off course.

Sociologists are great believers in the snowball effect when it comes to social problems. What once starts out as a few random snowflakes overtime becomes an emotional snowball the size of a mountain. Cruel cultures that mortify outsiders are accepted by locals as normal.

Harlem's endless tenements and hovels concealed a growing array of invisible poor, unreachable by government programs and immune to the countless neighborhood studies that largely defied logic. These were the "born" poor, their plight reinforced by a wretched environment and poor educational system, as good as a prison wall seemed to buttress their chances of failure.

With an unemployment rate twice as high as New York City itself, Harlem's frustrations slowly spilled over into the streets. There was little if any greenery in Harlem and no air conditioning. When people wanted to cool down they went up on the roofs to seek a stubborn breeze or massed on the building stoops to rehash recent agonies.

The most distressed individuals, of course, turned to dope, the great lubricant of the ghetto. Glassy eyed addicts roamed the street with only one objective in mind, another fix. Others drowned their sorrows in the Niagara of liquor stores that, not coincidentally, seemed to crop up on every street corner to capitalize on the abundance of people whose only wish was to forget their predicament.

By 1964 Harlem was 95 percent black, 230,000 people jammed into only 3½ square miles. Most of the businesses were mom and pop stores, holdovers from the Jewish days. They were still owned by whites who had long since moved their residence elsewhere. Fewer than 20 percent of Harlem's stores were black owned, so the majority of the money that was spent in the neighborhood left to the suburbs each night. The result-a perpetual decline in the state of the community.

The 5 percent white that had remained behind, mostly Jewish shopkeepers, were now in the eye of the black storm and would soon wish they had left with the rest. This would be a reoccurring theme in many future ghetto eruptions.

The anti-white animosity that saturated Harlem was quickly reaching lethal levels. Whites were regularly being taunted with racial epilates. The "Blue-eyed devil" was a marked man in Harlem. After dark his presence was an invitation to assault. Black and white policemen strongly advised whites to "take it back downtown." Black gangs which were formerly enemies now teamed up to "get whitey." Vulnerable whites were slashed, beaten and sometimes killed by black toughs out for revenge.

Library of Congress

This segregated drinking fountain outside a North Carolina court house depicts a typical Jim Crow discrimination. Jim Crow signs like this were not to be found in the North but the mentality was there. Northern discrimination was more chameleon-like. It had the capacity to take on different forms which allowed it to go unnoticed and blameless.

Photos courtesy Library of Congress

The endless rows of Harlem brownstones tower over two mesmerized little boys. With little greenery or playground space, Harlem was often bleak and depressing. With no place else to turn, kids invariably counted on the streets for entertainment. The streets, however, were a poor substitute and invariably contributed greatly to a child's delinquency and subsequent felonious future. Harlem children had little to look forward to except the perpetual misery of the ghetto.

Adam Clayton Powell - Harlem Crusader

Adam Clayton Powell Jr. was a charismatic and controversial black congressman from Harlem and the first black representative to wield any power in the U.S. Congress. A graduate of both Colgate and Columbia, he went on to become an ordained Baptist minister. An early crusader for civil rights, he took over his father's congregation in Harlem and inculcated thousands of parishioners to the necessity of civil liberties and the deportment of the police. Elected to the U.S. House of Representatives in 1945, he quickly became a lightning rod for controversy. His habit of bringing black constituents into the "whites only" congressional dining room earned the ire of many of his fellow representatives. Powell later confided, "When I came here, no downtown hotel would rent me a room. No downtown theater would even let a Negro sit in the balcony. When I heard that the dining room for Representatives' staff was off-limits to Negroes, I told my secretary and clerks to go down there and eat whether they were hungry or not!"

Much to his parishioners chagrin, the minister-politico was gaining a flamboyant playboy image by cavorting more in New York night clubs rather than contriving legislation in Washington. It was to cost him his marriage. In many respects his ostentatiousness made him even more popular among the Harlem masses because they saw one of their own "make it" and hold his own with the highest ranking whites. Despite his poor attendance records and Tammany Hall's repeated attempts to oust him in favor of their own, he always managed to survive and fight another day. It was once said of Powell, "He is only doing blatantly what many other congressman do quietly." In tandem with Malcolm X, they represented Harlem's Great Black Hope and lone voices from the ghetto.

Whether from the congressional rostrum or the preacher's pulpit, Adam Clayton Powell was going to be heard.

Malcolm X - "The Hate that Hate Produced"

In many respects Malcolm X was the quintessential byproduct of the ghetto. He was the recipient of untold sufferings which branded into his mind a hatred for those who oppressed him, the white race. As a troubled youth, the tempting vices of the streets were too much for him to refuse and he faced a life filled with incarceration. But a chance meeting in prison would propel him from an unknown con man into a legendary ghetto icon.

The Malcolm X of the 1960s came off as a young man consumed with towering rages and misguided hatreds, bent on starting a race war to make amends for the many indignities he had incurred. Upon further inspection of his tragic background, however, the foundation of his ideology becomes quite clear. He represented the black rage which reached a crescendo during the riotous '60s. Yet in his thirty-nine years, this self-educated militant became the dominant voice of the ghetto and a general to the multitude of black youth who grew up amidst the same urban hopelessness that had brought him down.

Malcolm Little was born in Omaha in 1925. His father, Earl Little, was a Baptist minister and strong advocate of civil rights. His outspokenness on that subject rankled many in the white community. The death threats finally caught up with Earl Little in Lansing, Michigan. The Black Legion, an offshoot of the KKK, burned his house down in 1929. Earl refused to back off. Two years latter his mutilated body was found across the Lansing trolley tracks, compliments of the Black Legion. Malcolm was six years old and the seeds of hatred had been firmly planted.

It would get worse. Malcolm's mother strived valiantly to hold the family of six together but as the years went by the family became more and more impoverished. She finally suffered a nervous breakdown and was committed to an institution where she would spend the rest of her life. The family was broken up and sent to various orphanages.

A respectable student, Malcolm told his 7th grade teacher he aspired to become a lawyer and was told in turn, "That's no realistic goal for a nigger." After being bounced around to several foster homes, he went to stay with his stepsister in Boston. After several junkets to New York City in the early '40s, he quickly became fascinated with Harlem and its dominant black culture. He became a street hustler, pushing drugs, running numbers and in the process became addicted to cocaine.

Malcolm's mug shot after his arrest for B & E/grand larceny, an offense in which he would forfeit the next seven years of his life. It was here that he began his transformation from a ghetto thug into a razor-sharp militant. He would emerge from prison more focused on an ethnic rather than a personal vendetta. Sometimes called "Detroit Red", the red because of his reddish-brown hair he inherited from a white grand parent and Detroit because of his extensive Michigan ties.

Malcolm X - a.k.a. "Detroit Red"

For years the street-smart teen managed to stay one step ahead of the law, but his luck ran out in 1946 when he returned to Boston and bungled the robbery of a jewelry store. He spent the next seven years of his life in Massachusetts reformatories. By his own admission he had a very limited vocabulary when he entered prison. But his desire for knowledge, while temporarily dormant, had not left him. He spent the majority of his stint reading vociferously, which greatly added to his future debating skills. He was now determined to fight white oppression with his intellect rather than his fists.

After his release in 1952, he became a strict disciple of the Nation of Islam (NOI) and quickly became their national spokesman under his mentor, Elijah Muhammad. He established mosques in Detroit and Harlem, spreading the word about the Muslim faith to urban blacks. But by 1964, Harlem was more interested in rumbling than rhetoric.

Typical of the dissension in Harlem prior to the riot, a longtime Jewish merchant noted, "It used to be that you would sell them (blacks) something for twenty-five cents they would say you were cheating them. But now when it happens they say you're cheating the black race." One day a Black Nationalist entered his store. "He was one of those Muslims and he pointed at the Negro girl who works for me and said, 'White man, see that girl there? In five years she will own the store and you will be sweeping.' So I told him they won't have to wait five years, that I have always done the sweeping here and I will still do it. I told him as a Jewish man that we have had troubles, too, but that you people want to start at the top and we are willing to start at the bottom." The stage was set.

A Day of Reckoning

By the summer of 1964 Harlem's anger was within a hairsbreadth of spilling over. On Thursday, July 16th a policeman's bullet shattered a lazy, sunny day and paved the way for the opening night riot that would be held over for some time.

As with most police incidents there are invariably two highly contrasting stories as to what happened. A group of black teenagers were sitting on the steps of an apartment house entrance when the landlord either intentionally or accidentally sprayed them with a garden hose as he was watering flowers. The angered youth chased the landlord. Off-duty New York police lieutenant Thomas Gilligan happened by. One of the teenagers, fifteen-year old James Powell, pulled a knife on him, successfully slashed the officer on the arm. Gilligan gave one final warning to the onrushing youth then fired twice, killing Powell.

The community furor was quick and focused. As numerous police cars arrived they drew a crowd. Several hundred teenagers began pelting police with bottles and cans. The crowd was dispersed but the anger wasn't.

New York World Telegram & Sun

On the Saturday following the Powell killing, community anger crystallized in the form of mass protest marches towards police headquarters. (Above) Marchers hold signs proclaiming "Save Us From Our Protectors" and "Wanted for Murder - Gilligan the Cop" with Lieutenant Gilligan's picture on them demanding his dismissal and trial. A longtime white store owner who witnessed the procession rasped, "If they bust Gilligan, no cop up here is worth ten cents."

POLICE

New York World Telegram & Sun

Officers of NYPD's riot-busting apparatus, the Tactical Patrol Force (TPF), administer the dose to a rioter after peaceful attempts to break up the crowd failed.

Saturday would be a day of reckoning. As young Powell was being mourned in a Harlem funeral parlor, a deluge of emotions spilled out into the streets. Distraught demonstrators marched towards the West 123rd Street police station, its ranks swelling as it went. When the vengeful crowd arrived, the police were waiting. The voice of a senior officer radiated over the bullhorn, informing the crowd that the district attorney was investigating the incident. The crowd would have none of it. A local leader was given the bullhorn to try his hand at diplomacy. A response was not long in coming as a shower of bricks from rooftop renegades pelted the police.

The police had seen enough. On a signal from a sergeant, the TPF raised their batons and waded into the crowd, flailing away at anyone unfortunate enough to cross their path. Shrieks of "killer cops" and "Murderers" filled the ether. The inflamed mob ran down streets breaking windows and looting as they went. The riot was on!

White reporters foolishly attempted to enter the area. They quickly found that the traditional journalistic immunity from violence was no longer honored in Harlem. They were early casualties in the War of Harlem. Police set up roadblocks but the rampaging crowd bowled right over them. The rooftop deluge of bottles, flower pots and Molotov cocktails, continued to reign down on New York's finest. To remedy the situation, the police began firing warning shots just above the rooftops. The sound of gunshots caused many rioters at street level to bolt: the young toughs just laughed and applauded. Off Lenox Avenue, the frenzied crowd formed a human chain of looters, passing garments from a clothing store to the street for speedy removal. Harlem's anger cascaded across the East River as crosstown rival Bedford-Stuyvesant began rioting in unison. New York Mayor Robert Wagner, who was in Europe vacationing, rushed home and was appalled at what he saw.

New York World Telegram & Sun

Law and order are the Negro's best friend – make no mistake about that. The opposite of law and order is mob rule, and that is the way of the Ku Klux Klan, the night riders and the lynch mobs.

– New York Mayor Robert Wagner

New York World Telegram & Sun

Harlemites taunt weary police.

Rioters, sensing police reluctance to kill, took every opportunity to taunt them. When local civil rights leaders tried to quell the unruly mobs, they were in turn jeered. At the behest of Mayor Wagner, Martin Luther King made his way onto the streets of Harlem and was heckled by the rioters almost as bad as the police were. It was a baptism of fire for King who greatly suspected he was not reaching the masses of the northern ghettos and the disheartening proof was now resonating in his ears.

There's a ragging tiger on the loose up here (Harlem) and the big cats in the Civil Rights Movement can't ride it and can't tame it.

- Harlem social worker

The generation gap was also becoming pronounced. Older blacks attempted to neutralize the crowd by preaching caution and reason. The rioters, mostly teens and young men, simply viewed them as Uncle Toms. Decades of bridled hatred of the system, the police and the never ending cycle of ghetto oppression were ignited and it would take four tumultuous days to play itself out.

New York World Telegram & Sun

New York police detectives examine the charred remains of a police cruiser, the target of a well-aimed Molotov. The license plate bears the laconic motto "World's Fair," a dream that had now gone tragically awry. But there were other dreams that also went unfulfilled. Northern blacks saw fellow southerners making progress and had for a century since the debacle of Reconstruction been told to trust in their government and the Constitution. With Harlem, that faith in the system had once and for all been shattered. Henceforth, ghettos seething with frustration, unable to get the attention of government and society to help them in their plight, would now resort to rioting as a fait accompli.

The Harlem Riot was over but it was just the beginning of five long years of urban riots that would tear the country apart. The term "long, hot summer" became synonymous with the riot season (May-August), as city after city sweated through the weather and held their collective breath at the sight of even the smallest police confrontation. Within weeks of Harlem the infamous Gulf of Tonkin incident would propel the country headlong into the Vietnam War. Now the country would be fighting a war on two fronts.

Urban Rene

1965

Aug 11-17	**Watts**
Aug 12	Chicago (Lawndale)
Aug 13-14	Springfield (Ma)
Aug 14-16	San Diego
Aug 17	Pasadena

WATTS: The Standard-Bearer

After the summer of '64 begrudgingly faded into memory and the East coast riots were just a byline on page ten, America hoped there would be only a mild aftershock the following summer of '65. But 1965 would be no aftershock, it would be an eruption of such magnitude it would shake the country to its democratic foundation.

The upheaval that detonated in Watts stunned the nation. The horrific violence and upheaval that defined Watts shattered one illusion. Rioting was no longer an East Coast phenomena, it was now a dilemma of national proportions. Watts would be the standard-bearer for the three hundred riots that would follow it. For every big city had a ghetto and every ghetto had for decades been experiencing the exact same grievances: hatred and mistrust of the police departments, unending poverty, discrimination, despair, hopelessness.

Once the Watts uprising got started it dominated the evening news across the country. The cryptic nature of Watts forced even long time Los Angeles residents to break out a map to find out where it was. By the end of the week it would be etched in the minds of every American.

Watts galvanized ghettos across the country, not only to rise up against their oppressors but to unleash their considerable pent up fury against them. Tiny Watts, a paltry two square miles in area, would become a national icon for rebellion.

University of California - Berkeley

The LAPD and National Guard set up this crude but effective roadblock for Watts rioters. Their hastily fabricated sign left no doubt as to what fate awaited transgressors. The colossus of Watts brought rioting to a new level of ferocity and would provide the blueprint for all riots to come: a spontaneous fuse, looting, targeted arson, sniping, mass destruction, anarchy. Future rioters became more "efficient" as a result of Watts.

The Gathering Storm

As news of the Watts rebellion trickled into Washington, government officials from President Johnson on down were aghast. How could this happen? The ink was hardly dry on the Voting Rights Act Johnson had signed just days previous to help empower the black community. "How is it possible," a visibly shaken Johnson pondered, "after all we've accomplished? How could it be? Has the world gone topsy-turvy?" At first, Johnson believed the information must be skewed and demanded conformation. The pall of smoke hovering over Los Angeles confirmed his suspicions.

By sifting through an abridged history of Watts a certain fatal pattern of events emerges. Linking them together readily illuminates this once dark and confused picture that President Johnson initially saw. With this in mind, one can rationally begin a countdown to conflagration and begin to understand why south central Los Angeles became a firestorm.

Watts came into being simply because the Pacific Electric Railroad created a junction in this once desolate area around 1900. Since the only ranch nearby was that of Julia Watts, the junction was dubbed the "Watts junction" and Watts was born. Mexican laborers followed in the railroad's wake and settled in the area with the sparse white population. Southern blacks, who had long dominated the railroad profession of porters and dining car waiters, began to flock to Watts around World War I. A force-field like segregation began at once.

Annexed by Los Angeles in 1926, Watts would see a drastic increase in black immigration during the post WWII industrial boom that hit Los Angeles. Whites fled in haste to the nearby communities of Lynwood and Huntington Park while blacks filled the void they left behind. But the wave of immigration was too much for Watts and numerous public housing projects cropped up to absorb the overflow so that by 1960 Watts was mostly poor and almost entirely black.

In the twenty-five years preceding the riot, Los Angeles County's black population had increased from 75,000 in 1940 to 650,000 in 1965, a near tenfold increase. Sensing disaster, the NAACP and L.A. Assemblymen Bryon Rumford sponsored legislation to end discriminatory real estate practices (redlining) in the form of the Rumford Fair Housing Act which was passed by the California legislation in 1963.

This enactment was a thunderclap in the realty world as whites came face to face with the possibility of having a black neighbor. Proposition 14, which would completely nullify the Fair Housing Act, was fabricated. Requiring 480,000 signatures to appear on the ballet, it easily exceeded one million. When Proposition 14 eclipsed the two-thirds majority in the 1964 election, the encirclement of Watts was complete, legally and democratically. The frigid isolation it spawned greatly accelerated the feeling in Watts for black solidarity and nationalism.

Los Angeles Public Library

The Watts Towers

Local residents tend to their yards in the shadow of the Watts Towers. Built between 1921-54 by immigrant Sam Rodia, he named them "Nuestro Pueblo" meaning "Our Town." For Rodia, the Towers were a gift to his adopted country, an artistic symbol of peace. The closeness that Our Town implied back in Sam Rodia's day would quickly dissolve amidst the ever changing postwar world. The economic boom that hit Los Angeles after WWII would drastically alter the ethnic make up of Watts.

Watts was a geographical antithesis of Harlem. Watts was a hybrid - part one and two story stucco houses sporting palm trees and wide streets, and part public housing with a smattering of junkyards to complete the landscape. While not Beverly Hills, it certainly wasn't the drab, cloistered ghetto that Harlem had become. But make no mistake, Watts could be a very rough place. The killer of a girl murdered near the Jordan Downs housing project could not be found despite the plethora of witnesses who were in the area. As always, the ghetto takes care of its own.

One of the most important ingredients for spawning riots is frustrated youths, and Watts had plenty of them. By 1960, 60 percent of Watts was under the age of twenty-five. These are the ages when young men's dreams are supposed to be coming to fruition. Instead, they were constantly reminded of their failure. In Watts, bankrupt of opportunity and stifled with oppression, life became a daily struggle just to keep the grim reaper at arms length.

In a gang and street corner society, it is of paramount importance for teenage boys to have adequate recreational facilities. When this is not the case, idle minds and considerable energies are certain to find a negative outlet. Opportunity, also, must be made readily available for all. Kids bare witness to the traditional escalator of American progress they see on TV but know their futile predicament excludes them from those basic Americanisms that most of us take for granted. The resentment turns into bitterness as young boys come of age and approach adulthood spiritually broken. A product of a poor educational system, and often, a broken home, he comes to the painful realization he does not have the skills to compete and looks to crime as an alternative. Technological automation and an ever shifting industrial base greatly eroded the employment picture in Watts over the decades, yet southern immigrants continued to enter Watts. With jobs locally in short supply, kids have to look elsewhere. Some may have to travel over an hour and spend $1.50 doing so for a job that pays only $6 or $7 a day. Without opportunity, the youth of Watts were doomed.

One post riot analysis underscored the terrible dilemma that unemployment breeds:

> **Unemployment and the consequent idleness are at the root of many of the problems. Many witnesses have described to us the overwhelming hopelessness that comes when a man's effort to find a job come to naught. Inevitably, there is despair and a deep resentment of a society he feels has turned its back upon him. Welfare does not change this. It provides the necessities of life, but adds nothing to a man's stature, nor relieves the frustrations that grow. In short, the price for public assistance is the loss of dignity.**

Los Angeles Public Library

1962 - The cornerstone for rebellion is laid.

In April of 1962, seven unarmed Nation of Islam worshipers were shot down by the LAPD during a raid on a mosque. Six men were seriously wounded; the man at the bottom of the photo is dead. Photographs previous to this showed this man with his hands still cuffed behind his back. They have since been removed. Malcolm X, the voice of the unheard masses in the ghetto, made much of this incident in the press and media:

> ***You've got some Gestapo tactics being practiced by the police department in this country against 20 million black people, second class citizens, day in and day out - not only down South but up North. Los Angeles isn't down South. Los Angeles isn't in Mississippi. Los Angeles is in the state of California, which produced Earl Warren, the Chief Justice of the Supreme Court - and Richard Nixon, the man who was Vice President of this country for some eight years and who wants to run for president again.***

All in all it was bad medicine for the community, ratcheting up tension and hatred between the two races and leading both down a gauntlet towards disaster.

LAPD Chief William Parker

William H. Parker joined the LAPD in 1927, going to school at night to obtain his law degree. There was never any doubting his intellect or capacity, he was a professional student who thrived on academic challenge. He became chief of the LAPD in 1950 and lasted sixteen years in that tedious post when most of his predecessors rarely lasted two. Considered a very rigid and inflexible personality, he molded his department with dogged determination until it was considered by many as the elite police force of the 1960s. As testament to this, the hit TV show *Dragnet* was modeled after Parker's LAPD. No doubt there were numerous similarities between the unyielding Parker and the combative Joe Friday. Parker firmly believed the police had few friends and as such, knew they had to be a close-knit operation. Parker was highly vilified in the black community, who saw him as the personification of the white power structure. A skilled orator, he never turned down a request to speak to the public, which he constantly imbued with the theme of the police being the underdog. He had seen much in his thirty-nine years on the force but nothing, not even the Zoot Suit Riots of '43 could prepare him for the Watts uprising.

The grim reality of a policeman - An overwhelmed Chief Parker laments the loss of one of his officers who was killed in a shoot-out. Parker expected and received a disciplined edge from his men. Despite his aloofness, he was well aware of the endemic evils the average beat cop encountered and the fallout which ensued: alcoholism, family conflicts, danger, high divorce rate and the perception, real or imagined, of too little community support. As a result, he was fiercely protective of his men and any criticism of them was generally met with a cold gaze from his steely blue eyes and an equally abrasive rebuke. His steadfastness did not win him any support with his legion of critics. During the riot, it was Parker and Mayor Yorty whom rioters pointed the finger at.

The End of Malcolm X

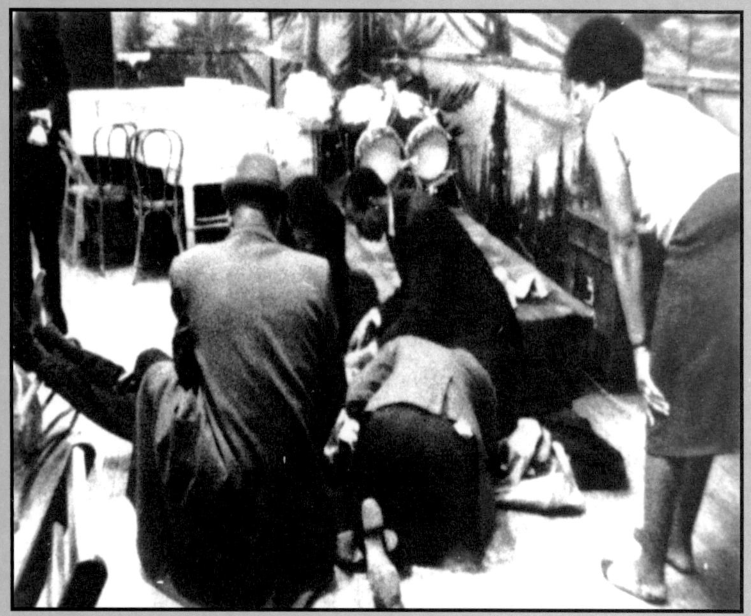

New York World Telegram & Sun

(Left) Friends of Malcolm X frantically attend to his bullet ridden body on the stage of Harlem's Audubon Ballroom. (Below) The NYPD rushes Malcolm X to the hospital but the steel will of this Harlem leader wasn't enough to ward off the massive amount of damage his assassins had inflicted. It was the end of Malcolm X and, for many ghetto teenagers who greatly admired him, it was the end of hope itself. Now leaderless, they fell in line behind any militant who had a grudge against the police department.

"I fought the best that I knew how."

- Malcolm X

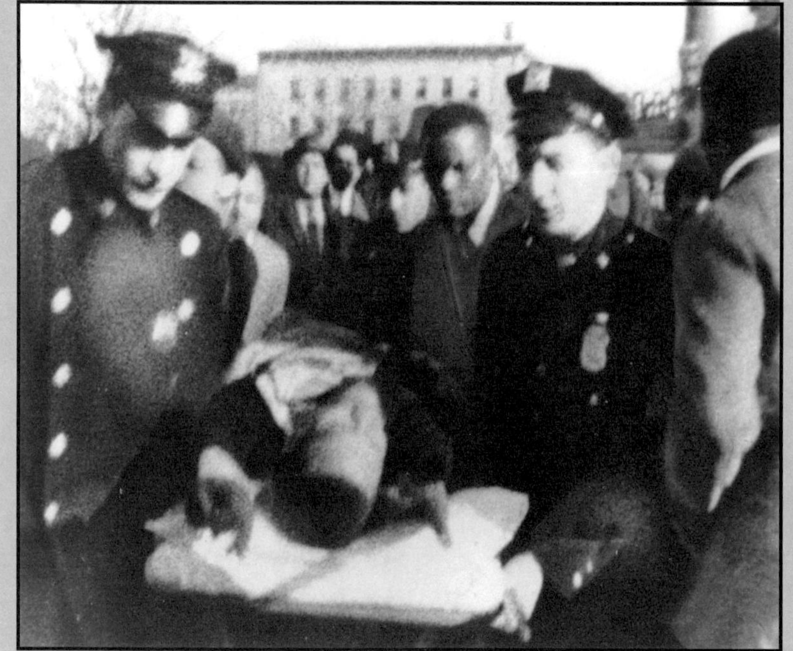

New York World Telegram & Sun

The assassination of Malcolm X at the Audubon Ballroom in Harlem on February 21, 1965 left a permanent void in the leadership of the urban, black world. Occurring only five months before the Watts rebellion, the legend of Malcolm X would hang over every ghetto long after he was gone. Ghetto teenagers had a special affinity for Malcolm X. In him they saw themselves. Among the many chants of the rioters to be heard throughout Watts, one seemed to echo a posthumous candor much louder than the rest: "Long live Malcolm X."

The Specter of Selma

While Selma, Alabama may be 2,000 miles from Watts, it was not far enough to keep racial animosities from reverberating all the way to Watts. Many of the inhabitants of Watts came from the Deep South and thus empathized with their brethrens' oppressive plight. It was a brotherhood that could not be broken by the endless scrub brush and barren desert that lay between them. In March of 1965, only five months before the Watts riots, Selma was the scene of a brutal police action against peaceful civil rights activists.

The specter of the old Confederacy cast a notorious shadow throughout the South. Despite guarantees by the 15th Amendment, black southerners were tricked or intimidated into not registering to vote. President Johnson would eventually set things straight by signing the Voting Rights Act in August of 1965.

Alabama State Troopers await marchers.

To set the stage, Dr. King picked Selma much like he chose Birmingham, because it was a fortress of segregation. A march protesting civil rights infractions from Selma to Montgomery was stopped by the state authorities.

Their second attempt on March 9th would become the apex of the civil rights movement. Some six hundred demonstrators started to march the fifty miles to Montgomery. Alabama Governor George Wallace would have none of it. As the group left the Selma city limits and approached the Edmund Pettus Bridge, a line of state troopers awaited with orders not to let them proceed. They didn't. Tear gas and billy clubs found their targets as a stampede ensued. Cameras recorded the debacle and beamed it into every living room in the country. The specter of Selma elevated hatred of white, authoritarian symbols in black, urban areas.

Troopers flail away at the defenseless marchers.

Detonation - "He Blew Up"

As is usually the case with riots, one of the triggering mechanisms is the aggravating summer heat and August 11th of 1965 found Los Angeles in the middle of a heat wave. The 92 degrees that the mercury registered made the air so hot you could smell the cement burning. In tandem with the oppressive racial atmosphere hovering over Watts, it took only a routine traffic stop to ignite the tinderbox that had accumulated for decades.

As California Highway Patrolman (CHiP) Lee Minikus was steering his big Harley north on Avalon, a black motorist pulled up beside him and warned of a drunk driver up ahead. Minikus spotted the suspect and pulled over twenty-one year old Marquette Frye and his brother Ronald just outside the Los Angeles city limits. Frye could not produce a driver's license and Minikus had to establish that the vehicle was not stolen. Satisfied on that issue, Minikus now addressed the odor of alcohol on Frye's breath. This required a sobriety test on the sidewalk which took more time. The multitude of street walkers which inhibit any big city on a summer day now began to stop and watch. As the minutes ticked by the crowd began to accumulate.

Initially Frye and Minikus had been getting along fine. It was a lively encounter as Frye was being quite animated in his explanations. So much so that not only was the crowd amused but so was Minikus. Frye's house being only a block away, one of the spectators went to retrieve Frye's mother, Rena. She was quickly hustled to the scene. According to Minikus, this is when the trouble started, "It was his mother who actually caused the problem. She got upset with the son because he was drunk." The embarrassment of his mother berating young Frye in front of so many onlookers was apparently too much for him. "He blew up," said Minikus, "and then we had to take him into custody. After we handcuffed him, his mom jumped on my back, and his brother started hitting me." The Fryes were forcibly arrested and hauled away but forty critical minutes had now gone by and a hostile crowd of two hundred had now accumulated. The seizure of the Fryes had greatly inflamed them and they would not be dispersed.

The LAPD had arrived, shotguns at the ready. A young black woman in the crowd allegedly spit on an officer. She too was forcefully arrested and hustled away. The fact that she was wearing an oversized barber's smock gave the erroneous impression to the crowd that she was pregnant. She was not. Too late, the crowd went berserk. After the police disembarked, the incensed mob began an orgy of violence at unsuspecting white motorists who, unaware of the danger, tried to drive through the hornet's nest. Cars were deluged with debris as they tried to run the gauntlet. Those who got through did so by the skin of their teeth. Those who didn't had their teeth knocked out and their vehicles turned over and set on fire.

"Get Whitey!"

The police left the scene and drove several blocks away to regroup, hoping the situation would diffuse itself and the crowd would disperse on their own with the police gone. They did not. In fact, the crowd had swelled to almost one thousand people, mostly irate teenagers and young men. The first indication of trouble came when a bus pulled up to the huddle of policemen looking like it had driven through a meteor shower. Its windows blown out and fraught with dents, it testified to the gauntlet of rock throwers the police had left behind.

For the mutinous mob back on Avalon, the freshly minted riot had become a convenient medium for settling old grievances. As the still unsuspecting white motorists naively entered the area, blood curdling screams of "Get Whitey" were accompanied by a torrent of bricks and rubble, anything to stop the vehicle and administer a beating. Even light-skinned blacks, having been tainted with white blood, were risking it. Local blacks who drove through the war zone gave the pass sign, one finger meant you were from Watts, two meant Compton and three meant neighboring Willowbrook. Anyone not hip to this code risked death.

AP/Wide World Photos

Charred automobiles litter Avalon Blvd, testament to the mob's fury.

"Burn, Baby, Burn"

Friday the 13th dawned on the streets of Watts as a calm before the storm. After the terrible spasm of violence Wednesday night there was a strange vacuum of activity on Thursday. Avalon Boulevard, covered with broken glass, glistened in the early morning sun as if it were made of diamonds. Community leaders huddled together, earnestly searching for answers to prevent a reoccurrence. Chief Parker was puzzled. Knowing that once riots started they don't stop voluntarily until the pent up fury is completely spent, he had expected more violence on Thursday. On Friday, his theory would prove correct. As dusk approached, the temporary peace was shattered by a tornado like frenzy of violence.

Six months before the riots, a Los Angeles disc jockey known only as the Magnificent Montague rolled into town. Fresh from gigs in New York and Chicago, he had tried to adopt the catch phrase "Burn, Baby, Burn" into the everyday ghetto vernacular. It was simply another hip way of saying "right on." The phrase never caught on out East but during the initial outburst Wednesday evening a teenager, caught up in the excitement, yelled the phrase as an afterthought. It quickly became a rallying cry amongst rioters throughout Watts against the white establishment. As white-owned businesses went up in flames, cries of "Burn, Baby, Burn" cascaded down the fiery streets of Watts.

Los Angeles Public Library

Friday the 13th lived up to it's ominous reputation as Watts burned.

Friday was Watts's Day as 10,000 rioters showed their community spirit by smashing, looting and burning their lifelong aggressions on anyone or anything that crossed their path. The riot area quickly morphed from the original two square miles into forty-six. Some 14,000 California National Guardsmen were on the way, but poor communications between agencies would cost Los Angeles dearly.

In 1789, an aide to King Louis XVI had the irksome duty of informing his majesty that his subjects had stormed the Bastille.

"Is it a revolt?" asked the King.

"No, Sire, it is a revolution!"

University of California - Berkeley

The LAPD cautiously enters a looted shop on riot scarred Avalon Boulevard.

One looter, elated with his choice of plunder, tried to rationalize his behavior. "Man! I give them people so much of my business they owes me a bundle of money they could never pay back. This ain't stealing! This is redeeming!" A woman smugly carting off a color TV, repeated his sentiments. "That's right," she said. "It just hit me I been paying $25 a month for three years on a bunch o' furniture that cost me no more than $300 to start with, so the least they can do for me is give me a TV."

The rampaging had become so contagious that even black owned stores were being pillaged, albeit at a price. One black store owner, wielding a shotgun, set a menacing mob straight when they tried to enter his store. "You may be my brother, but you're going to be my dead brother."

Corbis/Bettman

King addresses a hostile crowd during the waning hours of the riot.

King's nonviolent and multiracial methodologies were not endorsed by all blacks, as his visit to Watts during its last convulsions of anger demonstrated. His sequestered meeting with Mayor Yorty and Chief Parker was frigid and futile, Parker at times pounding his fist on the table to make his point and Yorty coldly suggesting that King "shouldn't have come here."

King arrived in Watts at the head of a ten car motorcade. The atmosphere in Watts was noxious with hate and King was greeted primarily with contempt by blacks who thought he was grandstanding. His attempts to reason with residents (above) were constantly interrupted with both sarcastic barbs and highly personal invectives. A rioter recalls towards the end of the disturbance, "We went down to 103rd Street. Martin Luther King is coming down the street on a truck with (a) P.A. system: 'My black brothers, why don't you go home?' People just ignored him, started throwing stuff at him." King left Los Angeles virtually despondent, believing in some way he had failed.

As the King entourage walked the litter-strewn streets of Watts they had a memorable conversation with a hostile youth. "We won," the youth exclaimed. King recoiled at the youth's ebullience. "How have you won? Homes have been destroyed, Negroes are lying dead in the streets, the stores from which you buy food and clothes are destroyed, and people are bringing you relief." The youth's answer both startled and enlightened King. "We won because we made the whole world pay attention to us. The police chief never came here before; the mayor always stayed uptown. We made them come."

Any lingering beliefs Dr. King may have had regarding any national solidarity were shattered. His excursion through Watts left him stunned. "We obviously are not reaching these people." For King personally it was a terrible defeat, not one of his own making by any means but one that would require significant soul-searching for yet another distant and unknown answer.

John Malmin - Los Angeles Times

California National Guardsmen retake the badly scarred 103rd Street after it was looted and systematically burned by the out-of-control mob. Now facetiously referred to as Charcoal Alley, 103rd Street took the brunt of the rioters' wrath. This was the former white business district of the area. According to a rioter who was amply familiar with the scenario on 103rd, "Everywhere I looked, I saw a fire. I was on the street till they called out the National Guard, and that's when I decided to go back to the pad, cause the National Guard, they weren't jiving."

LAPD Chief William Parker addresses a post riot Congressional committee regarding the causes of the Watts Riot. Two rows back Marquette, Rena and Ronald Frye listen on intently.

Was Watts simply an uprising of the criminal element or was it a dormant social volcano that finally erupted? To a degree it was both, but the endless cycle of failure which abounds in the ghetto produces a level of frustration few people in the suburbs will ever know.

It was, after all, only a small minority that stormed the Bastille. As was the case in Watts, only about 2 percent of the community participated in the uprising but the damage had been done. The rioters had succeeded in stigmatizing not only all of Watts as criminals but black society as well.

Watts sent shock waves through every big city in the country. Suburban whites peered out darkened windows, shotguns at the ready, carefully examining every unfamiliar car that entered the neighborhood.

The young toughs of Watts had not only crossed the line of defiance drawn by the LAPD, they had laid down a challenge to every ghetto in the country. One Watts rioter substantiated this theory when he barked, "We gonna have the biggest and best riot ever! We gonna show all those dudes in Chicago and New York we're bigger than they are."

Photo courtesy of Bob Sherman

The white backlash - After Watts, guns sales nationally rose to all-time highs for fear of a black invasion of the suburbs. Some gun dealers, as witnessed above, were anything but discreet. Watts was bad - 34 dead, 3,400 arrested and some 600 structures burned or damaged - but the worst was yet to come.

1966

July 3	Omaha
July 12-16	Chicago (West Side)
July 15-16	Dayton
July 18-22	**Hough**
July 22	Brooklyn (East NY)
July 25-27	South Bend
Aug 7	Lansing
Aug 11-13	Detroit (Kercheval)
Aug 27	Waukegan
Sept 6-11	Atlanta (Summer Hill)
Sept 27-28	San Francisco

Hough ...as in Rough Hough

Hough (pronounced Huff) is a neighborhood of Cleveland which mirrored an evolution that occurred in many a northern city throughout the 19th and 20th centuries. Like Detroit, Cleveland greatly benefited from the automotive boom in the early 1900s. That affluence quickly spilled over into neighboring Hough as palatial mansions epitomizing this newfound wealth quickly adorned the boulevards. But the star of Hough soon saw its zenith pass and by the 1950s prosperity had bid a hasty retreat, never to return.

Originally settled as a giant farm by Oliver Hough in 1799, Hough had expanded to become a tight-knit community by the Civil War. This was the height of the Gilded Age where many an unknown entity gained incredible fortunes seemingly overnight. As was the custom of the day, such affluence was to be displayed by the posh Victorian style mansions available during the period. Styles such as Romanesque, Italianate and Second Empire offered an incredible degree of individuality and splendor providing the owner with a custom, one of a kind residence that flaunted his personality.

Cleveland quickly became an industrialized, blue collar magnet. It grew exponentially to such a degree it eventually incorporated neighboring Hough. As Cleveland became a sooty, industrial eyesore, its coterie of blue bloods chose to flee towards neighboring Hough where their majestic manors lined Euclid Avenue to such a degree it gained the fitting moniker of "Millionaires Row."

Cleveland State University

If Detroit ever had a true sister city it would be Cleveland. Both owe their prominence to the Great Lakes and the automotive boom of the early 1900s. (Above) Cleveland's Republic Steel adorns the mighty Cuyahoga River during its industrial heyday.

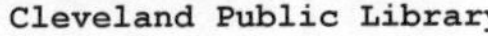

Cleveland Public Library

Cleveland Public Library

It was high old times in Hough during its heyday from 1880 to 1920. Hough was a place to see and be seen. Society's elite carved out a unique existence along Euclid Avenue making this Cleveland-Hough corridor the showpiece of the Midwest. Replete with topiary gardens and Grecian fountains, the name Hough came to symbolize prosperity. By the 1950s things would change drastically. Economic and social transformations began to chip away at Hough's wealth and luster. By the 1960s, with any vestige of prominence long gone, Hough had become an overcrowded, rat infested ghetto destined to have its star rise one last time as a dubious chapter in the riotous '60s.

Cleveland State University

Euclid Avenue - The fabled Millionaires Row.

Erieview - The Mistake on the Lake

Cleveland had numerous urban renewal projects on the board throughout the 1950s and '60s. Like many big industrial cities of the North, Cleveland had deteriorated significantly over the decades. Logic would dictate that the most blighted sections of the city should receive the most attention, but logic took a holiday and the fallout would cost the city of Cleveland.

Under the leadership of then mayor Tony Celebrezze, the city of Cleveland conjured up a new world entirely. It would be called Erieview and it would be located within a rock throw from the Great Lake itself. It was a grandiose plan indeed, encompassing some $140 million and the assistance of the indomitable architect I. M. Pie. There was one small oversight however. It wasn't needed. The city simply wanted a "showpiece" to bedazzle the public.

Library of Congress

Lost Opportunities - Cleveland squandered its last chance to circumvent the Hough Riot by repeatedly bungling its urban renewal plan. Hough was easily the most blighted section of the city yet only a paltry sum of money was thrown their way while the lion's share went into the shallow pipe dream of Erieview. By razing central areas of the city to make way for Erieview, poor blacks were pushed into Hough, setting up a severely overcrowded situation and a prelude for rioting.

Houses of Hough's former aristocracy, whom had long since fled to the suburbs, were divided and sub divided again to accommodate the masses uprooted by urban renewal, creating a terrible overcrowding.

Cleveland's Erieview debacle was symptomatic of a big city being administrated by the indistinguishable hand of private interest. A large tract of land towards Lake Erie was chosen even though the structures occupying this tract were in much better condition than the retched structures found in Hough. Many blacks who had lived in this area found themselves hopelessly caught in the vortex of Hough because it was the only place affordable.

Hough was not alone in being slighted. Euclid Avenue, which had always been the main artery through Cleveland, also suffered accordingly because Erieview shifted the focus away from the once prosperous downtown business district and towards the lake. Once again urban renewal, when guided by an inept hand, created more problems than it cured.

Now supercharged with federal dollars, Cleveland went about haphazardly leveling whole city blocks in preparation for the goliath of Erieview. Many blacks who had occupied this area abruptly found themselves scrambling for a roof. Despite the hollow ring of assurances from City Hall that they would be provided for, they were left to fend for themselves.

It was virtually impossible for blacks to buy homes in the suburbs because of the redlining practices of real estate agents. Hough was becoming a racial revolving door. As blacks began moving into Hough in the 1950s a parade of whites moved out. Owing to the high rent of the frequently absentee landlords, many blacks found themselves doubling up with relatives. Hough bulged at the seams with frustrated and angry people.

One irate tenant's reaction to the absentee landlords, who only showed up at the beginning of the month to collect rent and then disappeared, eloquently summed up the mood in the hood. "If I come back after death, I want to come back as a tiger and tear up Hough."

Despair lit the fuse

When Cleveland mayor Anthony Celebrezze accepted a position in the Kennedy administration in 1961, his office was filled by Ralph Locher (rhymes with poker). Like many of his contemporaries across the country during the 1960s, Locher inherited numerous problems that were not of his making but he nevertheless had to deal with. The disastrous after effects of urban renewal, the Civil Rights juggernaut and the ever growing quagmire of Vietnam made every day in the big city a potentially explosive one.

By all accounts Locher was a affable and quite capable man but his administration was renowned for gridlock. Locher's tenure, which he managed to stretch with great difficulty, lasted until 1967 when he was defeated by a black candidate named Carl Stokes. Stokes narrowly missed unseating Locher in 1965. To no ones surprise the voting was almost totally polarized. Such was the state of the city just prior to the riot.

Cleveland State University

Hough, once Cleveland's proudest neighborhood, had by the 1960s become a rat infested ghetto.

Affable or not, the Locher administration had badly bungled the urban renewal program to such a horrifying degree that the federal government froze the renewal money until the whole tangled mess could be sorted out. After years of stagnation it was too late. The fabled Millionaires Row had become skid row and Hough was so badly maligned in the press it was now mockingly referred to as Rough Hough.

By definition, a ghetto is a section of a city in which many members of a minority group live. In reality it is a prison whose inhabitants are trapped not by bars and concertina wire but by the invisible walls of poverty and prejudice. For the overwhelmingly black population in the ghetto, the warden becomes the only white people they come in contact with, namely the shopkeepers and the police.

Ghetto inhabitants harbor no illusions about their fate. With the last relic of hope gone, self esteem drains from the society like water out of a bath tub. The dehumanizing effect of a ghetto can not be understood from the pages of a book but rather by the people themselves.

Their faces tell it all. Thirty-year-olds look fifty; fifty year olds are nearing their life expectancy, old long before their time. Decades of pain permanently etched in their face, the always prevalent thousand yard stare gazes outwardly but often doesn't seem to register. Too many years of harsh distorted reality that in the end makes life itself a bitter illusion. As a death row inmate no longer fears retribution because he's conceded the fact that death is near and inevitable, so too are the ghetto inmates willing to flirt more and more with death because the alternative of life is so unpleasant.

Nobody knows you...
When you're down and out.

Cleveland State University

King took on all comers in an effort to get the word out in pre-riot Cleveland. Whether it was a white audience in a Grand Ballroom or a black audience in the park, he left no stone unturned if it meant keeping the peace.

Cleveland State University

Cleveland State University

In Hough, the only constants are poverty and frustration.

While there was a litany of leaders throughout the community, few if any were effective at reaching the troubled youths of Hough. "There is no Negro leadership," a black lawyer mused cynically, "The leadership in Hough today is the do-rag kid."

Hough's army of frustrated youths were easily inculcated into believing that violence and destruction against white people and white owned property was a form of civil rights advancement. No one had ever given them a reason to believe otherwise.

The increasingly disturbed social atmosphere surrounding Hough was like a headache that never went away. "It's the cheating by white merchants," said one black teenager. "People getting gypped all the time. High prices for relief people. The lousy credit buying. The bad credit ratings. The garnishes on the paycheck. If that ain't bad enough, it's the juvenile record following you around from job to job, from high school to the grave. It's just one insult upon another insult."

One Hough resident echoed these sentiments. "Riots are in the great American tradition. (President) Johnson is doing the same thing in Vietnam. The Negro is used to being in Hell."

Cleveland State University

The Cleveland Police Department had a bad reputation amongst the black community of Hough. Instead of protectors they were viewed more as oppressors. The fact that they were 94 percent white didn't help. The police department was on a collision course with the militants of Hough who in turn had a message for the police: "You can't stop the riot that's coming!"

Cleveland State University

To the outsider, Hough was like a grotesque fictional monster come to life. Even on a sunny day it seemed to be shrouded in gloom. Unemployment was always high in Hough. What few jobs that didn't take flight to the suburbs were low paying and dead end. Opportunity was a stranger. People idled away the hours on front porches, their faces, distant and forlorn, echoing their plight. Parents gamely attempt to hide the barren future from their kids, but in the ghetto reality is impossible to run from. It will find you.

The tenth of every month became disdainfully known as "Mother's Day" because that's when the ADC checks came in. It was also the same day local merchants habitually jacked up their prices, a grievance that was not forgotten as Hough's stores were being put to the torch in July of '66.

Library of Congress

Hough, it was once said, is a place were all the bad people were dumped into to join the melting pot poor who didn't have the resources to leave, creating a situation that can only lead to rebellion. Even by ghetto standards Hough had a nightmarish quality about it. By the mid 1960s some 70,000 people were jammed into two square miles. Hough had become an ungovernable hellhole for a city that simply wished it would just go away.

Havoc in Hough

Like Watts, the Hough uprising was ignited by a trivial incident. An argument in a white owned bar in a black neighborhood would touch off four crazed nights of hate-filled rioting that would make Hough a household name. The 79ers bar, located at the intersection of 79th and Hough Avenue, was the epicenter of the riot. This was the heart of Hough. The daily tension was thicker than the stack belch that blew in from the downtown steel mills. But the triviality of the incident suggests strong undercurrents of persecution and animosity that were desperately seeking an outlet.

There had already been numerous close calls in the area over the summer months and on the humid evening of July 18, 1966 Hough's last atom of luck would run out. The clientele at the 79ers was primarily black. The median age of the fifty-five guests that night was twenty-two, a highly combustible age especially considering the times. As is often the case in explosive situations like this, the details that emerged are murky at best and vary to such a degree one wonders whether the principles involved are describing the same event.

79ers Café – Epicenter for eruption

At any rate, on that Monday evening there was an incident between the white bar owners and a black prostitute who had been previously banned from the café. An argument followed for all the patrons to see. The prostitute left but the atmosphere became charged with tension.

Later that evening witnesses claimed a black male customer asked for drinking water but was refused. The owner claims the pint of wine the customer ordered was a carryout item and thus didn't warrant such service. The man became irate, shouting obscenities at the bar owner before he left, further augmenting tensions amongst the bars patrons. Shortly thereafter someone posted a hastily scrawled sign on the outside of the tavern proclaiming, "No water for Niggers." The fuse to Hough's long-latent powder keg had been lit and within an hour it would explode.

The two incidents circulated quickly through the community and a crowd gathered outside, eventually numbering some three hundred angry people. According to the bar owners, they made several phone calls to the police but got little or no response. Out of desperation they called the fire department, which made an appearance.

"What's the problem?" the firemen asked.
"You've got a riot out there," the owner screamed at the firemen.
"We don't have a riot; you have a riot," came the laconic answer and the firemen left.

When the police finally came they were too late and too few to quell the hostile crowd. The police were greeted with a hail of rocks and bricks which rapidly escalated into mass revolt. The Hough insurrection, which many felt for years was inevitable and unavoidable, was underway.

Hough version of urban renewal

Cleveland State University

As was the case in Watts, authorities had to escort firemen while they fought fires. Mobs cut fire hoses and showered firemen with bricks as sniper bullets whizzed by their faces. Shadowy figures danced amidst the flames as screams of "black power" filled the smoky night air.

Hough had crested in anger and the now overwhelmed police department could no longer carry the load. After much hesitation, Mayor Locher informed Ohio Governor James Rhodes that the National Guard would be needed. As 1,700 National Guardsmen flooded the hot spots, the rioters simply followed the old baseball adage, "hit em where they ain't." The riot spread to other neighborhoods which were not yet covered by the authorities.

The Hough Riot was following the typical pattern that had emerged across the country. By day the rioting was sporadic, at time even quiet. Cloaked under a cover of darkness, however, the riot flared unabated with the flame of rebellion. Gangs of rioters waged a viscous assault on the community, pillaging and torching a very selected group of stores. White businesses were ravaged while many black owned businesses right next door were left untouched.

Police ordered everyone off the street whether they lived in the neighborhood or not. One woman yelled out the window that she wanted to go check on her kids. Seconds later she was shot in the head by a sniper and died instantly. Another man sat in his car far from the riot scene. He was shot in the face with a shotgun at point blank range. He too did not survive. It appeared that vigilantes were using the riot as cover to avenge past grievances, which were numerous.

The ghetto doesn't have much respect for police, white or black. To be a black police officer in a large urban area during the 1960s could be a nightmare within itself. If you side with black civilians you're accused of not doing your job. If you do you're job effectively against black society you're accused of being an Uncle Tom. Either way there was little job gratification and much reason for despair.

During the riot, as a black police officer tried to clear the streets of black rioters, he fired off a warning to the enraged characters who were openly threatening him, "I'm telling you now, if anybody shoots me, I'm going to shoot you back." Another black patrolman was also given the business by the crowd. "Atta boy, Harry, you damned Uncle Tom. Hell, Harry, you got to live here too."

Hough had its share of black militants who were very adept at stirring up the teenagers. "(We) have to take whatever action is necessary to get them their civil rights. This thing is not just going to tear up Negro neighborhoods. These people are getting guerilla experience. We're going to take it right to Charlie's front door."

The National Guardsmen, bayonets affixed to their M-1 rifles, seemed to enflame the rioters even more because of their overwhelming "whiteness." Firemen fared no better. As was the case in Watts, police and Guardsmen were forced to ride along on top of the trucks and set up a perimeter around the engine. The Guardsmen pushed angry crowds back with their bayonets and were jeered in return, "Just keep pressing, you'll get yours."

Looters became profiteers as back alleys were converted to barter shops. Older residents berated the arsonist who burned businesses, "What are we going to do for food now?" One despondent merchant explained, "I can't and will not open again. I'm completely ruined. They say we are capitalizing on them. Well that's not true. When I first moved here nineteen years ago there were very few Negroes. They came to me, I didn't come to them."

The life of a black policeman in the ghetto was indeed a double edged sword. Does his baton land any softer?

AP/Wide World Photos

Cleveland police take a bead on a rooftop sniper. Police Chief Wagner (far left) brought along his deer hunting rifle and went roof to roof attempting to trap the elusive shooter. When that failed, a door to door search of the residents occurred. A police helicopter fluttered over the tenements, combing the darkened rooftops with its searchlight. When the snipers started shooting at the helicopter, it had to patrol the rest of the night with its lights out.

The Guardsmen also struggle under these strange, unfamiliar, circumstances. An apprehensive Guardsmen confided, "There were no lights and it was quiet. Too quiet. Looking out, you wonder who is on the next dark roof and does he have some kind of gasoline bomb." Another Guardsmen chimed in, "Geneva (a previous disturbance) was more or less a joke. It's not like that here. They mean business." Even though Hough is two thousand miles from Watts, the copycat rallying cry of "Burn, Baby, Burn" and "Get Whitey" could be heard with frightening regularity.

AP/Wide World Photos

A tense and uneasy quiet blanketed the scene as Ohio Guardsmen watch from a building top over a deserted Hough Avenue. After four brutal days of violence and anarchy the Hough riot was over but the tragic days of Hough and Cleveland proper would linger on for some time to come.

With four people dead, dozens injured and hundreds arrested, Hough had made a name for itself but for all the wrong reasons. Hough had raised the bar on revolution to a new level. One of Hough's irate black Nationalists offered his terse analysis. "The only weapon black people have is the violence and discontent of the young Negroes. We've got to get rid of the Uncle Toms and the white power structure keeping us down. All the city has been doing is trying to change attitudes, not conditions." As a result of the city's blind intransigence, Hough burned. After three years of rebellion across the scorched cities of America, rioting had become a red badge of courage among ghetto youth. Every year the bar of destruction was raised higher and higher as city after city that had not yet rioted was put under unyielding pressure to prove their warrior status. In 1967 the bar would reach its high water-mark.

U.S.A.
BLACK LEADERS
FOR
BLACK PEOPLE

Newark

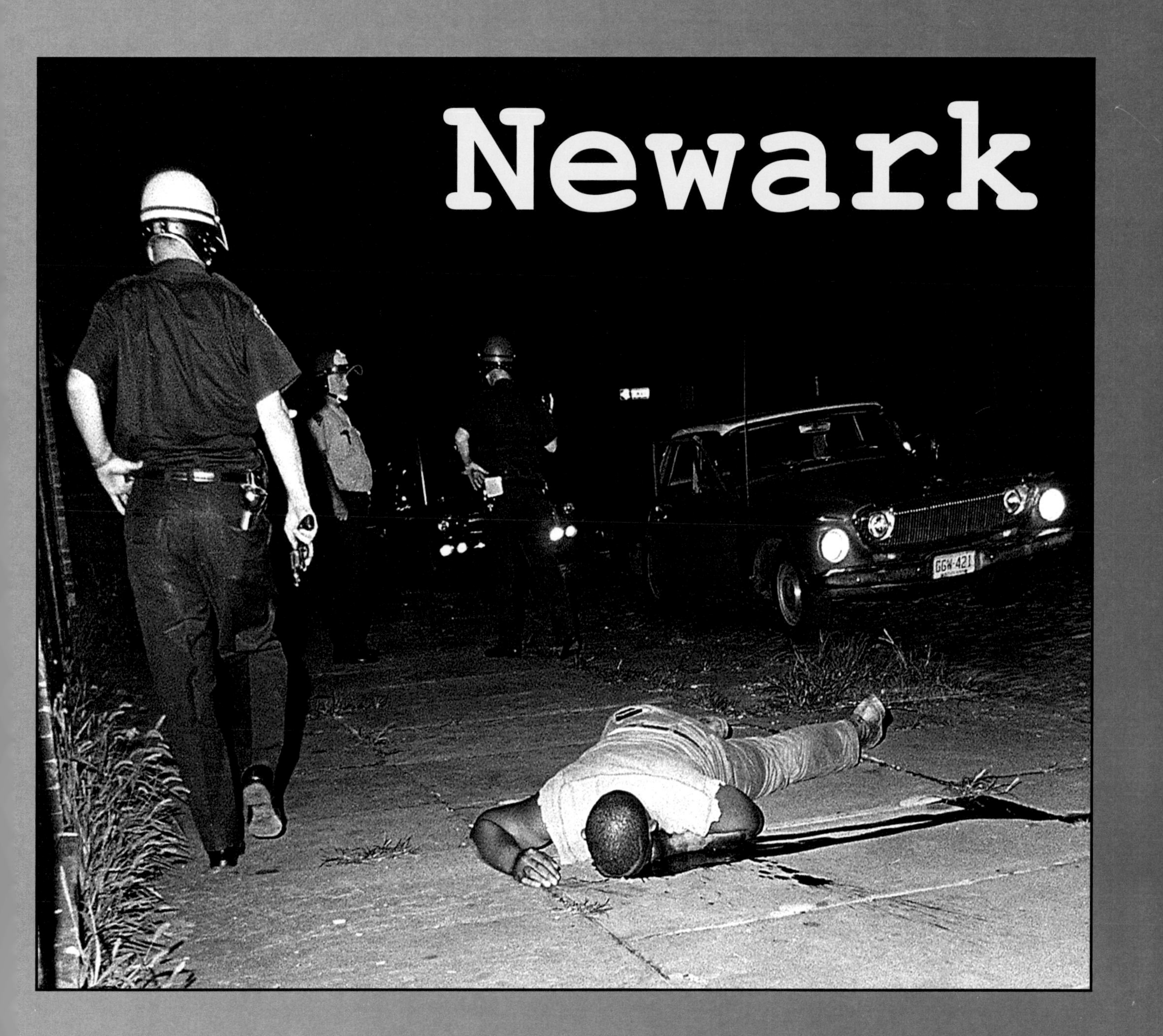

June	2	Boston (Roxbury)
June	11	Tampa
June	12-14	Cincinnati
June	14	Dayton
June	27-28	Buffalo
July	12	Erie
July	**12-16**	**Newark**
July	13	Harford
July	14	Plainfield
July	16-17	Cairo
July	19	Durham
July	20	Memphis
July	20	Minneapolis
July	**23-27**	**Detroit (12th Street)**
July	27	Cambridge
July	30-31	Milwaukee

Newark : The Anticlimax

Courtesy Newark Public Library

Newark Skyline

There was a time when Newark could boast of full employment, her municipal coffers bulging and her people fat and happy. But like the Charles Dickens novel *Hard Times*, depravity reared its ugly head upon "Brick Town" once too often. In 1964, in the wake of the Harlem riots, the cities of Elizabeth, Paterson, Perth Amboy and Jersey City all rioted in unison. While all of these disorders were worthy of note, New Jersey would save its biggest insurrection for last. Now the baton of insurrection was handed to Newark to demonstrate its version of ghetto one-upmanship. The Newark Riot of July, 1967 would equal the now legendary Watts in ferocity and destruction. With the country in its fourth year of rioting and with the magnitude of Newark on such a calamitous scale, many thought the storm of violence had finally blown itself out and calm would soon return to the country. No one at the time could have envisioned that the greatest insurrection of them all, Detroit, was only seven days away, thus making Newark the anticlimax.

Newark's agonizing tailspin into the abyss of depravity can be summed up in the city's application for Model City status that it submitted to the federal government in 1967. In it, the city described itself as "a basic training camp for the poor." Newark had become the poster child for urban decay. "There was a judge," a barbarous old saying goes, "who once sentenced a man to ten years in Newark."

The Long Shadow of Depravity

Newark was founded in 1666 by Puritans dissidents searching for a permanent home. Unwanted anywhere else, they finally settled at a niche on the Passaic River. In 1966, Newark celebrated its 300th birthday in grand fashion. Factory whistles shrieked a salute as a parade through downtown celebrated "Pride in Newark." Despite the fact that blacks and whites had heretofore got along in Newark, for many, the iconic motto "Pride in Newark" had a very hollow ring to it. As a plague of riots pinballed from one city to another, Mayor Addonizio announced that despite Newark's plethora of problems "I do not believe there will be any mass violence in Newark this summer."

Since 1900 some 100,000 blacks, refugees borne from Reconstruction, had fled the South in search of a better life and landed in Newark. Like the Puritans before them, southern blacks were dissidents from a place they were not wanted. The Puritans found peace in Newark. Southern blacks did not. One of the bitter ironies of the Great Migration was that millions of blacks left the poverty of the South for the bounty of the North just as the multitude of unskilled jobs were drying up for good. As a result the unemployment rate skyrocketed and with it the misery index of those who would become trapped in the bottomless quicksand of poverty.

The segregation blacks experienced was just as great. Newark's poor and trampled were herded by the magic of redlining into its cloistered Central Ward where for decades their shattered dreams were allowed to fester into a spearhead of anger that was pointed right at City Hall. The enduring fact that no one appeared to be acknowledging their tragic plight and no one noticed the indignation that flowed from the Central Ward simply put a finer edge on the sword.

The Negro has lived with the slave mentality too long. It was always 'Jesus will lead me and the white man will feed me.' Black power is the only basis for unity now among Negroes.

The rising tide of resentment climbed steadily across America as riot after riot left a scorched path to mark the spots where frustrations had erupted into violence. The civil rights movement, despite heroic efforts to effect positive change, was not making any difference to the people who needed it the most, the impoverished and hopeless of America's inner cities. The Stokley Carmichaels and H. Rap Browns now spoke for the ghettos.

Courtesy Newark Public Librar

The Crushing Sense of Nobodiness

One of many high-rise public housing projects which dotted Newark's Central Ward, the massive Edward Scudder Homes housed over 7,000 of Newark's poor in eight twelve-story buildings. Children of the projects were born under a dark star. Raised amidst extreme poverty, violence and crime, the world brands them with an indelible mark of inferiority. It is a emotional scar that will never heal.

Ghetto fathers, unable to find employment because the projects where built amidst an economic desert, find they have a cruel choice to make. Stay home and watch his kids starve or leave home so his kids can qualify for ADC and be fed. The result: an overabundance of one-parent families and broken homes with a stigma that sociologists refer to as "the crushing sense of nobodiness."

According to sociologist Dr. William Moore, "A project home is not one in which the individual tenants really make a choice to live. Rather, it is a place to live because they have no choice. The deprived child and his family become little more than human driftwood in the urban stream of social turbulence - never fulfilling, never being fulfilled."

Ass Deep in Corruption

Hugh Addonizio
Embattled Newark Mayor

Newark Mayor Hugh Addonizio was no stranger to flying bullets. As an army officer during WWII, he had stormed Omaha Beach as lead filled the air and survived the renowned Battle of the Bulge, earning himself numerous meritorious accommodations. In July of 1967 Addonizio would witness another battle of prolific proportions, on the very streets of the city he was charged with protecting.

But Addonizio was an embattled mayor long before revolt came calling. A seven term U.S. congressman, he was elected Newark's mayor in 1962 claiming he wanted to help his native city. There was a darker side to Hugh Addonizio, however. To a confidant he is alleged to have said, "There's no money in being a congressman but you can make a million bucks as mayor of Newark." These sentiments were buttressed by the fact that in 1970, after eight years as mayor of Newark, he was sentenced in a U.S. court to ten years in prison for extortion. According to the U.S. attorney who prosecuted Addonizio, he was guilty of "literally delivering the city into the hands of organized crime." His critics claimed during his tenure that he sold everything except the City Hall building itself.

It was under this felonious atmosphere that Newark began its tragic decent towards rebellion. Addonizio inserted a close associate, Dominic Spina, as head of the police department. Under his direction few officers got ahead on merit and the NPD quickly earned a reputation for being as corrupt as the crooks it was supposed to be subdueing.

Blacks had become the majority in Newark but held only a few token positions in city government, a transparent attempt by the mayor to exhibit solidarity. Addonizio's tenure had become too controversial - too many police incidents, unarmed blacks being killed, police guns mysteriously discharging, police brutality and City Hall corruption.

As 1966 turned into 1967, the final pieces of the rebellious puzzle would be put into place. The state of New Jersey was looking for a city to build its State College of Medicine and Dentistry. Newark leaped at the challenge, offering fifty acres from the black, Central Ward which was already undergoing an extensive urban renewal program.

The school's board of trustees recoiled in horror at the thought of building in Newark. Their hidden agenda was to build out in the spacious and tranquil suburbs. The political logrolling now began in earnest.

Addonizio was determined to land the medical school and use it as a springboard for his gubernatorial ambitions. Attempting to checkmate the issue once and for all, the school board insisted they must have 150 acres to build on. Anticipating this, Newark countered with a 185 acre bid, much to the dismay of the school board. In one last desperate ploy to keep out of Newark, the school board pointed out that the first fifty acres they wanted were not of the land already cleared for urban renewal but land across from the renewal area that had not been cleared, nor was it scheduled to be.

The black community, whose dwellings were to be razed, were livid. If it was their houses that were to be sacrificed then they wanted them replaced with more housing. It seemed like another case of "slum removal = black removal" and under the guise of eminent domain they were powerless to stop it.

With this atmosphere of anger hovering over Newark, the last piece of the puzzle fell neatly into place in June of 1967. The secretary to the board of education, Arnold Hess, was preparing to resign. The black community petitioned for Budget Director Willie Parker, a black CPA, to be appointed to the job. Since Newark public schools were predominantly black, it seemed like a logical fit. Instead, Addonizio made a decision that came to mystify many. He appointed a white crony of his, who possessed only a high school education, to be the new board of education secretary.

Sparks flew until 4:00 a.m. at the next board of education meeting to such a heated degree that a black community leader threatened, "Newark might become another Watts." Unwilling to cave, Addonizio instead convinced Hess to stay on for another year, which in effect pleased no one. City officials blundered on in ignorant bliss on these issues, still believing the black demonstrations to be nothing more than a speed bump along the road of progress.

The outrage should have been a warning sign. This was not the same passive Newark from years gone by. Typical of the newfound attitude among black teenagers was this quip from a sixteen-year-old Central Warder:

> ***Picketing and marching ain't getting us anywhere man. The whites got to face it man, this is a new generation. We ain't going to stand for the stuff our mamas and fathers stood for.***

Sticks and Stones

July 12th, 1967 was a steamy Wednesday in Newark. Around dusk that evening cab #45 double-timed it towards the intersection of 7th and 15th Street. Piloting it was John Smith, black, forty years old, an army veteran and trumpet player. As he approached the intersection he noticed a Newark police cruiser with two white officers inside seemingly double parked. Smith, who had a checkered driving record to say the least, flipped his lights and passed. The police cruiser followed and pulled him over claiming they were moving and he was tailgating. From here on none of the stories jive but what is known is that Smith was arrested by force (allegedly resisting arrest) and was taken into custody. Upon their arrival at the 4th Precinct, Smith's beaten body was dragged into the station (according to police he refused to walk on his own) as hundreds of roving eyes glared out the windows of the twelve story Hayes public housing towers across the street. This momentary lapse of discretion would cost the police dearly.

A volatile crowd from the Hayes complex began to accumulate outside the 4th Precinct. Their lifelong contempt for police was accelerated by the terrible tensions that had reached a crescendo in the previous months. Rumors began to circulate that Smith had died in police custody. Community leaders demanded to see Smith. They found him in his cell doubled over and groaning, his ribs stove in and cuts on his face. Realizing they had been "caught," the police started passing out riot helmets.

A ring of white and black police surrounded the station. Angry blacks from the Hayes Homes were giving them the business but, despite their unbridled hatred of the white police, saved their choicest comments for the black officers. "You Uncle Toms got to come home tonight." Smith was taken out the back exit to the hospital while leaders tried to calm the restless crowd still accumulating out front. It was too late. Shortly before midnight a well placed Molotov hit the side of the station house followed in short order by bricks and bottles, breaking almost every window. Club wielding police charged out the door to put down the insurrection. The battle for Newark was on.

Looting quickly broke out within sight of the 4th Precinct. One local leader who witnessed the initial looting was critical of the sluggish police response. "The radio cars were going back and forth and they saw them in there. They saw them in there getting whiskey and they just kept going. They didn't try to stop. As a result of that, all the people saw that the cops didn't care, so they went in too. A lot of stuff could have been avoided at this point."

By Thursday afternoon, with a relative calm restored, police Director Spina naively believed the riot was over. By 7:30 that evening the riot started anew, again in front of the Hayes housing projects. By 9:00 the Central Ward was in total rebellion.

Courtesy Newark Public Library

Newark's 4th Precinct, the epicenter of the riot, found itself in the ominous shadow of the city's Hayes and Stella Wright housing projects in the heart of the troubled Central Ward. The Hayes building pictured was one of eight, some of which offered a commanding view of the 4th Precinct and its everyday dealings. Snipers from the darkened roof would later duel with the police and Guardsmen a hundred yards below them.

Despite the plethora of ominous warnings throughout the long, hot summer, Newark police seemed poorly prepared for trouble. The New Jersey State Police, which was on standby since the alert sounded on Wednesday, noted in their log book:

> ***There is still no organization within the Newark Police Department. The Fourth Precinct appears to be running its own show. There are no barricades. No requests for State Police from Director Spina.***

"Like Laughing at a Funeral"

Late Thursday New Jersey Governor Richard Hughes imposed a 10 p.m. curfew in Newark, declaring that his largest city was in a state of open rebellion:

> ***The line between the jungle and the law might as well be drawn here as well as any place in America.***

At 2:20 a.m. Friday, Mayor Addonizio, who had been in a state of confusion and lethargy from the onset, finally called Governor Hughes to request the State Police and National Guard. When Colonel Kelly of the State Police arrived at City Hall an hour later, he found Addonizio in a virtual state of shock. "It's all gone, the whole town is gone," Addonizio moaned. "It is all over."

As the all-white New Jersey National Guard rolled through the white suburbs on their way to Newark early Friday morning, locals stood on the curb cheering them on, "Shoot the niggers," "Kill the bastards." In riot torn Newark, black teenagers who had looted a wig shop held up their plunder, yelling, "We've scalped the white man."

Springfield Avenue, the old Jewish thoroughfare which ran through the Central Ward of old Newark, bore the brunt of the rioters retaliation. As the looting commenced the projects spilled out onto Springfield Avenue and systematically ripped it apart in both directions.

The looters preference for furniture stores was revealed by the increasing array of ratty furnishings now appearing along the curb just outside the projects. The poor were not going solo however; even the middle class were represented as finely clad citizens drove their vehicles over to fill up on plunder. One middle class woman prudently decided to wait until the riot spread to the more upscale districts before she looted.

Early Friday morning Governor Hughes and Mayor Addonizio toured the devastated Central Ward in person. As their state police led motorcade meandered through the carnage, the despondent duo recoiled at the looting still in progress.

One couple in their new car stopped at a looted shoe store and skillfully packed their trunk as if it were a picnic basket. The looters paid little heed to the latent authorities, carefully plying their trade and coolly making off with their ill-gotten swag. Hughes particularly was aghast at the looting in broad daylight and the carnival like ambience which hung in the air. "The thing that repels me is the apparent holiday atmosphere I saw with my own eyes. It's like laughing at a funeral. And it could be the funeral of the city."

The riot flared to a fiery apex on Friday afternoon when Newark police were summoned to the Scudder housing project to investigate a reported sniper. What happened next depends on who tells the story. It is believed that several blacks from the project had been shot an hour earlier by the Newark police. Unaware of the hornet's nest they had entered, the police were beginning their investigation when a puff of smoke jutted out from an upper floor window of the Scudder towers. Newark police detective Frederick Toto, standing amongst his comrades, was felled by a bullet to the chest. He died on the operating table two hours later. It was after the death of Detective Toto that all semblance of restraint on either side was lost for good. From now on it would be an eye for an eye.

The Central Ward was now a flurry of unbridled outrage. An eleven-ton armored personnel carrier lumbered up to the entrance of the Scudder projects, Guardsmen and police creeping alongside its massive outline for protection. They sprayed the upper floors of the giant towers with a withering fusillade of bullets as shadowy figures danced for cover. After rushing the building, all that could be found inside was an empty, blood-spattered hallway.

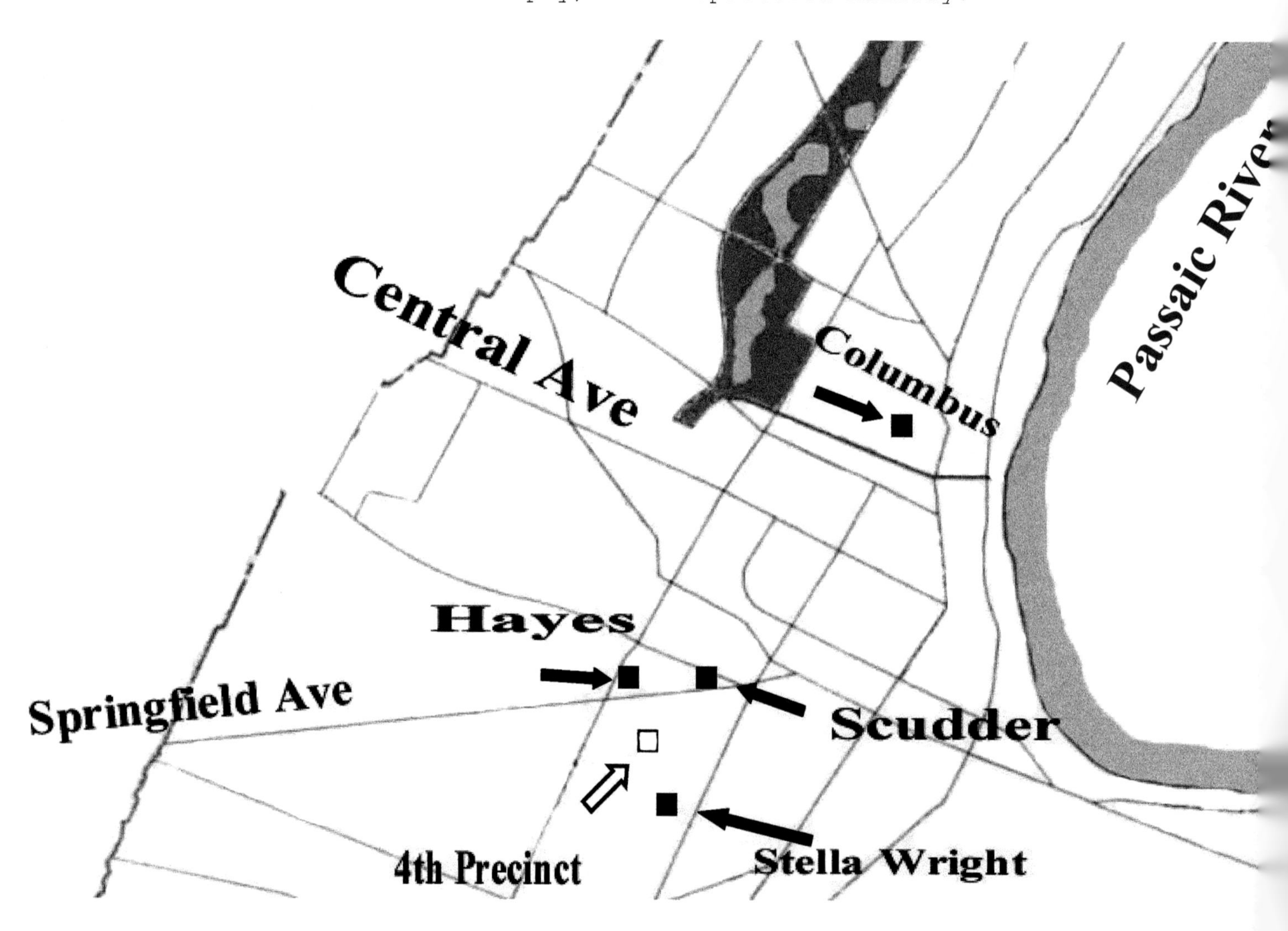

A map of Newark's Central Ward shows the precarious position the 4th Precinct was in.

Richard J. Hughes
New Jersey Governor

New Jersey Governor Richard Hughes tried to rationalize the devastation. "They (blacks) are not oppressed by government. They are oppressed by circumstances. There exists behind them one hundred years of discrimination and cruelty to them, in spite of the efforts of many sincere men to eradicate the cruelty and to bring a day when oppression will no longer be with us.

When one considers that, no matter what any administration - city, state or national can do, the roots of poverty and discrimination that have developed over a century can't be eradicated in a short time, even with all the good will in the world."

Manning the front lines of Newark's rebellion was a large contingent of Central Ward teenagers. Having known only poverty and deprivation their entire, miserable lives, it took little coaxing from adults to prod them into action.

Dr. Wyman Garrett, a prominent black doctor who hailed from Newark and fought his way out of the slums, never forgot the old adage about remembering where you come from. During the Newark Riot, Dr. Garrett traversed the treacherousness streets attempting to persuade the teenage rioters to return home. He later observed, "The veneer that used to cover up the hate is slipping. They're used to being rejected by the establishment of having committees formed to solve problems that don't have anyone on them that they know and trust. You know what really got me during the riot, when I was out trying to get them off the streets. Here were these fifteen-year old kids; I didn't see any fear in their eyes, not a bit of it. The cops and Guardsmen were scared, and I was scared. But not those kids. They say to me, 'Doc, you got some reason to live, you're somebody. You go on home. We don't want you to get hurt.'"

Photos Courtesy Newark Public Library

Newark's Central Ward ablaze - Arsonists targeted merchants whom they had bad dealings with over the years. Since the buildings were built so close together, however, it was like filling an ice cube tray. Fire simply spilt over to the next edifice until only the streets themselves could break the fire.

Civic leaders were quick to pounce on the concept that the riot was instigated, in part at least, by outsiders. It was a futile effort to cast the blame elsewhere as locally it fell on deaf ears. This riot was home grown, "Yes, it was agitation, agitation of neglect and harassment and prejudice," said one irate woman. "People want to blame outsiders so they can pretend that the niggers on their own plantation are too happy to riot."

The riot itself was like trying to cap a volcano in the middle of an eruption. It just wasn't going to happen. "There was only one man who could have walked on Springfield Avenue and said, 'Brothers, cool it.' That was Malcolm X. We have no such leaders now."

Getty Photos

A dead looter, perhaps seeking a pair of shoes or a stylish hat, paid for his foolishness with his life. The authorities that converged on Newark that bloody July week in 1967 gave no quarter. Looters were shot on sight. Another suspected looter, nineteen-year-old James Rutledge, was found shot to death inside a ravaged tavern. His autopsy revealed thirty-nine bullet

HUEY MUST BE SET FREE or
"THE SKY IS THE LIMIT"
GENERAL MEETING
EVERYNIGHT
AT 6:30 PM

Kercheval:

It Will Become You!

Kercheval: It Will Become You

"Ye shall above all things be glad and young" goes the opening line of the E.E. Cummings poem, "For if you're young, whatever life you wear, it will become you." On Detroit's far east side, this philosophy, although originally intended in a positive light, can readily be seen here in a negative one.

The neighborhood surrounding Kercheval Street is one noticeably lacking in revelment. It is a neighborhood like many in big city America of the 1960s that seems to have been left out of the progressive loop.

Kercheval seems hopelessly sandwiched between modern day prosperity and the urban poverty of the past. At the southwest end of Kercheval, the city's sparkling new Lafayette urban renewal project can be found. Now more than 15 years in the making, it quickly became the city's showpiece. To the east, just over the endless canopy of oak trees, can be seen the modern day high-rises of Jefferson Avenue that bristle with progress and prosperity. The showy concrete cathedrals seem to glower down arrogantly over the deprived of Kercheval, a street time has seemingly passed by.

Nowhere is the contrast between the haves and the have nots more self evident than off Kercheval on Detroit's east side. Perhaps this explains why the east side set the precedent in rioting a year before its west side rival. (Above) In the background, the opulence and luxury of Jefferson Avenue high-rises looms brazenly over the downtrodden of Kercheval.

Kercheval was a combination of poverty accompanied by it's close brother frustration. Never is one seen without the other. Houses decades past their life expectancy were desperately held together with tar, paper and hope. Some are so drafty that a candle sitting in the middle of the room can be extinguished when the wind howls at night.

It was here in the late summer of 1966 that frustration boiled over into anger. The Kercheval mini-riot was a third-rate riot by all accounts, but it was the first visible chink in the Model City armor. The administration attempted to downplay the mini-riot by referring to it as an "incident," but the undercurrent of anger was there and no public relations machine was going to dissipate it.

The poor look out into a different world, through a prism that reflects only poverty, turbulence and despair. They live in a constant state of want for the things they know they will never have. Impoverished scenes like the one above conceal a hundred different agonies. With opportunity lacking, the mood of the ghetto is poisonous and self-destructive. The seeds of despair take hold of the very young, drain them of their enthusiasm and replace it with fatalism. The poor do not look at life in terms of days, weeks or years but rather from a survivalist view of hours or minutes because they view their long-term future as nonexistent.

The old Annunciation Church off Kercheval was built in 1905 when it was a German/Irish neighborhood. Communities were built around the church, becoming the moral glue that held neighborhoods together. Spiritual solidarity was central to the family concept. While the presence of the church is still strong in black neighborhoods the sheer numbers pale in comparison to yesteryear, and, as a result, the moral compass that previously guided families through hard times is now seemingly canceled out by endless waves of moral degeneracy inflicted on our youth by the media and Hollywood. Churches, unfortunately, have taken on a secondary role in society today.

It was the dilution of these long-standing cultural mores, in tandem with economic barriers created by racial prejudice, that led to a rapid disintegration of the urban, black family.

Militant groups offered a cause or a philosophy to young teenagers who have never had anything to believe in. Harlem's Adam Clayton Powell, a preacher himself, cited "They [black teenagers] don't believe in the old line, fundamentalist preaching of the preacher who used to be the pivot of the black community." .

The Beat of a Distant Drum

Since 1964 the nation had witnessed several hundred riots of various magnitudes across the country. The Cavanagh administration had been sitting on pins and needles since it entered office in 1962. Every summer, as cities around them erupted in violence and mayhem, Detroit leaders took great pride that the chaos had passed them by. As a result of their anarchical abstinence, Detroit's reputation as the Model City seemed to be growing exponentially. At the conclusion of every summer, the administration congratulated themselves on another riot free summer, proof positive that their social programs were working.

But beneath the rosy headlines the veneer of civility which the Model City image exuded had worn down, and now the hostility was beginning to show through. Cavanagh's star, which once shone brightly in the black community, had now dimmed considerably. A Kercheval resident echoed these sentiments about the mayor. "Him and that urban renewal. Man, they steal my house, put those peckerwoods [whites] in it, then tell you to move to some worse house 200 years old. I'm tired of running, tired of being pushed. There's no place else to go. I hope to God it breaks out full scale. If I die, I'd rather die for something."

After Watts it would be too late to make amends. The line in the sand was now being crossed by every ghetto in the country. Time had run out for the pacifistic civil rights movement. Henceforth, it would be an eye for an eye.

Cleveland State University

The terrible Hough riot that inundated Cleveland occurred only one week before the Kercheval mini-riot. Riots being contagious, Hough was the tumbling domino directly in front of Kercheval.

It was the dirty little secret the nation refused to acknowledge or address. The societal boiler was way past its pressure limit and the relief valves were not working.

The Detroit Police Department, still almost 95 percent white, were seen in the black community as an enforcer of white power. Detroit was clearly going through a transitional phase by 1966. While the white flight to the suburbs steadily increased from a trickle to a steady rush, the white mantra of power that built the city refused to give in to the inevitable.

Kercheval seemed to abound with militant groups who loathed the white establishment, particularly the group known as the Afro-American Youth Movement. Its members were philosophically out of phase with the civil rights movement. Pacifism was great during massive demonstrations when the cameras were rolling, making people accountable. But in the dark shadows where back alley justice could be conducted, this concept didn't work. The Kercheval militants were bent on starting a riot as a springboard for their black revolution.

Riots of the 1960s generally followed certain unyielding patterns. They characteristically occurred between the hours of 6:00 and 9:00 p.m. on weekdays. They also were inherent towards hot, muggy days when people are suffering from sleep deprivation and are highly irritable. Only those generations that grew up before the era of central air conditioning can recall those "long, hot summer nights." The hot weather was a primer, as rioters habitually did not voice their grievances in freezing weather or rain showers, preferring rather to await more agreeable climate.

The area of Kercheval and Pennsylvania had been earmarked as a potential trouble spot by the city for some time. On the sultry hot evening of August 9, one of the "Big Four" police cruisers spotted seven black males loitering on the corner of Kercheval and Pennsylvania and asked them to disperse. Four of them did. But the other three, desirous of staging a rebellion, refused to yield.

Refusing to relinquish identification, the inevitable scuffle ensued. The militants, knowing this would draw a crowd, attempted to incite a riot, "This is our neighborhood and we won't be moved. Whitey is going to kill us." As desired, a restless crowd quickly formed and the Big Four radioed for backup.

As luck would have it, this being 8:30 p.m. on a Tuesday, the department was at full strength. Even better, owing to an anti-Vietnam demonstration downtown, the specially trained crowd control apparatus called the Tactical Mobile Unit (TMU) was monitoring the demonstration only three miles away. The TMU was formed in 1965 especially to deal with crowds but unlike their rival the Commandos, they were specially trained to endure crowd slander and provocation without reacting. Their skills would soon be tested to the limit.

Inspector Anthony Bertoni from the 5th Precinct was in charge of the TMU. As he watched the rather innocuous anti-war demonstration, he heard chatter over his radio about "rocks flying on Kercheval" so he decided to investigate.

As his cruiser headed east on Kercheval passing Mt. Elliott, Bertoni's instincts told him something was amiss. "We could sense something was happening because the street was deserted. There were garbage cans in the middle of the street. The next thing I know this kid came running into the middle of the street and busted the window on the passenger side of our car. He was not over twelve or thirteen years old. I called both (TMU) units in, we parked the cars away from the incident and on foot, we moved down the street."

As the scrum on the corner of Kercheval-Pennsylvania broke up, and the perpetrators quickly hustled off to the 5th Precinct, a crowd of teenagers began throwing rocks at unsuspecting white motorists (i.e. Watts) and breaking out store windows. Despite the rioters well motivated attempt to spread havoc, their moment would be brief. The TMU had arrived.

The TMU quickly disembarked onto Kercheval and went into their diamond formation. The front wedge of the diamond walks forward while the rear-facing wedge walks backwards, protecting the rear. In the middle of the diamond are free-floating officers who scan all directions for impending danger.

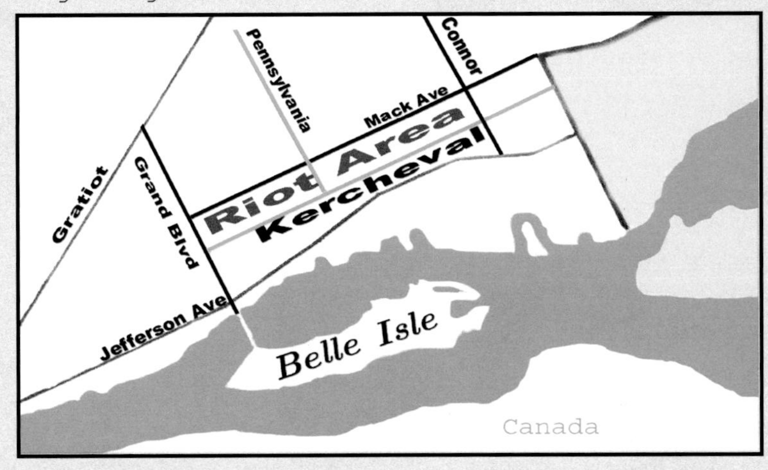

Courtesy Windsor Star

The Tactical Mobile Unit (TMU) of the Detroit Police Department, like the Big Four, was the terror of black neighborhoods. It was only a matter of time before the wrong policeman ran into the wrong civilian.

As the TMU continued heading east, sweeping all four lanes of Kercheval, they passed the corner of Pennsylvania where the melee started. Over 100 angry spectators were crowding the four corners, shouting threats at the heavily armed TMU as they marched by. "Wait till tomorrow night. It'll be just like Vietnam." The anger was certainly there but not the numbers or leadership. One bemused spectator just shook his head, "Hell, they did a much better job in Watts. They can't seem to get this riot off the ground."

Detroit police sealed off a mile-long stretch of Kercheval. As darkness descended on the troubled area, police search lights that had been set up on Kercheval probed the inky darkness for trouble. The flat, metallic voice of a police sergeant resonated over the loud speakers:

Please stay off the streets. We only want the troublemakers out of the way. Please go back inside. We don't want trouble.

The rioters, mostly frustrated teenagers "feeling their pepper," bid a hasty retreat as the sea of blue washed over Kercheval. By 10 p.m., Kercheval was curb to curb with police. Instead of direct confrontation, the teenagers implemented a haphazard, hit and run technique. Poorly fabricated and poorly aimed Molotov cocktails sailed through the air, landing harmlessly in the street. Store front windows were broken but little if anything was looted. "The most significant thing that's happening out there is that these kids who were taught all their lives to fear those crackers [police] can now stand up with a rock and say, 'I'm tired of this,' commented the leader of the Afro-American Youth Movement. "Things will never be the same again."

As Tuesday turned into Wednesday afternoon, the tension mounted. Both sides, the DPD and the militants, waited for the other to make the first move which would trigger a full-scale riot. Convoys of heavily armed TMU vehicles, with shotguns protruding out the windows, lumbered slowly up and down Kercheval as hundreds of piercing eyes watched. One of the spectators fumed, "Look at that bayonet on that cop's gun. Man, I'm buying a 16 gauge with my whole pay Friday." The anger resonated, "It's not just the police. It's the overpricing, the insults from Whitey. And that TMU. They call it 'crime control.' Hell, it's a riot squad, a Gestapo, the storm troopers. You don't need a riot force if everything is really as good as they're saying."

But the triggering incident never came. By the end of the second night the DPD was aided by providence as a cold, steady rain set in, dampening hostilities and sending the revolutionaries home frustrated. It was the end of the Kercheval mini-riot but not the end of rebellious activity. As the administration backslapped and toasted each other about the conquering of Kercheval, another storm of infinitely greater intensity was brewing on the city's west side. They had no way of knowing that providence and luck would soon part company with the Model City.

Bayonet equipped Detroit police are silhouetted on rain drenched Kercheval as the August mini-riot draws to a close. They managed to put down the riot without firing a shot, a feat that would earn the DPD national acclaim. For the administration, an air of complacency set in. Detroit had a riot plan, they put it into action, and it worked marvelously. Henceforth, they felt the city could handle anything with minimal force. By the time the Great Rebellion was over the following summer, they wished they had never heard of Kercheval.

"Men are both inner and outer beings. They must have some sense of their own worth and human identity. They also must find some meaningful place in their society. If they are denied and rejected by the world around them they have two basic choices. They can sink into despair and passivity, that resigned acceptance we often mistake for devotion to peace and order. Or they can create their own world and their own society: a black society."

Walter Reuther Library

"Being against violence is like being against sin.
It is right; it is popular; and it is easy.
However it will not diminish evil, unless you also provide alternatives to the temptations and desires which drive men towards wrong.
If the beginning of wisdom is understanding, the condition of effective political solution is knowledge of the problem."

Walter Reuther Library

Walter Reuther Library

"We know some things are not causes. This has not been caused by some mysterious and special defect in the black character. Few people have borne oppression and anguish with greater forbearance and patience. A hundred years of discrimination, poverty and often unspeakable brutality is only now erupting into sporadic insurrection, while the vast majority of blacks miraculously retain their faith that justice will be found within the orderly process of liberty."

"Men truly without hope or expectation do not revolt. Only when the door to possibility opens to a sliver of light do men hurl themselves against it."

AP/Wide World Photos

Walter Reuther Library

"Violence, although intolerable, has its roots in grievances that are also intolerable. If any man should deny this, let him also say he would be willing to have his child assume a black skin and grow to manhood in a black ghetto."

ECONOMY
PRINTING
CO

The Nether World of 12th Street

A Bizarre Amalgamation

When the pioneers of Detroit were laying out the city's boundaries, everything was included inside the giant inverted U shape of Grand Boulevard. This area was so large by 19th century standards that no one ever envisioned Detroit pushing beyond it. But the 20th century had arrived and with it came a voracious appetite for land to accommodate the automotive tempest that had blown into town and was redefining Detroit by the year.

To accentuate the "Grand" in Grand Boulevard, Albert Kahn's General Motors and Fisher buildings were erected. Just west of them could be found the cavernous Henry Ford Hospital. The area was bulging with new growth.

With the onset of the Roaring Twenties, the Jewish community would make the pilgrimage from the east side to 12th Street. From Grand Boulevard all the way north to Clairmount, 12th Street was dominated by a mile-long row of Jewish shops. Twelfth Street was a city within a city. It was no longer necessary to go downtown to shop; Jewish bakeries, fish markets and handyman stores filled the void. These two and three story brick buildings, each with their own unique ornamentation and configuration, were built so close together that 12th Street gave the appearance of a walled street. Even in peaceful times, the buildings always seemed to loom over 12th Street with an angry foreboding.

The area was no stranger to violence. Twelfth Street was once the home of the notorious "Purple Gang." A byproduct of Prohibition, this ruthless group of Jewish racketeers thrived on the illicit alcohol trade that flourished in Detroit. The Purple Gang baptized 12th Street with the blood of anyone who decided to go into business for themselves. Bullet ridden bodies of people who tried were a harbinger of the violent days to come.

With the gradual easing of housing restrictions in the 1950s, the complexion of 12th Street began to change. Middle-class blacks from the east side began to trickle over. For a few years there seemed to be a peaceful coexistence. However, when Black Bottom was razed for urban renewal, much of its displaced poor (including the more sordid elements) had little place else to go. Like the previous generations of blacks who followed the Jews into Black Bottom, blacks now followed the Jews over to 12th Street, the new Hastings Street.

Many Jewish residents began an exodus to the suburbs of Southfield and West Bloomfield. The Jewish Shaarey Zadek congregation had built a new synagogue in Southfield and sold its old 12th Street building to an incoming black congregation. The black minister was invited to the dedication of the new synagogue, after which he exhorted to the rabbi, "You take good care of the building, rabbi. We'll be wanting to buy it from you in 10 years."

Twelfth Street had deteriorated badly in the years preceding the riot. The fabled Jewish thoroughfare was now a far cry from its kosher days of gefilte fish and matzo balls. By 1967, the remaining Jewish shops now formed a bizarre amalgamation with the liquor stores, pawn shops, soul-food shacks and sleazy bars that had materialized. Greedy landlords divided and subdivided the once-spacious apartments and flats above 12th Street. The area now boasted the highest population density in the city and, not surprisingly, the highest crime rate. Twelfth Street had become a malfunctioning melting pot that was about to boil over.

The ill-fated 12th Street one week before the riot. One of the old 12th Street regulars described its twisted dichotomy: "There was a daytime 12th Street, and there was a nighttime 12th Street, and they didn't overlap. During the day the good citizens came out like your mother. All the hustlers that were out there knew that your mother wasn't into that stuff, so she just came shopping. But come dark, mama goes home, gets off the street, and the night shift comes on." Known as the Sin Strip, Avenue of Fun or the Pocket Ghetto, anything you wanted, legal or illegal, you could get on 12th Street.

As the sun went down over 12th Street, a nefarious underworld emerged from the darkness. Its dens of iniquity opened to the endless tide of revelers that swept into town from who knows where to indulge themselves in the shadowy nether world of 12th Street. The eerie neon glow emanating from the store signs completed the deviant circle of decadency that saturated the sinful strip.

"It's a place where a black man with a little money in his pocket can go and try to forget he's black."

But black men were not the only ones seeking to forget their worldly troubles. Despite being the most segregated city in the country, when it came to sex, racism was temporarily forgotten on 12th Street. White "Johns" flooded the thoroughfare, eager to partake in the army of black hookers who plied their trade up and down the street at the economical rate of $10 for 10 minutes. Prostitutes sauntered on street corners, cocked their hips in doorways or hung out of second and third floor windows advertising for the slow procession of prospective Johns that were often bumper to bumper on the street below. Decked out in yellow wigs and orange dresses, prostitutes were often verbally chastised by street-corner preachers attempting to save their souls. Others hopped in your car for a discrete sojourn around the block, an early form of drive-thru service, if you will.

Twelfth Street was a freak magnet, attracting the most sordid cast of characters known to man. Slick-haired pimps roamed the street adorned in shark-skins suits that changed color from gray to purple in the sunlight. Hustlers clad in bell-bottoms and shoes with jangling spurs picked through cars while their unwary owners satiated themselves in the brothels above the now silent 12th Street stores. Revelers sporting shiny gold pants and black silk shirts danced to the endless beat of Motown which blared from the neighborhood juke boxes.

On the Saturday night prior to the riot, 12th Street was lined with out of state cars bearing license plates from Ohio, Indiana and Kentucky. It was hardly a revelation to the locals, nor was it apparently to the entire Mid-west, that 12th Street was the best side show around.

But fornication was not the only vice available. Drugs and gambling bolstered the veritable treasure trove of vices offered to those who came seeking the outrageous. They were rarely disappointed. During Prohibition, thousands of blind pigs (speakeasy) honeycombed the city. While the failure of Prohibition was now only a laughable mistake of history, its legacy of blind pigs still remained scattered throughout the city.

Detroit Public Library

The infamous Economy Printing, which hosted the notorious party that brought Detroit to its knees, ironically managed to survive the riot virtually unscathed, while much of 12th Street burned to the ground. The police raid would prove to be, as one local appropriately phrased it, "the most expensive pinch in history."

Bill Scott always took an active part in the 12th Street community. The trouble was, people being what they are, no one else seemed too interested in dabbling in community politics. But Bill Scott knew that the world was changing, and with the civil rights movement in full force, the political stars would never be aligned this way again. Unable to spark his neighbors into action, he put his keen street instincts to work and conjured up a drawing card, the United Community League for Civic Action. It was formed in 1965 for the express purpose of backing local political candidates running for office and thus helping the neighborhood gain some badly needed political clout. To house his ambitions, Scott leased the upper floor of the vacant Economy Printing building in 1966 just north of Clairmount on 12th Street.

William Scott II

"They Call Me Bill"

Scott was well known in the 12th Street area. A sly sixty years of age, Scott was considered by those who knew him to have a PhD in street hustling, "A lot of politicians know me and they don't call me Charles or Jim or Tom. They call me Bill." Even Scott, however, had trouble getting through the bureaucracy. "Try to get them after election and they are always busy. If you want a street blocked off and a fire hydrant turned on for the kids, you might as well whistle up a tree."

Politicians often helped pay the expenses of the United Community League because Scott could get the word out. In off-election years the contributions, not surprisingly, slowed to a trickle. Nevertheless, Economy Printing was considered an ideal location in the heart of a burgeoning black populace. Scott had been told, "to hold onto this good location when political activity was slow, even if it meant running a speakeasy." On the weekends, this is exactly what Scott would do. It was a chance for the locals to blow off steam, gamble, have some soul food and, of course, drink. For Scott, it was a chance to indoctrinate patrons into the political process.

Since they had no liquor license, gambling license or permission to host such sordid activities, police departments are compelled to shut them down. The catch is that the illegal acts must be witnessed, and blind pig operators generally possess a real faculty for keeping this from happening.

Take Bill Scott's humble abode off 12th Street. Housed on the second floor of the defunct Economy Printing, it was impossible to observe illegal activity despite the obvious debauchery that could be heard from the street.

The membership card for Bill Scott's United Community League. To gain admittance to the blind pig, you knocked on the front door and the peephole opened. You either flashed the card or provided a password. If the doorman was the least bit suspicious, the peephole slammed shut and you went elsewhere.

MEMBERSHIP CARD

United Community League for Civic Action

9125 TWELFTH STREET DETROIT, MICHIGAN 48206

Phone 894-9349

THIS IS TO CERTIFY that:

Name ______________________________

Address ____________________ Phone__________

is a participating member of the UNITED COMMUNITY LEAGUE FOR CIVIC ACTION and is entitled to all of the rights, privileges and immunities accorded by this organization, subject, however to the Constitution and By-Laws of said organization.

Attested:

______________________ Office Sec'y

Detroit Public Library

The turbulent summer of '67 had already yielded over fifty insurrections across the country by the middle of July. The sacking of Newark made it fifty-one. As the God of calamity centered himself firmly over Detroit, a number of public officials huddled together at the behest of an apprehensive mayor. They were asked to stage a mock riot and then play it out in an effort to predict the city's state of readiness.

With a map detailing Detroit's black community spread out on the table, two intersecting lines were drawn arbitrarily to represent the epicenter where they would focus on their fictional exercise. The lines intersected, by sheer coincidence, at 12th and Clairmount.

Their prediction was to come within an ace of fulfillment. It was appropriate that the crosshairs of this riotous rifle were aimed at 12th Street. It was easily the most dangerous and crime-ridden section of town, teaming with unstable personalities and an array of vices that rendered analogies of Sodom and Gomorrah.

There was something in the air that July. As one militant veteran from the failed Kercheval uprising the previous summer bluntly forecast, "We weren't ready then. When we are ready, you'll know about it."

It was up to the Detroit Police Department's "cleanup squad" to prevent such illicit activity. This was a special group of officers whose task it was to ferret out, penetrate and bust blind pigs. It generally consisted of a sergeant and two or three undercover patrolmen. In the 10th Precinct, this meant Sgt. Arthur Howison and company.

The cleanup squad had attempted to raid the Economy Printing building on nine separate occasions in the year preceding the riot. They succeeded twice, the last time only a month before the riot, in which they netted twenty-eight prisoners. "We'd been trying to get it for some time," one undercover officer said. "Scott had a good thing going."

The pocket ghetto of 12th Street was easily within reach of some very respectable black neighborhoods. The highly esteemed Boston-Edison subdivision, with its cavernous mansions that once housed Detroit's auto elite, is only a bottle throw away. To the west of 12th is the noble LaSalle Boulevard with its manicured yards and trimmed hedges. In this respect, one could say the neighborhood was divided between the rich, the middle class and the felonious characters that flourished on 12th Street. Respectable citizens pulled their shades down to the 12th Street graft but to no avail. The vice was spreading and the commotion brought on by the night shift was enraging the legitimate citizens of the neighborhood.

The 12th Street regulars were a different breed however. Since many were transient in nature and generally did not own property in the area, they cared little that the neighborhood was rapidly eroding. They viewed the raids by the Detroit Police Department as an attempt by the white power structure to inflict their social mores on them.

The night of July 22 was, ironically, a full moon. Perhaps the old legend about a full moon causing strange behavior and violence (lunacy - Latin for moon) are true. There were, as previous chapters have spelled out in detail, plenty of reasons for ghetto rebellion, and they all came together on this moon lit night.

Tensions had been noticeably high of late around 12th Street. A local black man named Danny Thomas, an Army veteran, was brutally murdered less than a month before the riot by a group of white thugs as Thomas and his pregnant wife were enjoying a picnic in Rouge Park. Neither of Detroit's major newspapers even mentioned the murder yet had gone out of their way to avenge the murders of Marilyn Donahue and Betty James six years earlier. The newspapers claimed they didn't want to inflame an already tense situation, but the black community didn't buy it. It was viewed simply as yet another miscarriage of justice, further evidence that the civil rights movement was not working and they would have to take matters into their own hands.

Blood that Never Dried

Saturday July 22, 1967, found Detroit in the middle of an oppressive heat wave. It had regularly approached 90 degrees in a neighborhood where air conditioning was as rare as a presidential visit. It was eerily similar to the searing June day in 1943 that spilled the blood of Detroiters all over Woodward Avenue and opened a gapping wound in the soul of the city. It was, after twenty-four years, blood that never dried.

Bill Scott was hosting a party at Economy Printing for two returning Vietnam veterans and another who was on his way over. The 10th Precinct cleanup squad was looking for action too. Sgt. Howison, who is white, was sorely out of place in this virtually all black neighborhood. His two undercover operatives, Patrolman Charles Henry and Patrolman Joe Brown are black and in plain cloths. At 10:30 Saturday night, they knocked on the door of Economy Printing posing as University of Cincinnati basketball players. The peephole opened and the doorman, suspicious, challenged them. "We don't know you." Their story was too flimsy and he sent them away. The patrolmen departed for other game as Economy Printing's jukebox, blaring James Brown, echoed on into the night.

Acknowledging defeat, Howison took his crew and moved on; there were other blind pigs to bust. By 3:30 in the morning, however, they were still unsuccessful. Almost ready to call it a night, they found themselves coincidentally passing Economy Printing again when patrolmen Henry noticed three young ladies heading for the front door. On a hunch, he exited the car and quickly mixed in with the group. The peephole opened, and the very same doorman who had curtly refused him five hours earlier, now foggy-eyed from drinking, gleefully waved them by. The raid was on!

July 1967

Sun	Mon	Tues	Wed	Thur	Fri	Sat
						1
2	3	4	5	6	7	8
9	10	11	12	13	14	15
16	17	18	19	20	21	22
23	24	25	26	27	28	29
30	31					

Bentley Library

The stairwell of Economy Printing that led to the defining moment in Detroit's history. Note the police pry bar used to gain entry still sits at the entrance. To circumvent hostile crowds during raids, arrestees were normally led out the back door. In this case, the back door was a steel fire door impervious to sledgehammers. The padlock was of hardened steel and the key could not be located. Since the rear of the building backed up to a long, dead-end alley, Sgt. Howison had no other recourse but to disembark with his prisoners via the front door, right in front of the tempestuous crowd he so desperately wished to avoid.

Patrolman Henry, a future police commander, later commented on what transpired next. "I had trouble getting in. There was a pool table they'd use to shoot dice, a bar, a kitchen that served food. It looked like a third-rate bar. People were having a good time. There were different circumstances in those days. People were friendlier, they would drink and gamble, but there was very little dope. Customers had no fear of a jail sentence. Especially in the 10th Precinct, along Twelfth Street (a police raid) was a common occurrence."

Cleanup-crew procedure dictated that Henry had ten minutes to witness an illegal act before the front door would be broken down announcing the beginning of the raid. It was now 3:45 and Henry was running out of time. He went up to the bar and put down fifty cents, receiving a beer from Bill Scott himself. Scott later claimed it was on the house. It was a moot point. The dice throwing in the next room was enough for a bust. It was at this propitious time that Howison and company came crashing through the door, taking everyone by surprise.

Pandemonium ensued. Howison was as bewildered as anyone when he found not the usual fifteen to twenty party goers but eight-three! This presented him with a difficult dilemma. The 10th Precinct possessed only one paddy wagon which held fourteen prisoners at most. Phone calls were made to the adjoining 6th, 11th and 13th Precincts to quickly send their wagons over, but this would take time. In the interim, the prisoners were held upstairs.

Outside on 12th Street, the commotion of the police cruisers was beginning to draw a crowd. This was the norm on 12th Street as people wandered about from party to party in numbers all through the night.

At first there were only some twenty people watching from across the street, 12th Street regulars with wine clouded eyes, drinking a staggering path back home. As the first paddy wagon arrived and Howison brought down a group of prisoners, the streetwalkers directed some good-natured mocking towards the familiar faces. "We'll send you some cigarettes when you get to Jacktown." But as the first wagon pulled away, and the police awaited the painfully slow arrival of the second, the 12th Street jocularity would quickly come to a halt. "Green Sleeves" had arrived.

A Ford Motor Company employee, young Michael Lewis typified the plight of the urban black in many respects. Frustrated, depressed and weary of the white establishment foisting its morals on the black community while reinforcing it with their batons. Like the militant brothers on Kercheval the previous August, Lewis recognized the time for rebellion had come.

Michael Lewis, the ill-famed "Green Sleeves," was the man accused of inciting the crowd outside Economy Printing and starting the riot. At the time he was known to the police in attendance only as Green Sleeves because, despite the sweltering temperature he wore a long green-sleeved shirt. With his constant, belligerent diatribes launched at the patrolmen tending the paddy wagons on 12th Street, he was able to turn the jovial crowd into a tempestuous mob. While the police deny any charge of brutality, decades of aberrant behavior needed only a fuse. The raid itself was poorly executed, taking an hour in a neighborhood known to be seething with anti-police sentiment.

Michael Lewis

Like a ticking bomb, the agonizing minutes clicked by as the cleanup crew awaited the next wagon. Sgt. Harold Smith had arrived with some young police trainees. They were to receive an indoctrination of incredible proportions. The crowd outside, which originally numbered twenty around 4:00 a.m., quickly multiplied to fifty, then one hundred, then two hundred. The incensed Green Sleeves, maintaining a position well to the rear of the crowd, began lacing the air with invective, "Black Power, don't let them take our people away; look what they are doing to our people....Let's kill them whitey mother f-----s ... let's get the bricks and bottles going. Why do they come down here and do this to our people?" The crowd was quickly swayed. Howison, still on the second floor detaining the remaining prisoners, could hear bottles hitting the side of the building. He was quickly joined by one of Sgt. Smith's men, who had been outside guarding the entrance, now announced alarmingly, "It's getting kinda hairy outside, hurry up."

Green Sleeves would soon be joined by another angry young man, Bill Scott III, ironically the son of the blind pig proprietor. The younger Scott was present the last time Economy Printing was raided, frequently working the peep hole himself. He still bore a large chip on his shoulder about the way the police had treated his family and the never-ending frustrations of ghetto life were just beneath the skin. Now seeing his father and sister forced into the paddy wagon, he too was irrevocably moved towards rebellion.

The cleanup crew now anxiously awaited the arrival of the last wagon. It was 4:45; they had been there an ill advised hour! As the last wagon approached, some two hundred and fifty angry onlookers had pooled across the street. Led by Green Sleeves, the periodic missile throwing continued against the harried police standing guard outside.

The crowd could see the last prisoners upstairs emptying into the stairwell for the final load and when the wagon doors closed behind them, the final barrage of bricks and bottles showered the frenzied officers. As the frenzied flight back to the 10th Precinct began, two cruisers narrowly missed colliding with each other, much to the delight of the 12th Street regulars.

But the coup de gras was yet to come. As the police began to breathe a premature sigh of relief, someone from the crowd picked up a bottle and launched it high into the air. Like the home crowd at a football game watching a last chance hail Mary pass, the mob bridled as the bottle arced passed a streetlight, began its decent and crashed right through the rear window of the last police cruiser which wisely kept on going. Like scoring the winning touchdown with time running out, the crowd went berserk.
The Great Rebellion had begun.

Courtesy Windsor Star

Twelfth Street shortly after the raid. Economy Printing is past the light on the left.

AP/World Wide Photo

Twelfth Street looking south towards the boulevard. As daylight broke, this was the scene that greeted the Detroit police when they returned to the area in force. Their numbers, however, were dwarfed by a swarm of looters. A holiday of piracy ensued. Soon after this photo was taken, 12th Street would be on fire. The Supreme Linoleum & Paint Company on the right would burn for days.

Just past 5 a.m. on Sunday, as the city was just starting to awaken from its slumber, Detroit's 10th Precinct began to get a flurry of phone calls from residents who wanted to know why all the burglar alarms were going off on 12th Street. Lieutenant Raymond Good grabbed a man and went to investigate, unaware of the trouble his cleanup crew had encountered. The cleanup crew was also unaware of the ruptured beehive they had left behind. They police believed that, with their presence removed from the area, the situation would calm down on its own. It didn't. It was still dark as Good's police cruiser pulled up to the frantic scene on the corner of 12th and Clairmount. Good could see a swarm of people on the street, including Green Sleeves, who passed right in front of the cruiser. When Good got out to confront him he was immediately hit from behind with a piece of cement. Good staggered to the car yelling, "Let's get the hell out of here!" As the oblivious cleanup crew filled out paperwork back at the 10th Precinct, a startled Good burst through the door. "What did you do!?"

Like an A bomb detonation, the crowd surged down 12th Street, doing a dance of destruction as they went. A symphony of burglar alarms added to the carnival atmosphere. When the police did not return, the crowd grew. Between 8 a.m. and noon, the crowd ballooned to some 10,000 people. Some were looters, some were observers, some were older residents trying to stop it, to no avail. The rioting continued unabated. Inertia was now in charge!

Groups of looters, brandishing a wide variety of hammers and crowbars, feverishly began their assault on 12th Street stores.

According to an out of town reporter who witnessed the riot, "Detroit's second day of violence was aimed not so much at skin color as color television sets. In no other riot-sacked city has there been such wholesale cooperation between Negroes and whites queuing up like happy locusts for a running grab at life's luxuries."

Timeline for Tumult

Sunday - July 23

3:45 a.m.	DPD raids blind pig housed at Economy Printing, 12th Street/Clairmount. Angry crowd of locals forms outside.
5:00	DPD departs with prisoners under hail of projectiles.
5:05	Mob flows down street breaking windows. When police do not reappear, looting begins.
7:50	Commandos conduct sweep of 12th but proves ineffectual. At least 3,000 rioters present.
8:24	First fire is started. Detroit Fire Department arrives and extinguishes fire without incident.
9:00	Crowd on 12th Street between 8,000 - 10,000.
9:30	Black community leaders attempt to calm thousands of rioters on 12th Street and are stoned in return.
10:30	Police now find themselves under a barrage of bottles/stones. Character of riot is changing from carnival atmosphere to violence.
1:00	Fire Department returns to fight more fires but this time are stoned.
3:30 p.m.	Fires raging on 12th Street.
4:00	Turning point of riot: now spreads west to adjacent Linwood, Dexter and Grand River. Twelfth Street given up for lost.
4:20	Mayor Cavanagh calls governor to request National Guard.
5:25	First reports of looting on Grand River. First contingent of Guardsmen arrive at staging area (Central High School on Linwood). Main body of National Guard is on annual two week training in Grayling, 200 miles away.
6:31	Police at Grand River and Joy radio that situation is "out of control."
6:57	Governor Romney officially authorizes use of National Guard which now begin to appear on streets of Detroit from staging area.
9:07	First report of sniper fire (at Police helicopter).
9:37	First report of sniper fire at fireman.
10:35	Riot spreads to east side, Kercheval and Mack area.

Monday - July 24

12:15	Detroit Fire Chief Charles Quinlan requests suburban assistance after fighting 300 fires on Sunday, forty of which are still raging. Detroit will celebrate this its 266th birthday with the most arsons any city has ever seen.
12:25 a.m	First riot fatality, white store owner shoots white looter. Looting is wide spread throughout city.
1:33	Police log: "Dexter & Davidson - entire block on fire."
3:00	Cavanagh and Romney contact Washington and request federal troops.
9:00	Cavanagh and Romney renew request for federal troops.
12:00 p.m	President Johnson authorizes federal troops to Detroit but sends Cyrus Vance ahead to determine if troops are really necessary.
3:50	Federal troops land at Selfridge Air Force Base but are ordered not to disembark. Johnson hopes riot will subside before they have to be committed. Until then, 5,000 Guardsmen and police patrol both East and West sides of the city. The police arrested 2,931 people on Monday and seventeen of the riots forty-three dead would meet their maker on this day.

Tuesday - July 25

12:00 a.m. President Johnson goes on TV to rationalize his decision to send U.S. Troops into Detroit and cites Romney's "inability to restore order" seven times.
For the next three hours the snipers unleash a barrage of attacks across the city on unsuspecting targets.

12:20 Detroit fireman Carl Smith shot and killed by sniper.

1:10 U.S. Army begins deploying on Detroit's east side.

3:30 Detroit police officer Jerome Olshove shot and killed.

Wednesday - July 26

1:00 a.m. Three black teenagers found dead of gunshot wounds at Algiers Motel. Originally thought to have been sniper victims, suspicion is quickly cast upon Detroit Police Department. Fallout from this incident will be a source of consternation in the city for years to come.

The sniper finale gets under way as the west side is again inundated with bullets whistling through the air.

Thursday - July 27

State police are withdrawn from city as hostilities lessen.

Friday - July 28

Largest riot in nation's history is over. Thousands of sightseers are bumper to bumper in the riot areas, anxious to marvel at the wounded city.

Saturday - July 29

As the week draws to a close, the last shooting fatality is recorded. Nineteen-year-old Ernest Roquemore is killed by a paratrooper who was aiming at a fleeing felon. Roquemore inadvertently crossed into the line of fire.

Sunday - July 30

U.S. Army musters out of Detroit; Guardsmen leave the following weekend.

Dead: 43
Injured: 657
Arrested: 7,231
Damage to buildings: $50-75 million
Damage to city: Incalculable

Owing to the success in putting down the Kercheval mini-riot in 1966, it was decided by Cavanagh and Girardin to follow the same parameters of police restraint, meaning no looters would be shot in hopes that the lack of provocation would cause the crowd to self-liquidate. One must also weigh the value of not shooting into the crowd of spectators, many of whom (as can be seen lining the sidewalks) were women and children. Their deaths at this early stage would surely have brought about a full fledged race riot. So, much to the disdain of the police, they cordoned off the area and waited. But the fury never subsided. An avalanche of humanity poured onto 12th, at some points over 10,000 people joined the melee.

It was former Commissioner Herbert Hart, however, who had warned years previously that no two incidents were alike and it would be imprudent to prepare for one based on the outcome of another. He was right. Twelfth Street was drastically different from Kercheval. The population density of 12th was the highest in the city, as was the crime rate. The dwellings were multi-storied as opposed to single-story and the street itself narrower and constricted. With no resolution seemingly in sight, the Commandos were hastily assembled and prepared to conduct their sweep at 7:50 a.m. They were more outnumbered now than at any time since the raid. But the situation had reached a critical mass and all hopes of stopping the riot were now pinned on the Commandos. It was now or never.

As their twenty-four man, V-shaped wedge started forward, their bayonet tipped carbines glistening in the already suffocating July sun, the burglar alarms still clanging away after having been tripped hours earlier, the crowd began to part like the biblical Red Sea before them. But owing to the geometrics of 12th Street, many rioters simply exited down alleyways and reappeared again behind the Commandos, a tactical stalemate. This is the same thing that happened in Watts two years before. The success of Kercheval would not be repeated here. No miracles would come from the sky either. With the DPD at its lowest manpower of the week, the rioters could not have selected a better time to rebel.

By 9:30 a.m., community leaders asked that the Commandos be withdrawn all together so they could enter the area and attempt to settle the rioters down on their own terms. It was a disaster. A Detroit congressman, atop a car with a bullhorn, was heckled badly as missiles landed at his feet. They were forced to bid a hasty retreat. “You try to talk to those people and they’ll knock you into the middle of next year.”

Some 12th Street shopkeepers always gave their customers the full measure. Others took advantage of the economic plight of the poor. Since many locals had no transportation, they were essentially forced to shop on 12th Street, where unscrupulous merchants habitually sold rotting meat, sour milk or cheap, shabby furniture at a substantial mark up. Some were quite liberal with extending credit to low-income blacks knowing the debt would be paid five-fold upon completion. It was a grievance of long standing with the locals. A fervent hatred of 12th Street merchants grew to alarming proportions over the years. With the riot now in full swing, shady merchants became the first target of the rioters rage. In a desperate attempt to ward off rioters, black merchants hastily scrawled "Soul Brother" on their windows.

With the failure of the Commando sweep, 12th Street was given up for lost. The riot area was cordoned off in hopes that they could contain the riot. In effect, looters were given a moral holiday. Rioters quickly learned the police were told not to shoot and began assault by mouth and missile against their old foe. "They won't shoot," said one young looter. "The mayor said they aren't supposed to." The police gritted their teeth for the time being but would soon pay the rioters back with their own coin. (Below) Still adhering to the no-shoot order, Detroit police watch in disgust as rioters' loot and burn their way unabated down 12th Street.

Detroit Public Library

Just north of Economy Printing, the first contingent of Guardsmen assemble outside St. Mark's for their initial assault on 12th Street Sunday evening. Several hundred Guardsmen were on drill status in the Detroit area and thus quickly made available.

The majority of the National Guard were on their annual two-week training in Grayling when word of the disturbance reached them. On their trip south they could see Detroit burning from as far away as Grand Blanc. "It was at that point," said a Guard officer, "that we decided to issue ammunition." Nothing, however, could prepare them for the conflagration they were about to encounter.

The authorities were again one step behind the rioters. In the early afternoon hours the DPD believed they were gaining control of 12th Street. The lull may very well have been the aftereffects of looted whiskey. Unfortunately, the rioters' energy and focus had moved on. Neighboring Linwood Avenue and Grand River would now feel the wrath of thousands of rampaging rioters, now intoxicated with "success" and alcohol. Dexter and Davidson would fall soon after. The disturbance had become a rolling riot, spreading so quickly and to such an extent that both Romney and Cavanagh immediately began contemplating a request for federal troops.

Bentley Library

LBJ and Gov. Romney in happier days. The tumult of the riot would strain their relationship considerably. Johnson had previously offered army assistance to Govs. Brown of California and Hughes of New Jersey to put down their rebellions. Both men, like Johnson, were Democrats. No such offer was made to Romney who at the time was the leading Republican candidate for president. When Romney requested troops, he was given a bureaucratic cold shoulder. Johnson sent his personal envoy, Cyrus Vance, to Detroit to act as a liaison and to stall for time. After touring the devastated area with Romney and Cavanagh, Vance transparently quipped, "Is doesn't look too bad to me." Cavanagh scornfully fired back, "Usually the city isn't burning."

Again, as in 1943, there was political wrangling between federal and state officials about the legalities involved with such a request. Romney refused to declare a State of Insurrection which would have nullified most insurance policies covering Detroit's multitude of fire victims. President Johnson went on TV at midnight, Monday, to rationalize his decision to send U.S. troops to Detroit. He tried to make up mileage against Romney, mentioning him fourteen times and constantly citing the "clear, unmistakable and undisputed evidence that Governor Romney of Michigan and the local officials have been unable to bring the situation under control." It was a political cheap shot Johnson would soon come to regret.

Political saber-rattling aside, President Johnson had yet another powerful concern about sending troops to Detroit. Daily anti-war demonstrations branded him as the sole cause of the Vietnam War. He feared the media would "charge that we cannot kill enough people in Vietnam, so we go out and shoot civilians in Detroit." Johnson insisted that a common-sensical, disciplined soldier be selected to command. This was no time for a rogue cowboy.

Lt. General John Throckmorton was a seasoned veteran of three wars and a polished soldier through and through. Prior to deploying his troops onto the streets of Detroit, Throckmorton received a call from the White House. It was Johnson, brooding over what he perceived as the inevitable. Throckmorton tried to allay his fears. "Mr. President, we will only shoot under the most severe provocations." With the army now taking over, this meant the federalization of the National Guard troops, who would now be under Throckmorton's command. There would be considerable post riot fallout as to why the vastly experienced paratroopers were given the less turbulent east side while the less experienced Guardsmen were assigned the hellish west side.

Lt. General John L. Throckmorton
Commander - Task Force Detroit

When Throckmorton first met his counterpart, Michigan National Guard General Cecil Simmons, he asked him what his orders were pertaining to looters. Simmons replied, "We are to use as much force as necessary. If we are unable to stop them any other way, they will be shot." Throckmorton countermanded the order, adding that all Guardsmen were to unload their weapons and to fire only on an officer's command. Simmons bristled, "You mean you want them to get away?" Throckmorton nodded, explaining it was the lesser of two evils. Simmons attempted a rebuttal but Throckmorton stopped him in mid sentence. "You have your orders," snapped Throckmorton. "Yes sir!" bellowed Simmons, "and they will be obeyed."

Throckmorton did not want his men mixing with the unpredictable Guardsmen. The New Jersey Guardsmen had fired 13,326 rounds of ammunition during the Newark riot. By riots end the Michigan Guardsmen would expend an astonishing 155,576 rounds on the west side to the Army's 202 rounds. Whether the Guardsmen either didn't receive the order to unload or intentionally abrogated it, they continued to fire at snipers, real or imaginary, that appeared in the darkness and just as quickly disappeared.

The U.S. Army troops, finally given a reluctant O.K. by President Johnson to go to Detroit, landed at Selfridge Air Force Base north of the city around 3:50 p.m. Monday. And there they sat on the tarmac for the next twelve hours awaiting orders to disembark while the political saber rattling between Washington and Detroit continued. Vance appeared to be buying time, hoping the riot would blow itself out and the troops would not have to be committed. But the constant haranguing by Romney and Cavanagh finally seemed to melt even the hard-core Throckmorton who believed he had seen enough and in turn prodded Vance into acquiescing.

Of the 4,700-man Army contingent, 1,800 were immediately air lifted to the staging area of the state fairgrounds. From there they took DSR buses to Eastern High School (above) and, henceforth, onto the east side streets of Detroit.

The paratroopers, more than half of whom had already done tours in Vietnam or the Dominican Republic, were seasoned combat veterans. Almost half were black, which was not a coincidence, as opposed to the Guardsmen, who were 99 percent white. They stuck out to say the least. To say the most their 'whiteness' inflamed rioters.

Courtesy Windsor Star

Frantic Guardsmen scramble to restore order while the city goes up in flames around them. While the Guardsmen were heavily criticized for their performance, some omissions should be brought to the forefront. As elite as the Army paratroopers were, they did not even enter the city until early Tuesday morning after the two worst days of the riot were already over. This left the beleaguered Guardsmen and the overwhelmed DPD to canvass the entire 144 square miles of the city by themselves.

While General Throckmorton could afford the luxury of ordering his men to "unload all weapons" and "return fire only against snipers on the command of a commissioned officer," there was simply no comparison to the nightmare the Guardsmen were experiencing on the infernal west side.

Were the Guardsmen trigger-happy; yes! Yet had the seasoned paratroopers found themselves on the west side, with ten thousand rioters on the loose and block after block on fire, it stands to reason even they would have been tested to the fullest.

The Guard is out
The Guard is out
See them going by
The muzzles of their guns are black
And someone's going to die

The Riot of a Thousand Arsons

Courtesy Windsor Star

Linwood Avenue goes up - The anarchy that ripped 12th Street apart on Sunday morning would drift two streets over and visit Linwood Sunday evening. The Detroit Fire Department handled three hundred fires on Sunday. By midnight, forty were still raging out of control. It was at this point that Chief Quinlan put out the call to the suburbs for assistance.

One black woman claimed she set fire to a furniture store that she considered a career price-gouger. Because of the interest on her original dept of $285, her final tally wound up being $910. "Yes, I burned the damn Jew store down," she said. "That's one bill I will never have to pay. I made sure the office and all the records went up in flames first." One of the early morning arsonists approached a black schoolteacher on Sunday evening saying, "We have 12th Street in flames, Linwood is next!"

Shortly thereafter Linwood was a curtain of flames, bathing the darkened city in a devilish glow. Transformers and electrical lines crackled as fire did its ugly dance and the power went off for good. The Detroit riot gained worldwide acclaim as the riot of a thousand arsons, far exceeding all insurrections that preceded it.

Walter Reuther Library

Detroit police, in tandem with their Guardsmen comrades, disembark into the tinderbox of Linwood Avenue. The smoke was so thick, at times it blotted out the sun, embers raining down on rioters and police alike. The nation's fifth largest city was in open rebellion and burning fiercely. Detroit was in a fight for its life.

As fires raged in the area, the Guardsmen began a curb to curb sweep of Linwood, forcing rioters from the area who had been looting and pelting firemen with rocks and bottles. Dozens of Guardsmen assembled shoulder to shoulder, bayonets at the ready, and swept southward towards Grand Boulevard. Shadowy figures could be seen on the rooftops showering the Guardsmen with debris. The rioters cursed the Guardsmen as they passed while the non-rioters cursed the rioters. As the Guardsmen approached each intersection, a squad would break off and position themselves to restore order. A young but determined Guard officer leading the formation barked a warning into his bullhorn:

Everybody off the street and back to the alleys or you will get hurt. Go back to your homes and protect your property.

MANICURING
FACIALS
Soul
BRO.
SHOP
BRO.

Police commandos patrol ravaged Grand River Avenue. Note the streetlights have all been shot out by the police and Guardsmen who wanted to minimize their silhouette at night against the deadly snipers.

Overleaf: Stunned Canadians stop their cars and gaze in disbelief as Detroit burns.

The Quiet Man

Like many European immigrants of the 18th and 19th century, Krikor Messerlian came to America not seeking riches or glory but simply to be free. Messerlian came to Detroit from Armenia, where he had narrowly escaped the Turkish slaughter of hundreds of thousands of Armenians, only to be beaten to death on the streets of Detroit. His is one of the litany of tragic stories that made up the horror of the Detroit riot.

Locals called him "George" because it was easier to pronounce than his native Krikor. He was known as the quiet man. A shoemaker by trade, he eked out a living as a shoe repairman in his dingy Linwood Avenue shop from which he lived a very frugal existence for thirty years. But Krikor didn't mind. In his tortured eyes his freedom made him a very wealthy man.

The neighborhood surrounding Messerlian's store had been deteriorating for years. Despite the fact he had been robbed and beaten in his shop twice and despite the fact he was only five feet tall, the sixty eight-year-old Messerlian had the Old World warrior mentality about him. He did not know how to back down.

Krikor Messerlian

When the riot started on Sunday, Messerlian's neighbors at the cleaning establishment next door cleared out and begged him to do the same. He refused. They called him periodically to check on him. The last contact was at 4:00 Sunday afternoon. Krikor Messerlian had thirty minutes left to live.

A marauding pack of rioters chose the cleaners next door to loot. Messerlian, who stood much taller than his unimposing stature, went after them, slashing away with a twenty-inch saber. He managed to cut one, temporarily scattering the crowd. One of the rioters vowed revenge. "I'll get that old man for you." He chased Messerlian with an ax handle that he had been using to smash open stores and now used it to smash open Messerlian himself. After knocking Messerlian down, he continued beating him ruthlessly as he lay prostrate on the barren street. Horrified bystanders who were watching the spectacle unfold cursed the violence. "Someone stop him, someone stop him!" It was too late. The mortally-wounded Messerlian lay unconscious on Linwood Avenue for a half hour before help arrived. It would be of no use to him now.

Little remained of the fiery Armenian's existence. On the wall of his looted shop hung a faded document signed by the British High Commissioner of Constantinople, dated July of 1920, his permission come to the United States. It was his proudest possession.

Messerlian's cousin, who came to America with him in 1920, could not comprehend what had happened, "He came to this country, a free country, and they killed him."

As the sun set on Detroit Sunday evening, an orange glow pulsated for miles. A greasy pall of acrid smoke hung over the wounded city as rioters continued to dance amidst the flames.

After sharpening their skills on 12th Street and then Linwood, looters descended on Grand River stores, smashing them open like a piñata at Mardi Gras. A two mile stretch from West Grand Boulevard to Livernois was picked clean and put to the torch. Integrated packs of looters, completely unabashed, worked with the feverish determination of Noah in dismantling stores, as hundreds of baseball fans from the Tigers-Yankees doubleheader drove by in astonishment.

Perhaps the most outrageous of the looting stories, a group of rioters could be seen dragging a two story circular stairway down the street. Others brought the family car and tied furniture securely to the roof. Another looter stole an over-sized armchair and hailed a cab to help him get it home. When the two struggled unsuccessfully to fit the chair into the trunk, the cabbie left the disgruntled looter by the wayside.

Walter Reuther library

Flames and smoke boil out of the S.S. Kresge Department Store on Grand River, as the last of the major West side thoroughfares goes up in flames. Right: Guardsmen approach the railroad viaduct off Grand River where more damage was done than the entire Newark riot combined.

46
IR 146
27

NO
LEFT
TURN
7AM-9AM
4PM-6:30PM
MON THRU FRI
NO
STANDING

Detroit police, state troopers and Guardsmen return fire on a sniper in the shadows of a burned and looted Grand River Avenue.

Walter Reuther library

The New Front Line - With the orgy of looting that took place the first day of the riot subsiding, the DPD relinquished center stage to the DFD on Monday. The new front line was now manned by an army of weary firemen who steeled themselves to quench the firestorm that threatened to engulf the entire city. Scenes like this seemed reminiscent of Dante's Inferno:

Through me the way into the suffering city
Abandon every hope, yee who enter here.

Monday found Detroit on the verge of incineration. The Detroit Fire Department answered a staggering 617 alarms on Monday alone. Their job would get tougher. Rioters now directed their rage at the firemen. The radio constantly crackled with the sound of desperate voices:

Engine 46: "They're shooting at us. What'll we do?"

Chief Quinlan: "Pick up and get out of there if there is no police. Leave the line where it is."

Vigilante groups sprang up out of necessity to protect personal property. At Davidson and Dexter on the west side, flames threatened to consume the entire block. Many black owned businesses were already on fire. A black resident named Loften grabbed his rifle and urged his neighbors to do the same. Loften caught the attention of a big fire rig that was ordered to leave the area. "I hollered at the firemen, 'Aren't you going to put out the fire?' They said not til the police came to protect them from the snipers. I told them go ahead and we'd shoot any SOB that tried to stop them."

A Family Affair - Without the assistance of the brotherhood of firemen, it might very well have been a repeat of 1803 when fire destroyed the city of Detroit. Some forty-three different communities assisted the beleaguered Detroit Fire Department in attempting to extinguish the conflagration that engulfed the city, including an engine from Windsor, Canada.

Birmingham
Clinton
Commerce Twp.
Dearborn
Dearborn Heights
Ecorse
East Detroit
Eloise
Ferndale
Flint
Garden City
Garden City Mut. Aid
Gibraltar
Highland Park
Grosse Ile
Grosse Pte. Park
Grosse Pte. Woods
Harper Woods
Harrison Twp.
Lansing
Hazel Park
Livonia
Madison Heights
Milford Twp.
Newport
Plymouth
Plymouth Twp.
Pontiac
Redford Township
River Rouge
Roseville
Royal Oak
Royal Oak Twp.
South Rockwood
Southfield
St. Clair Shores
Sterling Twp.
Taylor Twp.
Warren
Wayne
Westland
Windsor, Onatario
Wyandotte

On the east side, Army paratroopers close in on a sniper who has wreaked havoc in the area. Many of Detroit's police and fire stations were under attack by snipers during the riot. The early morning hours of Tuesday were the worst. There were eleven sniper attacks on the east side and thirty-eight on the west side during this time. The only confirmed sniper killed was Jack Sydnor, who blazed away from his third-story apartment on Linwood. Detroit police rushed Sydnor's apartment. Sydnor managed to shoot two police officers before his bullet-ridden body tumbled through the window and landed three stories below. It stayed there for hours while the authorities battled other snipers in the area who were bearing down on them.

By Tuesday the looting had gradually receded and the snipers moved in. Denuded mannequins could be seen grotesquely twisted over the pavement or hanging ominously from a lamppost. They stood as a sign of the rampaging army of looters who had sacked the city in the first two days of rioting. The young toughs had had their day. Now the professional revolutionaries were taking over, the snipers. The sniper activity under cover of darkness was especially dangerous. Snipers quickly learned to stand back from the window when firing, making it very difficult for authorities to pinpoint the telltale muzzle flash.

Rifle and small arms fire of various calibers could be heard throughout the city. As two Guardsmen waited in the shadows trying to get a line on a sniper that had pinned them down, they could hear a wounded voice in the distance calling, "Help me, help me." Then it stopped for good. An M-48 tank rumbled up, its turret and 90 mm gun rotating wildly in search of snipers. The tank's menacing presence managed to silence the snipers until it departed, then the shooting started anew.

The brilliant display of stars above glistened over the madness below. From a building rooftop, a bewildering spectacle could be witnessed below. With the nine o'clock curfew came darkness and, almost on cue, gunfire. Shadowy figures used the night to mask their sniping but the authorities countered. An army spotter plane flew in low over the trees, combing the rooftops for shooters. Now loud shots could be heard coming from the Lee Plaza. Frightened residents turned lights off. Sirens. Police bullhorns. The authorities shot off a signal flare to mark the spot of trouble and the spotter plane dove abruptly to investigate. A .50 caliber machine gun burped a lethal dose against the building. Apparently the Guardsmen found their mark because the shooting stopped.

But the silence was not to stay. A dull explosion off Lawton brought a Guard troop transport. It was too dark now for the spotter plane so a helicopter hovered over the rooftops, its eerie Cyclops headlight scanning the roof of every building, street by street as if it were mowing the lawn. Dogs barked in confusion, adding to the chaos. It sounded like a European city under siege during WWII but it was Detroit. The peaceful blanket of stars in the sky made the situation by contrast surreal.

Two reporters from Chicago showed up at police headquarters enquiring as to where the riot was. The weary police sergeant advised them to simply go out the front door and head in any direction.

The west side had become an open supermarket. Brazen looters even drove their cars or trucks into the riot zone and loaded up, then went home and quickly unloaded their booty into their garage to go back for more. While they were gone, their garage, in turn, would be looted.
There was little hint of embarrassment exhibited by the looters but rather a warped pride seemed to show through. Knowing their holiday of piracy would be brief, they enjoyed the moment. Bold young men slung TVs under each arm and coolly walked away from the scene. Others, with the police in hot pursuit, ran a very respectable hundred yard dash between alleys, price tags fluttering as they went.
One determined female looter announced, "I got me six chairs. Now I got to find a table." Another looter, having picked through a ravaged department store, came away perplexed, "Can you imagine? Big place like that and no TV sets."
Despite appearances to the contrary, only about one percent of Detroiters took part in the looting. There were many instances of Detroit's older residence, white and black, attempting to stop the riot. One Guard officer remembers stepping off the truck into the riot zone, the adults approached him, "I live here. I work to pay for my house here. This is my home. We'll tell you who the troublemakers are." The officer cited other support by the locals: "They brought us food. I'll tell you, our guys ate like kings. We got orders not to accept food, but I held onto the letter. I hope we never have another one (riot), but I learned a lot about the citizenry of Detroit. They're great people."

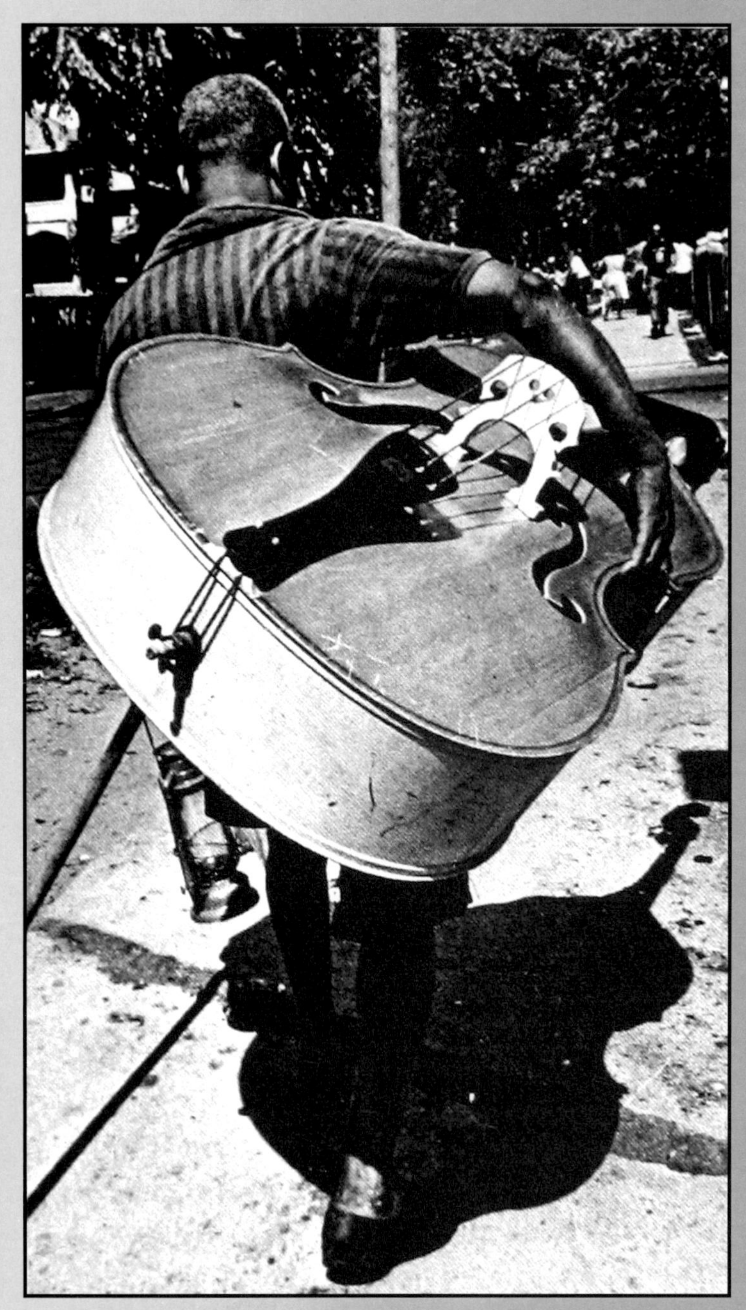

Typical of many looters who simply stole for the sake of stealing or thought it was owed to them for past grievances, this man heads home with a most illogical accumulation: a mop, a lantern and of all things, a bull fiddle. Another looter, caught red handed with a stolen saxophone, claimed it was his. When the officer demanded he play a tune, the ruse was over.

"Now I know nobody in here has any loot, Oh Lord no.

I know none of my people would do a thing like that.

But just in case some of you wake up one morning and find that a color TV just happened up on your porch or a radio just stopped by to say hello, I'll help you get it back to where it belongs."

12th Street preacher to congregation

Anarchy @ the Algiers

The Algiers Motel as seen from Woodward Avenue with the three story annex in the background.

Of all the grim episodes that occurred during the riot, one incident would remain infamous above the rest. During the early hours of Wednesday morning, three black teenagers were shot to death in the annex of the Algiers Motel and their deaths remain unsolved to this day. The incident has lived on primarily because of the inability to piece together the terribly scrambled accounts of police and civilians alike.

Here is what is known:

- Just after midnight on Wednesday, someone at the annex was shooting off a starter's pistol loaded with blanks simply for amusement, a foolish thing to do during the course of a riot.
- A National Guard unit nearby believed it was a sniper and radioed Detroit police.
- Detroit police arrived immediately and in tandem with state troopers and the Guardsmen, stormed the motel annex in search of a sniper.
- By the time the sun rose that morning, three black youths staying at the annex were dead and the authorities tried to pass it off as a sniper attack.

Surviving witnesses from the Algiers tell a different story entirely. They talk about a "game of death" that Detroit police initiated in an attempt to find out who the sniper was, tragically unaware of the fact that there was no sniper at all.

The police, who were told (erroneously) by the dispatcher that the Guardsmen were "under heavy fire," entered the annex in tandem with state troopers and Guardsmen. Victim number one, Carl Cooper, was apparently killed during the initial rush into the house. Perhaps the authorities mistook him for the sniper or a fleeing felon. At any rate, Carl Cooper was in the wrong place at the wrong time. A shotgun blast killed him instantly. Fred Temple, victim number two, was killed moments after Cooper. As the authorities crashed through the back door, they must have encountered Temple. What he was doing and why he was shot we will never know.

Detroit police were informed at roll call on Tuesday of the shotgun death of Detroit Police Officer Jerome Olshove who was killed by a looter. The news hit the DPD like a lightning bolt. Olshove (Ol'-shoh-ve) was highly respected and well known, having earned numerous meritorious citations. His father and brother were career Detroit police officers. He had planned to leave the department for a job at IBM after nine years on the force. His last day was to be Thursday. Some officers wept openly after the news broke while others bridled with anger, a suppressed anger that would not stay down for long. Perhaps this was the emotional trigger that spawned the death game. As was the case in Newark with the death of Police Detective Frederick Toto by a sniper, the violent death of a comrade may have pushed Detroit police over the edge.

Jerome Olshove

As the authorities began a floor to floor search of the house, all the occupants were flushed out of their rooms and told to spread eagle in the first floor hallway. An aggressive interrogation began in search of the gun and when no response was forthcoming they were beaten. Still no response. It was here that the game of death ensued. A Detroit police officer grabbed one suspect and marched him into another room. He discharged his shotgun into the floor, intentionally missing his suspect while trying to convince those out in the hall that he had killed the suspect so the guilty party would reveal the gun. Still no response. The death game continued. A National Guard Warrant Officer brought another suspect out of the lineup and marched him into another back room, then fired into the ceiling. Still no response.

The first police officer, envious of continuing the game, tossed his shotgun to another officer, loudly asking if he wanted to "kill one." Only apparently the second officer was unaware that this was only being used as a scare tactic to evoke confessions. The third victim, Aubrey Pollard, was then led into a back room. As the Warrant Officer walked past he saw a "flash of clothing" indicating a shotgun blast into the victim. Realizing the game had now gone terribly awry, he collected the other Guardsmen present and as they walked out the door informed a Detroit police officer that this was strictly a police affair. The senior state trooper had already collected his men and left because "he didn't like what he had seen there."

As the remaining officers pondered their next move, a convenient exit strategy emerged. Gunshots could be heard emanating from down the street and some of the officers took off in hot pursuit. The remaining officers cleared the annex, warning the survivors to leave immediately. Most ran for their lives. Another took it upon himself to inform Carl Cooper's parents that their son was dead. The pendulum of guilt quickly began to swing in the direction of the Detroit Police Department. The bolder witnesses began to contact political representatives about what they had seen, setting in motion a chain of events that would drag on for years.

The rear of the Algiers annex where a neighbor testified he heard shots fired before the authorities arrived and that he saw "a Negro man standing on the lower left rear of the Algiers Manor Motel, and saw the man fire a shot in the direction of Woodward and Euclid: It appeared that the man had a revolver."

The police initially tried to pawn off the killings as the work of a rogue but elusive sniper. But the witnesses and evidence they left behind indicated otherwise. All the autopsies indicated the youths were killed inside the house at close range by a shotgun using double "O" buckshot, the same kind used by the police department for riot control.

A week after the riot it was clear that the police department was heavily involved in the killings. Three officers and a private guard were arraigned on a variety of charges. Owing to the publicity generated by the best selling book by John Hersey, "*The Algiers Motel Incident*," published in 1968, the defense asked for the trials to be moved out of Detroit. Their petitions were granted. Trials were held in Lansing, Ann Arbor and Mason. In the end all were acquitted and the rage in black Detroit ratcheted up even further.

It must be remembered who the state senator representing Detroit was at this time. Coleman A. Young, D-Detroit, was outraged, "This latest phase of a step by step whitewash of police slayings demonstrates once again that law and order is a one-way street; there is no law and order when black people are involved. Especially when they're involved with the police." Young's stance would play an important role 18 years later when, as mayor, he fired two white police officers for their roles in beating a black motorist who eventually died. His quick response in accusing and firing the officers were in part dictated by the ghastly memories of the Algiers Motel incident.

This peaceful vacant lot bears no hint of the nightmarish events that took place here forty years ago. Both the Algiers Motel and its annex were torn down in the 1970s, successfully ridding the city of its most haunting icon of the riot. The psychological scars of the community, however, have never healed.

Igor Beginin, an Eastern Michigan University Art professor, witnessed the riot and put his recollections on canvas. Beginin was no stranger to tumult. He had lived in war ravaged Yugoslavia during WWII, and out of the smoldering ruins of Detroit, the painful ghosts of war would begin to re-emerge.

Courtesy Igor Beginin

The Shape of Unrest.

"The mid day sun was hazy behind a canopy of smoke and ashes giving the environment an eerie appearance of moon-lit medieval ruins. As I worked, the ruins in front of me took on the appearance of a face, a fearsome symbol of the God of Madness which seemed to be brooding over us all."

Igor Beginin

The riot did not cause Detroit's problems, rather it catalogued them. In the space of one horrific week, Detroit had gone from being the Model City, a pennant of progressivism, to having the dubious distinction of hosting the most devastating civil disorder the country had ever seen. Between the Michigan National Guard, U.S. Army paratroopers, the Michigan State Police and the Detroit Police Department, it took some 17,000 men, armed to the teeth, to put down the Great Rebellion.

For many, it seemed incredible that "only" forty-three people had died during the riot. With tens of thousands of bullets filling the air and fire engulfing entire neighborhoods, it seemed a peculiarly low number, but it is the number that stands to this day. It is impossible to determine with any degree of accuracy how many snipers there were, but if even a fraction of the police reports were correct, sniping was more prevalent in Detroit than all previous riots combined. Fortunately, they were poorly equipped with little training for their intended purpose or the death toll would have been frightfully higher.

The heart-wrenching stories range from a police officer killed two days away from retirement to a four-year-old girl whose world of dolls and tea parties ended in a hail of bullets meant for someone else. They are all a tragic part of a bigger element - the death of a city that once held world prominence.

A lone Guardsman stands watch over the remnants of Bill Scott's United Community League. The overturned bar and smashed jukebox bare mute testament to a party that was crashed by the DPD and would forever change the soul of the city. It would be a long time before Detroit was in a revelrous mood again.

Lesson's Learned: The Kerner Report

SPEED
LIMIT
30

Lessons Learned - The Kerner Report

It wasn't supposed to happen in Detroit - the city that had been the prototype Model City, the national yardstick for social progress. Detroit was the only city in the country that had two black U.S. Congressmen. Detroit had the largest chapter of the NAACP in the country at a staggering 18,000 members. Despite the mercurial nature of the automotive industry, Detroit industrial wages were the highest in the country. "Detroit has opened the golden door to the Negro," said a black poverty worker after the riot. "But only a relatively few Negroes can get through that door at any one time. That's the real trouble. In Jackson Mississippi, no Negro can get through the door, and strangely enough that can be kind of reassuring. He can always say it's a white door and so there's no use a black man even trying. Some call it Negro laziness or apathy, but it's the disease of the ghetto."

With Newark in cinders and Detroit a bombed out shell, President Johnson had seen enough. The devastation of the uprising in Detroit had stunned the nation, and yes, even the world. Johnson appointed Illinois Governor Otto Kerner to form a highly diversified committee and put this appalling puzzle of American history under the microscope. America needed answers. Johnson instructed them:

Let your search be free. Let us be untrammeled by what has been called conventional wisdom. As best you can, find the truth, the whole truth, and express it in your report. This matter is far, far too important for politics. Only you can do this job. Only if you put your shoulders to the wheel can America hope for the kind of report it needs and will take to its heart.

Detroit's violent convulsion directly and indirectly brought about the Kerner Commission. Its members were charged with finding the answers to three basic queries: 1) What happened? 2) Why did the riots happen? 3) What needs to be done to keep this from happening again? We have already covered 'What' happened.

With marathon-like stamina, the commission members toured the riot-scarred areas that pockmarked the country, interviewed hundreds of witnesses from all layers of society and, despite the successes of the civil rights movement and its accompanying legislation over the years, came to one basic conclusion:

"Our nation is moving toward two societies,
one black, one white - separate and unequal."

The Kerner Commission

Otto Kerner

Chairman: Otto Kerner - Governor - Illinois

John Lindsey: Mayor of New York City
Roy Wilkins: Director - NAACP
Fred Harris: Senator (D-Oklahoma)
James Corman: Congressman (D-California)
William McCulloch: Congressman (R-Ohio)
Edward Brooke: Senator (R-Massachusetts)
I.W. Abel: President - United Steelworkers
Charles Thornton: Chairman - Litton Industries
Herbert Jenkins: Chief of Police - Atlanta
Katherine Graham Peden: Chairman of Commerce - Kentucky

Otto Kerner, Democratic governor of Illinois from 1961 to 1968, was chosen to lead the commission because he was once a judge and a U.S. District Attorney and thus knew something about obtaining the naked facts. Having attained the rank of Brigadier General in the U.S. Army also spoke volumes about his leadership capabilities. Kerner's initial response to the daunting task that lay before the commission:

We are being asked to probe into the soul of America.

It was a sick soul at that. The Kerner Commission found fault at every level of society, but the lion's share of the fault was an answer America didn't want to hear, not then, not now:

Segregation and poverty have created in the racial ghetto a destructive environment totally unknown to most white Americans. What white Americans have never fully understood - but what the Negro can never forget - is that white society is deeply implicated in the ghetto. White institutions created it, white institutions maintain it, and white society condones it.

The resounding cry of outrage that had been emanating from the black community for decades had been legitimized by the Kerner Report. The soul had been laid bare for all to see but salvation was still light years away.

Kerner: The Flowchart of Blame

- The frustrations of powerlessness have led some Negroes to the conviction that there is no effective alternative to violence as a means of achieving redress of grievances and of moving the system. These frustrations are reflected in alienation and hostility toward the institutions of law and government and the white society which controls them, and in the reach toward racial consciousness and solidarity reflected in the slogan "Black Power."

- A new mood has sprung up among Negroes, particularly among the young, in which self-esteem and enhanced racial pride are replacing apathy and submission to "the system."

- The police are not merely a "spark" factor. To some Negroes police have come to symbolize white power, white racism and white repression. And the fact is that many police do reflect and express these white attitudes. The atmosphere of hostility and cynicism is reinforced by a widespread belief among Negroes in the existence of police brutality and in a "double standard" of justice and protection – one for Negroes and one for whites.

- Pervasive discrimination and segregation in employment, education and housing, which have resulted in the continuing exclusion of great numbers of Negroes from the benefits of economic progress.

- Black in-migration and white exodus, which have produced the massive and growing concentrations of impoverished Negroes in our major cities, creating a growing crisis of deteriorating facilities and services and unmet human needs.

- A climate that tends toward approval and encouragement of violence as a form of protest has been created by white terrorism directed against nonviolent protest; by the open defiance of law and federal authority by state and local officials resisting desegregation; and by some protest groups engaging in civil disobedience who turn their backs on nonviolence, go beyond the constitutionally protected rights of petition and free assembly, and resort to violence to attempt to compel alteration of laws and policies with which they disagree.

Courtesy of National Archives

Fatherless children in the ghetto face a never ending handicap of misguidance and privation. It is all part of the crippling culture of poverty which inhibits the ghetto. Having been born without special skills or luck of birth, they are condemned to the economic and cultural underworld of the ghetto which will eventually maim their spirit.

The ghetto creates and sustains crippling circumstances for children to overcome; principle among them was fatherless children. In the period from 1960-65, female headed households rose from 23 percent to 32 percent. In Watts it went from 36 percent to 39 percent. This point was not lost upon the Kerner Commission:

With the father absent and the mother working, many ghetto children spend the bulk of their time on the streets - the streets of a crime-ridden, violence-prone, and poverty stricken world. The image of success in this world is not that of the "solid citizen," the responsible husband and father, but rather that of the "hustler" who promotes his own interests by exploiting others. The dope sellers and the numbers runners are the "successful" men because their earnings far outstrip those men who try to climb the economic ladder in honest ways. Young people in the ghetto are acutely conscious of a system which appears to offer rewards to those who illegally exploit others and failure to those who struggle under traditional responsibilities.

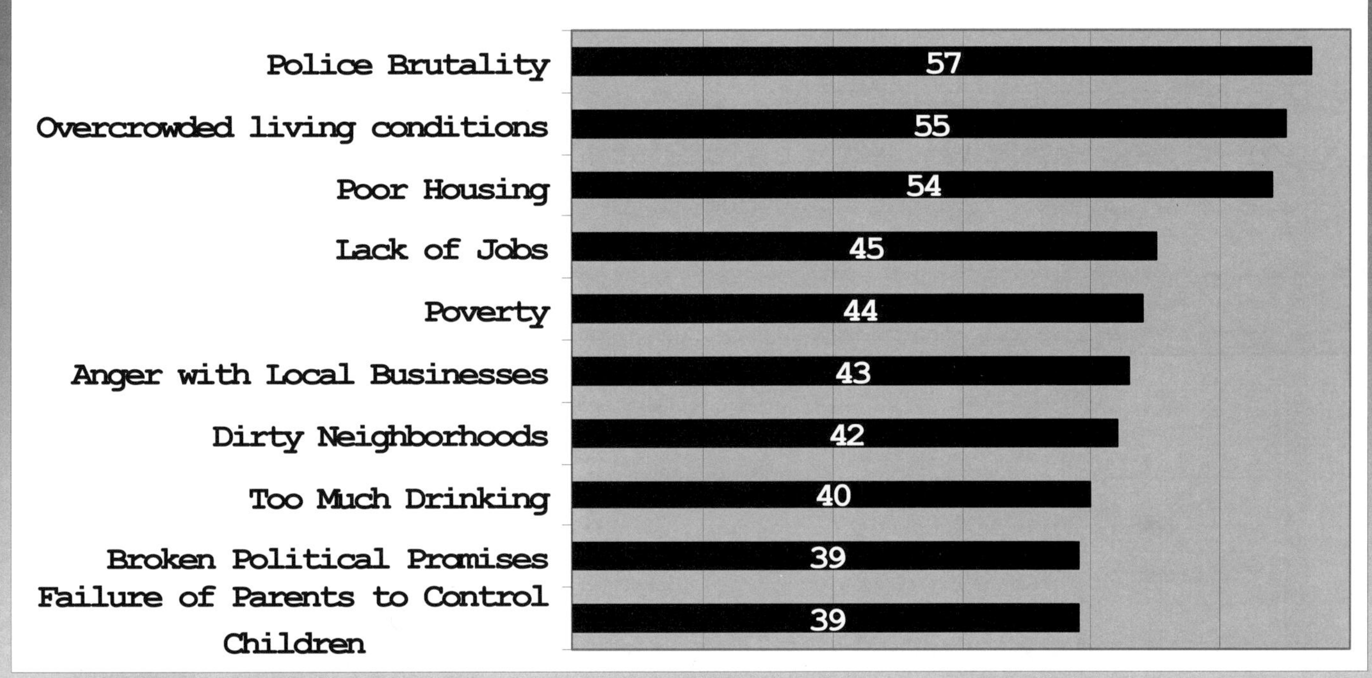

Statistics courtesy of Detroit Free Press

Militant blacks believed riots of the '60s were uprisings against poverty and racism and that by mass rioting they were abandoning the concept of integration for black separatism. Moderate blacks believed riots were caused by poor housing and unemployment. Most whites believed rioters were criminals and should be shot on sight. Above, a poll taken from post-riot Detroiters lists what they believe triggered the riot.

The principal measure of progress toward equality will be that of employment. It is the primary source of individual or group identity. In America what you do is what you are: to do nothing is to be nothing; to do little is to be little. The equations are implacable and blunt, and ruthlessly public. For the Negro American it is already, and will continue to be, the master problem. Employment not only controls the present for the Negro American but, in a most profound way, it is creating the future as well.

- Daniel Patrick Moynihan

The DPD: The Good, The Bad, The Ugly

The Detroit Police Department withstood a firestorm of criticism after the riot but Commissioner Ray Girardin stood by his men, slowly whittling down the denunciations with his own assessment of the situation:

Does the public expect a policeman to be a public executioner who can inflict capital punishment for misdemeanors? It is one thing to shoot back at snipers, and it is another thing to shoot down a child who is looting a pair of shoes or even a television set. Property can be restored, but not life.

Society looks at policeman and blames them for the unrest. This is unfair. Society has neither dealt with its problems nor equipped policeman to deal with theirs, and it is time to get police work back into focus. In Detroit, for instance, we have 4,500 officers to deal with a population of 1,640,000, but also more than 700,000 civilians, some of them criminals, moving in and out of the city every day. The role of urban police must be redefined, and, obviously, better training and equipment will be needed.

The horror of a riot is easily visible, but the question of what force police should exert applies to a wide variety of situations. On any summer night in a major city like Detroit, the radio in my car may report, within five minutes, that a woman has been knocked down, a suspicious person is roaming an alley, a candy store has been robbed with one person shot, a baby is about to be born in an automobile and a crowd is gathering in a ghetto. In each case a man called policeman is supposed to solve the problem, just as he was supposed to deal with the rioters.

Many Detroit police officers were wounded emotionally and many would leave the force in the years following the riot. James Bannon stuck it out and made it a career, eventually rising to Deputy Chief of the department under Coleman Young, but there were some early misgivings:

It (the riot) damaged a great many officers psychologically. I ended up going to church and praying and wondering what this job was all about. I went from supreme confidence in my own ability to saying to myself, "Hey, this isn't what I signed up to do."

A Scarred Giant

Bentley Library

J.L. Hudson Jr. begins his laborious task of sifting through Detroit's ruins.

Even while the last plumes of arsonist smoke were dissipating, Romney and Cavanagh enlisted the help of department store heir J.L. Hudson Jr. to lead a group christened New Detroit to reach consensus objectives for rebuilding the city.

The elite and the egalitarian, all enamored with a flush of altruism, attempted to put aside differences and set things straight. But it wasn't meant to be however. The cast of characters was, despite its altruistic intentions, just too diverse, their backgrounds too different and their objectives too varied. Little by little it became a series of prolonged quarrels over how to go about helping the city. The elite eventually appointed stand-ins to take their place and the militants quit in disgust, believing they were underrepresented. The foundation for the new Detroit was being built on quicksand.

PT 111

There was a pride of métier amongst rioters in the 1960s. The thought that "our" riot was more destructive than "your" riot became the predominant theme and a ghetto badge of honor.

As the riot subsided, the eerie, vacuum-like silence that follows a tornado seemed to make time stand still, if only for a moment. The gangs that had gleefully and with great disdain ripped open 12th Street and its environs were nowhere to be seen. As one merchant reasoned, "They're probably at home watching their new color TVs."

A jewelry store owner who the locals called Bizon lost everything, "They cleaned me out like an army. I was good to them. For three days they told me, 'Bizon, tomorrow we'll get your safe.'" It took looters three days to chisel through the hardened cement walls, but, good to their word, on the fourth day the safe was gone.

When the smoke of rebellion cleared, gruesome store skeletons began to emerge, their basements rapidly filling with water from broken or melted pipes, carrying with them the flotsam of someone's livelihood. Roofless and open buildings, giant steel girders twisted like licorice sticks from the intense heat. One of the 12th Street merchants, Samuel Lipson, looked at the blackened, knotted wreckage that was once his variety store. He vainly conceded, "I'm wiped out. I'm sixty-three. At this age, I lost everything. We didn't expect any trouble. As a matter of fact, I was consulted by different civic groups about whether we felt there was any trouble. In our opinion there wasn't a sign of it."

Lipson's insurance company felt otherwise. They refused to renew his insurance when it ran out a month before the riot, certain Detroit would fall sooner or later. Lipson, along with a consortium of other merchants, cite the city's lackadaisical response for their dilemma, "Cavanagh, he couldn't run for street cleaner right now as far as the businessmen are concerned. The whole thing was mismanaged."

Joel Zack's, owner of Zack's drug store that had been located at 12th and Seward for twenty years, watched his store burn out of control for two straight days. When it was finally safe to enter, he found two badly charred bodies floating in his flooded basement. More than likely they were looters who were caught in the back of the store when an arsonist decided to torch it. They retreated as far as they could until the flames themselves past the final judgment.

One local merchant, who retreated to his home in the suburbs, didn't dare go downtown to check on his store. He couldn't stand not knowing and decided he would call his store instead. The phone rang, someone picked up:

Merchant: "Who's this?"
Looter: "Who's this?"
Merchant: "I'm the owner."
Looter: "You were the owner."

Who Started the Riot?

When you see a furniture store being looted, and a black man comes out the front door carrying one end of a sofa, and when the other end emerges there is a white man carrying it, you have to stop and scratch your head and say, "This is a race riot?" The Great Rebellion was many things to many people but it was not a race riot. For rioters, it was a rebellion against circumstances.

The color of segregation is not always white or black; sometimes it is green.

One local priest lamented, "We had fits last year because nobody could talk to the activists in the Kercheval-Pennsylvania row. Both the block clubs in the area and the police were completely out of touch with them. That should have been our warning sign."

Police Commissioner Ray Girardin also relayed his fears:

One group that always worried me was the 16 year olds who had been kicked out of school, rejected by their parents, and had nothing to do but roam the streets. No one was reaching them.

The average rioter was a black male, somewhere between fifteen to twenty years of age, underemployed or unemployed, and carried with him an unending rage. He had great pride in his race and rejected the stereotype of blacks as shiftless and ignorant.

While extremely hostile towards whites, he also exhibited a significant hostility towards middle-class blacks whom he believed deserted the ranks. He believed he was being held back not because of education or ambition but because of his color.

He more than likely was born during WWII, grew up during the Korean conflict and came of age during Vietnam. American involvement in war had inadvertently legitimized violence and greatly desensitized his society.

The civil rights movement, despite its great efforts, created great expectations for the rioter it could not fulfill. Bobby Kennedy took it a step further:

Too many Negroes who have succeeded in climbing the ladder of education and well being have failed to extend their hand to help their fellows on the rungs below. Civil rights leaders cannot with sit-ins change the fact that adults are illiterate. Marches do not create jobs for their children.

As Detroit buried its dead in the days following the riot, an intensely personal view of the tragedy began to hit home. (Right) Patricia Smith, the wife of slain Detroit Fireman Carl Smith, clutches the flag which adorned her husband's casket.

Fireman Smith, who had been recuperating from previous surgery and was officially on sick leave, didn't hesitate to return to duty to help his exhausted comrades fight the infinite blazes that were consuming the city. As Smith darted across a darkened Mack Avenue to get back to his rig, a snipers bullet cut him down.

Over 1,000 firemen from forty communities marched in the funeral procession to the cemetery. The minister's calm, reassuring voice could be heard reciting the 23rd Psalm as they walked, "The Lord is my Shepard, I shall not want..."

Walter Reuther Library

The funeral for four-year-old Tanya Blanding, the youngest of the riot's victims, was held before a packed house at Central United Church of Christ on Linwood. She was hit by machine-gun bullets when Guardsmen mistook the lighting of a cigarette in a darkened room for a muzzle flash. The Rev. Albert Cleage took the pulpit, "Tanya is the symbol of an end of a period we won't stand for any longer. We'll keep this alive. When they say this is a good city we'll say 'What about Tanya?' ...We'll find ways to make this town, this city, a place in which black people can live with dignity. We've got to see that it doesn't happen again."

"I wouldn't go back to 12th Street

if they paved it with diamonds."

Looted 12th Street merchant

Walter Reuther Library

This inferno off Linwood consumed almost the entire block. It was started when an irate local threw a firebomb into the corner store to avenge the way the proprietor had been treating people. The strong winds pushed the fire onto adjacent houses, eventually destroying the home owned by the bomb thrower himself. Of the many vehicles destroyed in this blaze, one belonged to Detroiter Charles Dees who was away fighting in Vietnam. His mother's house and his car burned to cinders. Gov. Romney, aloft in a helicopter, thought Detroit looked like bombed out Berlin at the end of WWII.

State of Michigan Archives

Detroit Public Library

A typical scene on the streets of post-riot Detroit, a local woman who did not participate in the riot, witnesses first hand the stark reality of the rampage. Like most Detroiters, she now realizes she has to deal with the senseless destruction of a few and scoffs away in disgust.

Detroit Public Library

Wayne County Prosecutor Bill Cahalan, who had only been in his new position a month, was dealt a nightmarish hand. After the county jail was filled to overcapacity, authorities were forced to improvise by creating makeshift lock ups. Prisoners were stuffed into buses, parking garages and even the walled bath house at Belle Isle. When those filled, the remaining prisoners were shipped to the correctional facilities at Milan, Jackson and Ionia. Cahalan later recalled:

I was surprised. The leadership was surprised. We didn't think it was going to happen in Detroit. We felt that, with the Cavanagh administration, that the blacks had a voice in the government. So there wouldn't be any need for a race riot. This was not a race riot though. It was something other than that. I don't know. It was a period of lawlessness. The people involved were not protesting some injustice - they were out looting and burning.

It was something, maybe, you would have expected under a different administration, but not under the Cavanagh administration. It was a civil disturbance. But it didn't have any purpose.

We weren't prepared, perhaps because we thought it wasn't going to happen in Detroit. We were totally unprepared. We ran out of space for prisoners. There were no plans for that. There was no idea what was going to happen. I mean, the whole city could have gone up in flames, as far as we knew. We'd go up to the roof of police headquarters and it looked like the whole city was on fire.

An indignant Guardsman keeps a watchful vigil over his prisoners. Unable to sequester the army of detainees in the traditional manner, authorities had to quickly improvise. Here a garage near the 10th Precinct was quickly converted to a holding pen for some of the over 7,000 arrestees which the week long dragnet captured.

Courtesy Windsor Sta

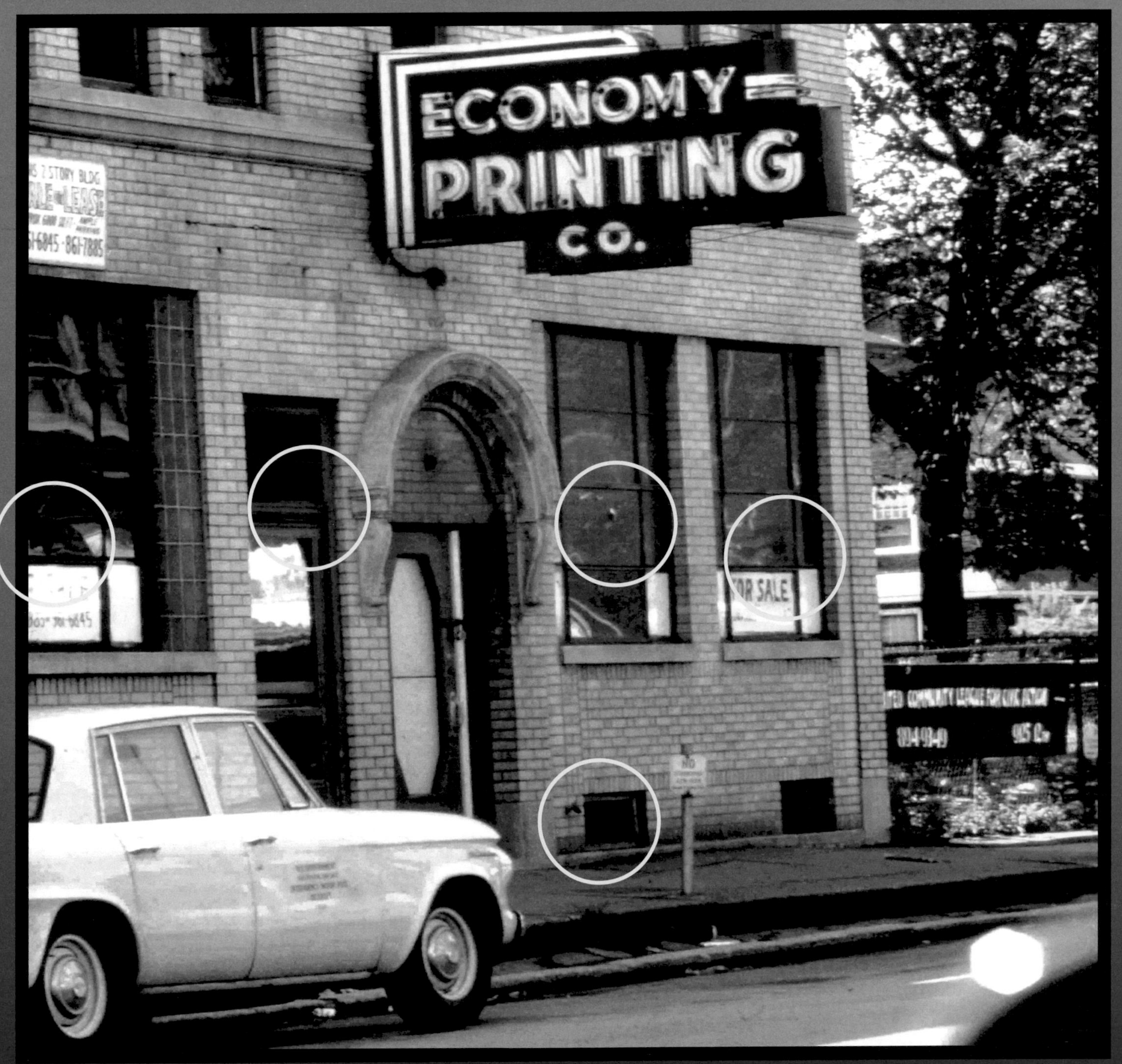

Detroit Public Library

A post-riot photo of Economy Printing showing damage incurred from the raid. Note the broken windows from the deluge of bottles and rocks that were hurled at the police as they loaded the last paddy wagon. Much more debris reigned down on the sidewalk and police vehicles at the curb. The front door, which the police broke down to gain entrance, has been hastily repaired but still bears their padlock. Note also the proximity of the house in the near background. According to police it was after all a citizen complaint about the building that brought them there to begin with.

After the most hectic week of their young lives, bleary-eyed Guardsmen sleep the sleep of exhaustion on Detroit's Kern block.

The statue of Jesus, which adorns the front lawn of the Sacred Heart Seminary off Linwood, was painted black during the riot. It has remained that way ever since.

"There is a huge section of our society that is not really a part of it," a despondent Cavanagh lamented. "The people feel left out and get committed to complete lawlessness at the slightest excuse. They see affluence all around them but do not share in it. And they find it frustrating."

In the final analysis, America's Model City succumbed to the same demons that befell its predecessors. The volcanic fury that accumulated over the decades could not be quenched in a single generation. Typical of the hidden frustration found in Detroit, one irate rioter ripped open his shirt, revealing to the police his scarred body, "I got this scar fighting the Germans in WWII, I was in Korea too. I'm forty-two years old and I can't find a job." The most dangerous person in any society is the one who believes he has nothing to lose.

It was not a raid on a blind pig that set in motion the worst riot in American history but rather the inability of Americans to gel as a society. There was no abridging the anger that permeated Detroit in those days, it simply had to be expended. Now that the demons have been exorcised and we are forty years wiser, perhaps a rebuilding can begin.

The view from defeat - A haggard Mayor Cavanagh inspects the ruins of his city and is confronted by a youth. Cavanagh had no answers for him, nor should he have. He did everything possible to diffuse the time bomb his predecessors had handed him but in the end there were too many fuses and too many sparks to curtail.

"Look upon these ruins, citizens of Detroit, and make your unbelieving eyes grow accustomed to them. For they will doubtless be with us for a long, long, time."

State of Michigan Archives

Rosa Parks Blvd
12th
DONT
WALK
ONE WAY

Hope
is the last
to die

Hope is the last to die

Less than a year after the Detroit Riot another lightning bolt of tragic news dealt a mortal wound to the civil rights movement. Martin Luther King, champion of civil rights, was cut down in the prime of his life. America's cities rioted their response in unison this time, one last massive urban convulsion in the waning days of a decade that U.S. historians have deemed the most internally disruptive to date.

The cities that lay in ruins would be frozen in that degenerative state some time. Despite impassioned pleas for help, Congress turned a deaf ear, believing if they flooded these cities with money, it would be seen as a reward for rioting. In the meantime, the Vietnam War raged on unabated with no end in site, taking with it the flower of a generation.

As the decade of the 1970s loomed on the horizon, many believed better days were ahead. They were wrong. The 1970s would be the worst decade of all for the riot cities as the snowball of urban abandonment continued to grow to unimaginable proportions and nothing was going to break its momentum once it started rolling. The controversial issue of busing further opened the floodgates of white flight to the suburbs leaving a vastly weakened tax base.

With so many black people killed in '67, the lesson before all of us is very, very clear... Nothing can be gained from the senseless loss of life and destruction of property. Blacks literally ... burned down their own city. I think the lesson has been learned. I don't think you will see that occur in the same manner.

- Coleman A. Young

All of the riot cities hemorrhaged population and tax base during the 1970s but everything is cyclical and by the 1990s the magnetic attraction that the big, urban environment offers returned, enabling them to come out of their economic funk and initiate a rebirth. It was a long and tumultuous road back, however. Many of the riot cities voted in their first black mayors during the 1970s, causing momentary elation in the black community. Unfortunately these mayors found themselves heirs to an economic disaster, overlords of empty shells.

As one economics professor commented, "When the blacks get Newark they're getting in on a bankruptcy sale. There's just nothing there. We've reached a time when the capacity of cities to upgrade their inhabitants is at a dead end." Yet like a Depression-era hobo, down on his luck in a society that has turned its back, the riot cities made due with the resources at hand. America's riot cities are indeed a story of hope. When things are bad, sometimes hope is all you have left.

LBJ reacts to the tragic news of Dr. King's death in April of 1968. The two were titans from different ends of the political spectrum who meet in the middle to forge a much needed societal progress. While both departed the scene with their visions unfulfilled, in the end they planted the seeds for future generations to have a better life.

The Death of King

A Los Angeles teenager cringes at the newspapers headline. King's death brought yet another wave of rioting across the country. One hundred and thirty cities crested in anger for the now-martyred leader. Irregardless all of the accolades Martin Luther King received during and after his life, he would have traded them all for a better universal understanding of what he was fighting for. His journey through the civil rights movement from 1955 to his untimely demise in 1968 was one of the greatest feats of leadership in American history.

Los Angeles Public Library

A final salute for the peacemaker as the plane carrying Martin Luther King's body prepares to depart Memphis for the final journey home to Atlanta.

Walter Reuther Library

On a warm spring day in 1968, Robert Kennedy, himself now a declared candidate for the presidency, stands in the heart of 12th Street, only yards from where the riot started. If there was any white man alive that black society trusted, it was Bobby Kennedy. It was he who prodded his brother John to initiate civil rights legislation. This photo was taken only a month after the assassination of Dr. King, an event that caused more rioting in this very area and across the country. As seen on the faces of his greeters, they are inquisitively happy to see him. This would be Kennedy's last trip to Michigan as he himself would succumb to an assassin's bullet only a month after this photo was taken.

The poor have become nearly invisible and with that invisibility the sense of community has disappeared... We can face our difficulties and strive to overcome them with imagination and dedication and wisdom and love. Or we can turn away-- bringing repression, steadily increasing human pain and civil strife, and leaving a problem of far more terrible and threatening proportions to our children.

- RFK

The Moynihan Report

Daniel Patrick Moynihan

In March of 1965, a controversial report by Assistant Secretary of Labor Daniel Patrick Moynihan kicked up quite a row in Washington circles and it cascaded all the way to the grass roots of urban America.

As riots raged on the East coast in 1964, Moynihan's report broadcast the naked truths that no one wanted to hear - that urban black families were crumbling and that the ghosts of white institutions, ranging from slavery to Jim Crow, created this situation.

The statistics he unearthed were staggering. Less than half of America's black teenagers had lived their entire life with both parents, 21 percent were fatherless and somewhere between 25-40 percent were illegitimate. President Johnson drew heavily on the Moynihan report in a highly-acclaimed speech he gave to Howard University graduates, "When the family collapses, it is the children that are usually damaged. When it happens on a massive scale, the community itself is crippled."

Moynihan was no grandstanding hypocrite, however, but rather a unique hybrid of enlightened experiences. His father walked out the door when he was eleven, never to return. Moynihan grew up on the very edge of despair that he later analyzed, including the New York slums of East Harlem and the notorious Hell's Kitchen. But Moynihan persevered. He clawed his way out of the ghetto and earned a Ph.D. from elite Tufts University in 1961. His unique blend of formal education and street smarts made him a highly credible social critic.

Moynihan bluntly pointed out in 1965 that, "The gap between the Negro and most other groups in American society is widening. The fundamental problem, in which this is most clearly the case, is that of family structure. The evidence, not final but powerfully persuasive, is that the Negro family in the urban ghettoes is crumbling. A middle class group had managed to save itself, but for vast numbers of the unskilled, poorly-educated city working class the fabric of conventional social relationships has all but disintegrated. There are indications that the situation may have been arrested in the past few years, but the general post-war trend is unmistakable. So long as this situation persists, the cycle of poverty and disadvantage will continue to repeat itself."

As the urban riots drew to a close, Vietnam continued to rage on. Yet another reason for discontent, blacks represented a higher proportion of soldiers drafted based on their percentage of population. Ironically, many blacks felt the service offered them a much better chance for equality. They learned that through hard work they could rise through the ranks and achieve distinction. Returning home, they once again became a second-class citizen, prisoner behind the invisible walls of prejudice.

Birmingham

Birmingham has paid the price over the decades for the "Cotton Curtain" that once divided its communities. One long time city leader recalled, "You can't believe how bad our image was. You'd finish speaking at some convention up North and the first question they'd ask you was, 'How many niggers did you get before breakfast?'" It got so bad in the late 1960s that leaders contemplated changing the name of the city. But Birmingham has "come to Jesus" since then.

In 1979, Birmingham elected its first black mayor. Richard Arrington, son of a sharecropper and holder of a Ph.D., was a witness to the chaotic demonstrations in 1963. Even in the time frozen South, old ideologies have begun to thaw. The "whites only" signs were euthanized, the obnoxious (c) which appeared after a black persons name in the phonebook denoting "colored" has been deleted and the schools were integrated, with curious results.

Birmingham Public Library

Birmingham's Kelly Ingram Park - where it all started.

Kelly Ingram Park is quiet now. Ferocious police dogs are now only an apparition of the poisonous days when this community was guided by the powerful hand of ignorance. The giant magnolia trees which dominate the park still stand their stoically. They were much smaller in 1963 when they bore witness to this pivot point in civil rights history. Like the community of Birmingham, they have grown considerably and with the passage of time comes wisdom.

White southerners have an intense pride in their lineage and can easily trace it back many generations from memory. While there are some who see the Confederate flag as an icon for slavery, many southerners simply see it as the flag their forefathers fought under and, as history has noted, very bravely so. Southern communities are like no other. Towns of 5,000 people are so close knit they are more akin to a family of 5,000. As such, the acceptance of blacks into the community was bound to take some time, but a current inspection of the new South finds that the civil rights seeds that were planted long ago have taken root and now bear the fruit of more recent generations.

Harlem

Harlem was originally developed in the late 1800s as a hideaway for wealthy and middle class whites, a retreat from the confines of lower Manhattan. Developers built and built until the banks would loan them no more. Their greed would be a windfall for the black community. Realtors were forced to sublease to blacks to stave off receivership and the black Mecca was born. It was the first chance blacks had ever had to build a community in above average conditions and they would make the most of it. Blacks began to trickle into Harlem around 1900. By 1919, the black population of Harlem had quadrupled.

Black servicemen coming back from France in 1918 had been profoundly influenced by the various cultures they had encountered overseas. Instilled by Uncle Sam with a "fight for democracy" attitude, they brought this same will to fight back to Harlem. Blacks had been cut off from their African lineage because of the slave trade and were now attempting to reconstruct their culture.

This new found black pride and solidarity would culminate during the 1920s with the Harlem Renaissance. Harlem became the world stage for the "New Negro," who had made the transition from cotton field to concrete jungle and found a white audience that embraced the song and dance they brought with them. For the first time, blacks had established a solid middle class.

But the Roaring Twenties would come to a crashing halt when the Great Depression put America in an economic death grip from which Harlem would not recover. While the Renaissance did not stop abruptly, the talent that built it slowly retreated to more stable climates.

The 1940s brought WWII and even though the war produced a bounty of jobs in New York, ugly race riots in 1935 and 1943 would bring an end to whites flocking "up town" and the beginning of white flight. Even black migrants who continued to arrive from the South chose to skip Harlem. Since many of Harlem's black entertainers relied heavily on white audiences, they now had to move to downtown Manhattan to survive, further draining Harlem of talent.

By the 1950s, Harlem had deteriorated significantly. Harlem had become an economic Dust Bowl and with this depravity came a drug epidemic. Harlem streets were inhabited by an army of heroin addicts who stole and mugged to feed their habits.

By the 1970s, Harlem was in intensive care and fading fast. Many proprietors found it more prudent to burn their building for the insurance money than continue to lose money. Since 1950, Harlem had lost 60 percent of its population. Wholesale abandonment of buildings, burned-out cars and burned-out people now defined this once colorful neighborhood. Without investment, Harlem could not recover.

The 1980s found Harlem a no-man's land. With the crack cocaine epidemic draining away lives and resources, men were given a lower life expectancy than those in third world Bangladesh. Harlem became the most notorious slums in the country. But the 1990s began to change that. In league with skyrocketing real estate prices in Manhattan, the Fifth-Avenue types suddenly discovered it was once again hip to live uptown amidst its mystic surroundings, and the gentrification of Harlem began.

The affluent have been reclaiming Harlem, chipping away at the outer edges of this cultural black Mecca with their monopolistic wealth and prominence. Longtime Harlemites, who spent grievous decades experiencing the most violent and desolate of times, are now back peddling for their very existence as the shadow of gentrification advances house by house, block by block closer.

In league with the rich is a wave of latte-toting yuppies who think The Savoy was a bowling alley and Duke Ellington was a quarterback for the Giants. It has become, in essence, the Harlem Renaissance II. The battle for Harlem is no longer black vs. white but rather the princes against the paupers. One lifelong Harlemite was baffled at the reversal, "People used to work three jobs to get out of Harlem. Now they're working three to get in."

"Thousands of tourists come to Harlem churches to hear the gospel..... They want to know how it is that you may not have food on your table or money in your pocket and sound so happy."

AP/Wide World Photo

As the white community prepared itself for a black invasion of the suburbs after the Watts uprising, one suburbanite had the compunction to address the problem. Budd Schulberg, Hollywood writer of the Academy award winning *On the Waterfront*, was born in Los Angeles and still felt a sense of community there. Although unfamiliar with Watts, Schulberg, who is white, was miffed as he began his journey into the unknown. Flower beds and palm trees punctuated the small but neat single-family homes of Watts. Reality quickly took hold as Schulberg turned his car onto the fire ravaged 103rd Street, more recently dubbed "Charcoal Alley." Schulberg had a flashback to his days in the OSS during WWII when he witnessed one bombed-out German city after another.

Watts was another world to Schulberg. It was the "other America," an asylum with the gatekeeper missing. But a more personable inspection revealed Watts not to be an asylum but a society that was painted deeply into the corner of failure. Schulberg decided to offer a creative writing class as an outlet. Days turned into weeks as the sign-up sheets remained embarrassingly naked until finally a recruit, (a scout really) a young teenager named Charles sent to query the white man's intentions. "I got things to write about," Charles reflected, "only I don't know if they're stories." Schulberg put his young student at ease, "Stories aren't fancy things like the Arabian Nights. They're the things you've been doing, what you're thinking about now - that's what writing is."

It was as if the literary flood gates had opened, albeit a trickle at first, and a class began to take shape. It was an odd collection of misfits, bound together by adversity and a writer's edge. Charles brought with him a homeless teen named Luke, who, because of his retardedness, had a penchant for staring at Schulberg only inches from his face. Luke couldn't write but expressed himself in the only way he knew how, he sketched.

Other characters gravitated to the writing class. Another homeless teen named Leumas presented Schulberg with a scrap of paper featuring one of his prized poems. Schulberg, a Dartmouth graduate, winced when he saw the grammaticism of the first line, "Never know a begin of me." Rather than chastised the young teen, Schulberg instead instituted his class maxim, "Write only what you know," thus sparing the class future discouragement, an experience they had known their whole lives.

They were all veterans of the hard life that Watts offered in abundance but as Schulberg was to discover, their traumatic experiences brought a simplicity to their writing he had never witnessed before. Perhaps no one had ever shown them how to write. Perhaps no one cared. The Watts Happening Coffee Shop, an abandoned building filled with life's abandoned people, was for them the first place they could call home.

"I have been asked," says Schulberg, "if I am not afraid of the angry young men of Watts who are said to contemplate guerrilla warfare. I am more afraid of the greed and selfishness and the blind intransigence and the appalling ignorance of social dynamics that build concentration camp walls around enclaves like Watts."

Courtesy of National Archives

The Watts Happening Coffee House on 103rd Street, the infamous Charcoal Alley. It housed Schulberg's Shakespeare's and their crystallization of life in Watts.

Anger turned inward is depression. Anger turned outward is Watts. But adversity is a great teacher and post riot Watts turned its anger inside out in 1966, creating the annual Watts Summer Festival. Since then it has become the oldest African-American festival in the country. The festival does not celebrate the anniversary of the horrific event but rather uses it as a stepping stone towards creating a better society.

The Watts Summer Festival touts community pride, cultural and political awareness as well as a remembrance of the thirty-four who perished during the riot. During the inaugural parade you could look through the refreshment tents and still see burned out stores, a constant reminder to local residents not to trod the path from whence they came.

If Watts is anything, it is resilient. Like a boxer sent to the canvas a dozen times, Watts refused to stay down for the count.

I am a little hurt, but I am not slain;
I will lay me down for to bleed awhile,
then I will rise and fight with you again.

Los Angeles Public Library

The Other America

Civil rights has come a long way since the 1950s and continues to make commendable progress. But now national attention needs to shed light on another dark secret Americans have coldly ignored, the homeless.

Greater Los Angeles itself is a blur of contrasting worlds. Career yuppies in $2,000 a month penthouse apartments avoid the human wreckage of Skid Row below them, shielded from the screams and moans by a vertical buffer. Los Angeles has become, unwillingly, the homeless capital of the country. Peering from the shadows of Skid Row are the glazed and frightened eyes of thousands who have no one to turn to. Skid Row is like a human landfill, full of discarded objects that no one else wants. Known as the "broken down brigade" there can be found among the faceless flock amputees in wheelchairs, schizophrenics, prostitutes and runaways. Seventh Street and San Julian have taken on the image of a third-world country, while the glitz and glitter of the Hollywood Hills is just a short limo drive away. Skid Row is, simply put, the dark side of the moon. It's a side that few people see, nor do they want to see. We shield our eyes, pretending not to notice the human flotsam that drifts in, and when it is unavoidable, we convince ourselves their plight is of their own making. On the contrary, any one of us could fill their ranks.

One veteran of "the Row," who has been in and out of juvenile centers and prison since the age of ten, laments about the disparity of his situation, "I can't read. Can't write. That's something I just don't tell people. To get a job, at fifty-years old, what am I gonna do? I don't wanna go back to prison."

Los Angeles Public Library

America's homeless – The Next Great Crusade.

It is impossible to accurately gauge the depth of despondency on the Row. Paramedics beat a steady path there attempting to save the overdose victims who seek an end to their immeasurable anguish. On the flip side, one woman who has been on Skid Row for ten years still says the rosary before she falls asleep in her makeshift tent.

The America that was reared in the deprivation of the Great Depression and blooded during WWII not only learned the lessons of humility, they lived them. The Greatest Generation voted and worked for what was best for the country and the community.

A sickening obsession and devotion to wealth and indulgence has weakened the bonds of compassion that once held the country together. The top 1 percent of wealth in America has amassed 44 percent of the financial assets. That's equivalent to the bottom 120 million Americans combined. On judgment day they leave behind not respect or admiration but only the disgraceful legacy of having accumulated the most while having given the least.

Like the hobos of the Great Depression, the homeless have become invisible, doomed to share a gloomy existence on a parallel with the rats that boldly nip at their feet at night. Americans have grown cold to the concept of humanitarianism. Upper classes view the poor as almost subhuman. The erosion of public sympathy towards the plight of the anonymous has greatly weakened the social fabric that was once America. We pull down our shades and change the channel out of ignorance that a comfortable upbringing has imbued us with. We blind ourselves to the reality that had fate played the same cruel game, it could just as easily be us sleeping out in the cold. As Martin Luther King once said, "Our lives begin to end the day we become silent about things that matter."

ONE
WAY
CURLIFE

Present day Cleveland has witnessed a tremendous resurgence from the moribund metropolis in its death throws, but it required three harrowing decades to set things straight. The white flight that hit Cleveland after the Hough Riots left it "black, brown and broke." The city would lose over a quarter of its manufacturing jobs through the 1970s and '80s. Through improved governance, the city has strived and has succeeded in becoming a tourist attraction in the archaic rust belt of the Midwest. Cleveland stands today as the leading light of urban regeneration.

Hough too has come a long way. Visitors to the area would be hard-pressed to imagine the fury that went on here forty years ago. Block after block of deteriorated buildings have been razed. The new Hough portrays a unique blend of ethnic and economic cultures quite contrary to the old ghetto. A large and modern medical center, along with the expansion of Case Western Reserve University, has reestablished credibility to a neighborhood that clearly desired and deserved a second chance.

Courtesy of National Archives

Legacy of the Hough Riot – Abandoned businesses and a shattered economy.

Like the aspirations of the community, the Hough obelisk reaches skyward as a reminder to all that Hough has finally jettisoned the ghosts of its once turbulent past

Newark

The 1970s were perhaps the cruelest of all to Newark. One Newark resident, who had seen many changes over the years, saw the post riot years in Newark with a very disparaging eye, "Newark used to be a city where they manufactured everything, now it's the car theft capital of the world... there was a factory where somebody was making something on every side street. Now there's a liquor store on every street - a liquor store, a pizza stand and a seedy store front church. Everything else is in ruins or boarded up."

Newark elected its first black mayor, Kenneth Gibson, in 1970, in a racially-polarized election that further divided the community. While Gibson's election was a huge moral boost for the black community, Gibson inherited an economic shell that would paralyze his attempt to right the stricken city.

Library of Congress

Barren expanses and weed choked lots are constant reminders of Newark's costly rebellion. By the 1970s, Newark's streets became ghost towns as industry and enterprise steered well clear. The economic desolation created from looted and burned-out businesses that never returned exacted a fearful vengeance on not just the few who rebelled but the entire city.

Public Housing: The Scourge of Newark

An aerial view of pre-riot Newark would reveal to the outsider a startling array of public housing towers, stranded in a barren and forbidden landscape in a part of town that was to be avoided. The great slums of the 1800s were torn down during the massive urban renewal projects of the 1940s and '50s and replaced with high-rise public housing projects, the newest innovation.

High-rise public housing was the federal governments answer to the critical post-war housing shortage that overwhelmed many of the big northern cities. It would prove to be a failure of catastrophic proportions. It was a thinly veiled attempt to house as many impoverished people as cheaply as possible on the smallest parcels of land by stacking them one on top of another. Since these projects were built over the ruins of old slums, tenants found themselves in an economic no man's land, setting the stage for high unemployment, crime and a permanent underclass on a mammoth scale.

To circumvent over inflated land prices and meet the stingy federal cost regulations, designers had no other recourse but to build straight up, often twelve to eighteen stories. The dreary, monolithic appearance was also intentional to remind its inhabitants that they were indeed underclass. Sociologists were aghast at this new governmental strain of logic. They had prophesized about the perils involved with a beehive-like concentration of poverty-stricken people under one massive, hastily designed roof. But the projects were cranked out in cookie cutter fashion. In some cities, as many as 33 eleven story buildings were haphazardly jammed together. Detached from the rest of society in their own cultural vacuum, failure was almost assured.

The idea germinated from French architect and visionary Charles Le Corbusier. Initially contracted by French authorities to help deal with the overcrowded slums of Paris, he believed cell-like apartments stacked on top of each other would raise the quality of life for the poor.

This could also be done, reasoned Le Corbusier, with entire cities but on a much grander scale for the wealthy. He referred to his utopian enterprise as Villa Contemporaine. Immense buildings sixty stories high would house the wealthiest in society. The unsightliness of transportation would be placed below ground where a multi-leveled transportation hub containing highways, rail and a bus depot cold thrive. At ground level there would be vast open spaces for parks. Congested sidewalks would be a thing of the past. An airport would dominate the middle, although it was never explained precisely how a pilot would circumvent sixty story buildings with any degree of safety. On paper, of course, it was the perfect world.

Le Corbusier's vision - Villa Contemporaine

Newark's Central Ward - Monuments of human despair

AP/Wide World Photo

Newark's tragic triangle - Decades of disgust and resentment finally give way to demolition as the Scudder Homes are reduced to dust in 1987. Off in the distance, Stella Wright (back, right) and the hulking mass of the Hayes project (far left) await their turn at oblivion. It was the fitting end to the nightmare of high-rise public housing.

Courtesy Implosion World

Columbus Homes – A misplaced piece of Hell.

The last of the Columbus Homes heals over in 1984, taking with it the stark, bleak world that was indicative of the projects. Grim and menacing in appearance, the Columbus Homes looked more like a maximum security prison and in some respects were probably worse. Honest poor were lumped in with hostile criminal elements. Projects became havens for gangs that dealt drugs and turned the buildings into a fortress that even the police couldn't approach without being noticed. The open fields surrounding the projects became fire zones for anyone who didn't belong. High rise public housing was a government experiment that turned into a Frankenstein's monster. Elevators broke down and tenants who lived on the upper floors were forced to take the poorly-lit, windowless stairwells where assaults and rapes were common. Legitimate businesses nearby often left for safer harbors. The vacuum was replaced with a multitude of liquor stores and schlock shops that preyed on the economically illiterate and those desperately seeking an escape from reality.

Courtesy Implosion Worl

May 2000 - The Hayes projects, which had figured so prominently in the riot, withered under the force of 1,500 pounds of explosives. A few traumatic seconds later and the agony of the Hayes Homes was mercifully brought to an end. It was the final, sad chapter in the history of high-rise public housing. Built in 1954, when segregation was still enforced, the Hayes projects were originally segregated white tenants. Then Mayor Leo Carlin declared at the christening that those "who live in bright and cheeried surroundings, such as those provided in this project, will lose the feeling of futility of existence and discouragement which breeds crime." A stigmatic qualification to say the least. In 1958, a law was passed barring discrimination in public housing, right on the heels of the great post-war migration which inundated Newark with southern blacks. As blacks moved in, the whites moved out. The physical condition of the complex quickly took a nosedive. Boilers went cold, lights went dark, and the police took a holiday. The Hayes complex, like that of the Scudder, Stella Wright and Columbus Homes, were the scourge of Newark. Surrounded by social and economic blight, thousands of blacks were trapped in a vacuum of poverty, and, like inmates in a great prison, they grew to hate their keepers. They were tragic icons which represented the utter failure of high-rise public housing and the end of a disastrous social experiment.

After decades of languishing near total insolvency and unwillingly becoming the butt of many sordid jokes, Newark has of late managed to gain a toehold on the ladder of progress. Tanks no longer rule Springfield Avenue as they did during the riot but have relinquished their grip to a citizenry that inhabits Newark by choice and not by default. Most of the illicit buildings which solicited Newark's youth are history. The notorious housing projects were once and for all laid to rest, never again to offer shelter to gangs, drunks and felons. The economic rollercoaster that Newark rode for decades has finally leveled off. Some businesses have returned, Rutgers continues to maintain a viable campus in the heart of downtown, and the Newark Bears, the city's double-A baseball team, offers a reason for families to pay a visit downtown.

We All Lost
We All Failed

FAIRWAY MARKET

Detroit Detroit

The Tailspin of Decline

Detroit, as the birthplace of the automobile, was seen as the symbol of the American dream. Immigrants came to Detroit, procured a good job, bought their first house and retired in peace. Post riot Detroit, in turn, became the poster child for social and economic decay, an urban museum inventorying all that has gone wrong with rust-belt cities after they peaked in the 1950s.

The invisible scars from the Great Rebellion have never healed. Former Detroit Mayor Coleman Young, who was elected seven years after the riot and was forced to deal with the city's depleted resources, commented, "The riot put Detroit on the fast track to economic desolation, mugging the city and making off with incalculable value in jobs, corporate taxes, retail dollars and plain damn money."

Post Riot Pullout

1967	-67 000
1968	-80 000
1969	-46 000

The Razing of 12th Street – For years following the riot, 12th Street looked like a mile long jagged scar, a constant reminder of the five day war that ravaged the area. Twelfth Street, Linwood and Grand River, once colorful thoroughfares, became grim and empty corridors, a checkerboard of weed choked empty lots. Concrete slabs marked the graves of looted and burned-out stores that once represented the livelihood of hard-working immigrants. Fire gutted buildings were razed and salvaged buildings were bought out by the city so the street could be turned into a boulevard. Other area businesses began to take on a fortress like appearance as their showcase front windows were bricked up in preparation for the next disturbance. Proprietors left their stores at night with guns drawn, got in their cars and headed for the suburbs. Perhaps the irony of ironies is that 12th Street was slated for urban renewal years before the riot, so this 'sin strip' would have been razed, riot or not. It is doubtful but possible that had 12th Street been razed years earlier that a riot might have been averted all together.

When Detroit was King

For decades Detroit was the greatest manufacturing city in the world. It was unmatched in its industrial capacity. Today, abandoned factories like the old Studebaker plant in Detroit's Milwaukee Junction are now standing mockeries of their former glory. Now cold and silent, only periodic cornerstones mark the spots where legendary names once made their mark in life. The white building just past Studebaker is Henry Ford's Piquette Avenue plant, birthplace of the Model T.

The year 1950 was the high-water mark of prosperity for Detroit. In those days, Detroit was building one out of every two cars in the world. Now it builds one in every thousand. Detroit's population spiked at 1.8 million and was king of the automotive world. As such, the city brought in millions of dollars each year to its economy as elite hotels like the Statler and Book-Cadillac were filled with out of town automotive conventioneers.

Now Detroit's Depression-era high-rise hotels are either dust or derelicts. Conventions, which were always more monkey business than company business anyway, have found more appreciable climates. Las Vegas, which was a mere speck of dust when Detroit was king, now owns the convention world. Northern cities like Chicago, Detroit and Cleveland will never be able to distance themselves from the fact that for six months of the year the weather is cold, frozen and dreary.

Coleman Young was not the sole cause of Detroit's decline. The arrogant and implacable automotive leaders of the era must also bear some responsibility for the city's predicament. Big Three complacency, white flight and unemployment all hit Detroit hard during the 1970s, capsizing the city and leaving an overturned hull of desolation and bitterness. With Detroit's ever-dwindling resources, it would take decades to right the ship.

The near total collapse of the Big Three automakers in the 1970s is a lesson in unprecedented arrogance and complacency. In their distorted world of reality, they saw themselves as untouchables. An auto analyst from that period recalled, "I remember Henry Ford II talking about how the Ford Pinto would push the Japs back into the Pacific Ocean."

Leaders of the Big Three led their companies off a cliff, choosing to ignore obvious signs and exhibit the usual "you'll have it our way" attitude. Even after the Arab oil embargo in 1973, American car companies continued to crank out poor-quality, gas-guzzling land yachts that exhibited bland and unimaginative designs. The time when the Big Three could sell cars as quickly as they could make them was over. They still believed themselves to have monopolistic powers over American consumers. The Japanese shattered that myth forever.

Labor unions, with their dictatorial attitudes, drove many a Detroit business out of town, out of state and out of the country. H. Glen Bixby, who was president of the mammoth Detroit based Ex-Cell-O Corporation, blasted the city's union atmosphere in 1960 stating that:

> ***Militant and venomous attitude toward industry has and will continue to limit job opportunity. Industries, like people, will not go where they are insulted and vilified daily. If Michigan labor union leadership is seriously interested in job opportunity for their members, they must change their attitude from one of conflict to one of cooperation.***

The economic aftershock was devastating as Detroit's economy unraveled like a cheap sweater. Since 1970, a staggering 75 percent of Detroit's manufacturing jobs have left the city or have been eliminated. The economic after shock decimated the city to such an extent that it can never be the same again. The most obvious physical symbol of decay is portrayed by the city's houses. People lose their jobs and have to choose between eating or house maintenance. Detroit has borne witness to the largest home demolition the country has ever seen. Between 1970-2003 Detroit has razed 166,992 housing units. This is one-third of the city's housing stock, i.e. enough to house the city of Cleveland. No other big city in the country has ever encountered such devastation.

The 1970s – Rock Bottom

The upheaval of the 1960s help set the stage for an even worse period in the city's history. With businesses and citizens frantically leaving Detroit at a record rate, city coffers quickly emptied, leaving a barren desert of resources without even a mirage of hope. The result was predictable, a desperate city with desperate people. Detroit began a total emotional meltdown with a runaway murder rate which gave it a national black eye and the lingering moniker of the "Murder City."

The rage was there. The frustration was there. I think we see it. The more widespread use of narcotics today is an escape. Even the violence, including the shooting, is another release I think of this anger, this ongoing rage and frustration. For the moment, the black community has turned inward on itself.

– Coleman A. Young

In the space of a short, tragic decade Detroit went from the automotive capital to the murder capital. It wouldn't have mattered if Franklin Delano Roosevelt was mayor of Detroit in the 1970s. This city, like the other riot cities, was headed for some hard times.

As downtown shoppers went about their business, police warnings blared over the loudspeakers: "Walk in twos after dark, keep your hands on your purses, stay away from the alleys and have a merry Christmas."

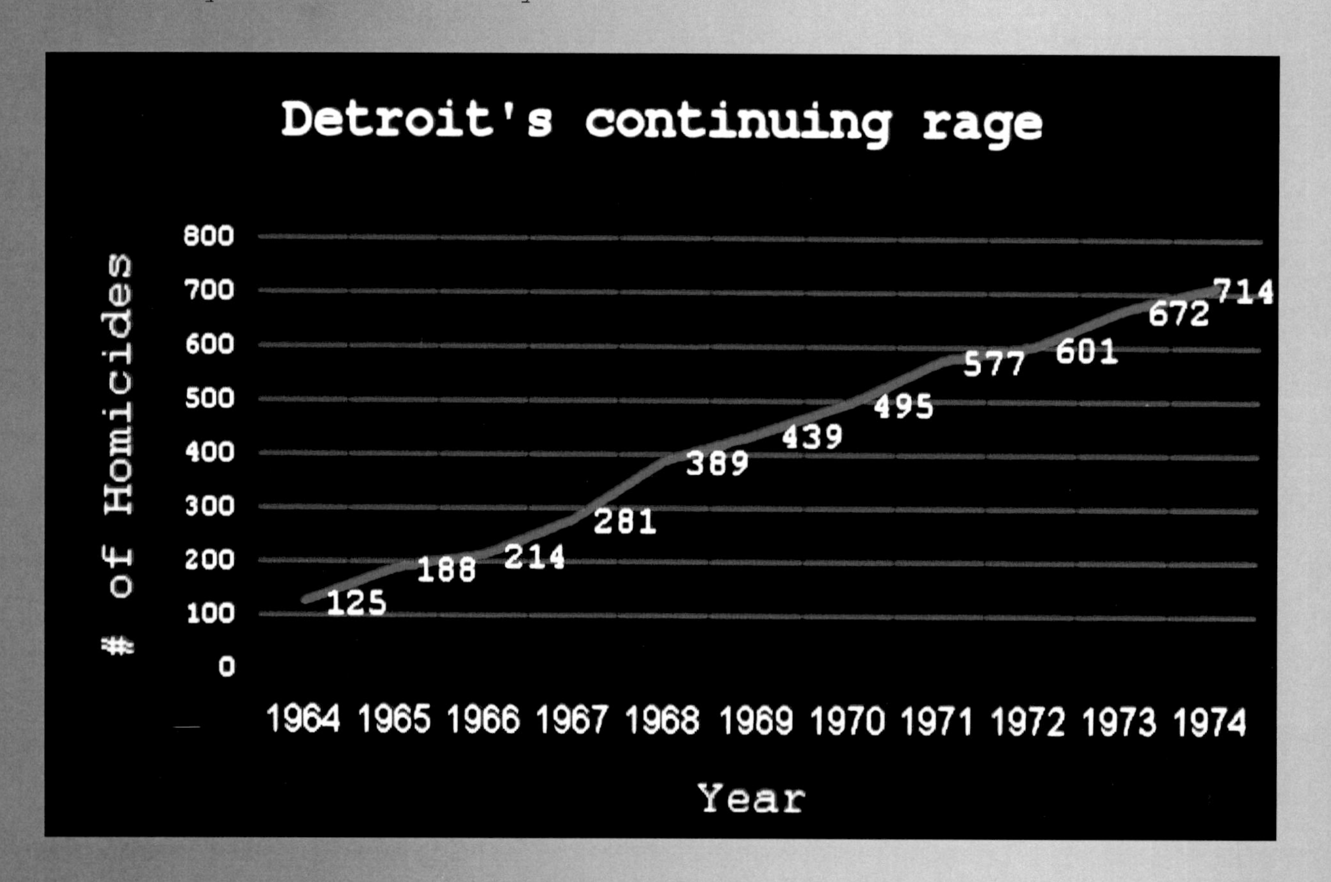

Young's Town

Detroit's fiery mayor Coleman Young. He became the Great Black Hope.

I issue a forward warning now to all dope pushers, to all ripoff artists, to all muggers: It's time to leave Detroit. Hit Eight Mile Road.

And I don't give a damn if they are black or white, if they wear Superfly suits or blue uniforms with silver badges - Hit the road.

- Detroit Mayor Coleman Young
Inaugural speech - 1974

Detroit elected its first black mayor in 1974. Coleman A. Young, a former Tuskegee Airman and longtime civil rights crusader, would run the city for the next twenty years. The man they called "Big Time" was legendary for his outspoken, confrontational style and no holds barred sense of humor. His reign over Detroit would be a journey few locals, white or black, would ever forget.

Young was born in Alabama in 1918 at a time when blacks were, by custom, supposed to stare at the ground when addressing whites as a sign of respect. His father refused, and counseled his son to do likewise, "Look any man straight in the eyes, but particularly a white man." The elder Young's attitudes did not endear him to the white community and they got out of town just ahead of the lynch mobs; destination Detroit.

But Detroit waters held the same riptide of prejudice as did the South. Young constantly found himself the victim of prejudice growing up. The pivot point of his life was the Bob Lo (an amusement park in the Detroit River) boat incident. As the only black member of his Boy Scout troop, he was told by park officials he could not go because of his skin color. With humiliation coursing through his body, Young watched the boat pull away from the dock with all his friends on it and would remember the sting of prejudice for the rest of his life.

As mayor of Detroit, Young took over a scarred and divided city in 1974 that had been hemorrhaging thousands of jobs, businesses and people for years. He proceeded to impart his attitudes on a city that was still unwilling to yield the fact that Detroit was now in the hands of black leaders. The city's white flight continued unabated.

Young had a black belt in street smarts and the temperament of a street fighter. His mastery of four-letter words came in handy when dealing with his legion of critics. He made it eminently clear, with his trademark bluntness, that he was not a man to be trifled with. Anyone who had previously crossed his path knew that already. For those who hadn't, he made public examples of anyone naïve enough to challenge him. He regularly cussed out white reporters whom he felt were trying to assassinate his character or that of his city. One of his arch enemies was local columnist Pete Waldmeir:

That sonofabitch Waldmeir once followed me down to Jamaica to investigate my goddamn vacation. I wish that mother------ had caught me. I'm mayor of nothing down there. It would be just two crazy Americans fighting in the alley.

Walter Reuther Library

1975 - The Livernois incident was another near-miss riot at a time when Detroit was at rock bottom. When a white store owner shot and killed a black teenager, Young walked up and down Livernois for two nights trying to quell the vengeful crowd. He made it known he was on their side, but he also made it eminently clear they were not going to burn down his city.

One of Young's main priorities was to integrate the police department so that it was racially proportional to the city's population. The police department was often seen as the last bastion of white privilege left in a city that was losing what little was left of its white citizenry. It was a battle Young unflinchingly accepted, but he spent much of his twenty years in office on a war-footing with his own police department.

Young trusted few people, and his constant flashbacks to prejudicial indignities of his youth could be triggered easily:

Beware of any benighted son-of-a-bitch who says he's going to help you pull yourself up by your bootstraps.

The FBI, who had bugged Young's townhouse, seemed to be ever probing his affairs for irregularities. The fact that they never charged him with anything made Young's claims of harassment and conspiracy seem that much more credible.

Young's defiant mentality didn't always win him friends. For example, he openly referred to Ronald Reagan as President "Prune Face." While many of his constituents appreciated his outspokenness, for the sake of the city he should have put his personal differences aside.

Walter Reuther Library

Young as a state senator just prior to becoming mayor. Here he enjoys a cold one during an informal soiree amongst old comrades in the Detroit ghetto of Black Bottom from whence he came. Young never forgot where he grew up. For him, hardship was a great teacher. Many of the critics who misunderstood him did so out of ignorance because they were spared such adversity.

A playground now stands where an inferno once raged.

Detroit was in a constant state of transition after the riot. Many businesses refused to build or rebuild in the city because crime was high, insurance (if you could get it) skyrocketed, parking was poor and large tracks of land were no longer available for the modern, mega-sized shopping malls now appearing on the scene. Merchants whose stores survived the riot were essentially trapped since no one was willing give an equitable price for a building in a riot area.

Walter Reuther Library

1954 - The opening of the first suburban mall, Northland, gave suburbanites yet another reason to not go downtown and eventually led to the end of big city department stores.

For decades, Detroit was the economic standard for all other cities to measure themselves against. With its Herculean economic might pivoting on the auto industry, both blacks and whites enjoyed a comfortable standard of living and a high rate of home ownership.

Detroit's Brush Park, the city's oldest subdivision, still reigns as a fallen example of the Gilded Age and as a before/after indicator of what the city has gone through in the last century. The Victorian mansions of Brush Park once housed Detroit's nobility. They are a time capsule of Detroit's past. They mirror a time when lumber barons, railroad tycoons and shipping magnets, the very men who set the stage for the gasoline aristocracy, left their unique stamp on Detroit with their one of a kind stately manors. The few that survive are symbols of Detroit's heyday and a barometer of the radical change the city has undergone.

But yesterday's Detroit is no more. Half of the city's residents have left since 1950 as well as more than half of the jobs. You can chart the path of abandonment left in their wake. Modern factories, once bustling with life, have been deserted for decades, slowly being picked clean for their copper or anything else scavengers can turn a buck on.

Today, Detroit is principally two cities. The inner core, which flaunts modern sports stadiums, refurbished attitudes and a sputtering nightlife receives the lion's share of the resources. Guided by profiteers who had envisioned a quasi resurgence, it is the latest attempt to lure suburbanites back downtown to unload some of their considerable revenue. Then there is the outer core, a no man's land of destitution and decay that the city has essentially abandoned to its fate.

The former mansion of Detroit lumber baron Lucien Moore accurately depicts Detroit's last 100 years. From prominence to privation to promise, Detroit has gone the cycle.

1890s - Prime

1970s - Abandoned

Today - Reborn

Renaissance Center - Monument of Hope

Detroit Public Library

The focal point of Detroit's rebirth was the massive Renaissance complex anchored on the Detroit River. Led by industrialist Henry Ford II, a consortium of companies became the post-riot conscience of Detroit, attempting to make amends by giving the city a new symbol of hope. It replaced the Spirit of Detroit statue of a crouching man who is either rising to his feet or sinking to his knees, depending on the state of the city. This suburban island in the middle of the city erased a wino filled junkyard of warehouses that represented Detroit's rust filled past. The Renaissance Center was not designed to single handedly pluck Detroit out of it's economic funk but rather to act as a catalyst to draw other investment to the area. Below, the "Ren Cen" as seen from the Canadian side.

Detroit Public Libra

The Good Shepherd

Detroit's Mother Waddles, "I read the Bible. It didn't just say go to church. It said do something."

When the down and out of Detroit's homeless garrisons find themselves at the end of the line, when there is no place left to go and no one else to turn to, there is always Mother Waddles. Like the Good Shepherd tending her wandering flock, Mother Waddles offers a rare but constant sanctuary. She has been feeding, clothing and sheltering Detroit's downtrodden for forty years.

Charleszetta Waddles is a veteran of the hard life herself. Her father died when she was twelve and she had to quit school. She was married at fourteen and a widow at nineteen. Remarried and subsequently divorced, Waddles found herself with ten kids to support and no visible means to do it, "I put tubs in front of my house on weekends and sold barbeque. You learn how to survive."

Mother Waddles, herself an ordained Pentecostal minister, became Detroit's patron saint for those in distress. Her one woman assault on Detroit's impoverished is the DNA that true heroes are made of. She has never asked for, nor has she ever received, any money from any tier of the government, a fact she is perpetually proud of. While her coffers always flirted with exhaustion, her formidable skills and magnetic charm seem to draw charitable works from well endowed community leaders.

While Waddles does not accept money from those few who can pay, she does expect an attentive ear on Sunday morning while she preaches to her flock. Among Waddles diverse congregation can be found an alphabet soup of destitution: chronic alcoholics from Skid Row, junkies, current and former prostitutes, panhandlers and confidence men. To her flock she preaches perseverance and enlightenment.
To society, she preaches the helping hand of humanity, "We're trying to show what the church could mean to the world if it lived by what it preached. We (Christians) got a long way to go. We think prayers get answered by a far-away God. We think we can pray to God without being involved. That's not true. We don't realize we have to answer prayers as well as pray. We must have prayer and prayers don't get answered unless we become involved in the business of loving each other."

For I was hungry and you gave me something to eat,
I was a stranger and you invited me in....

- Matthew 25:35

"Replacing Despair With Hope - This is the Nature of Americans"

Father
William Cunningham

Eleanor M.
Josaitis

Focus:HOPE

The last chapter written out of the ashes of the Detroit riot would be authored by an unlikely duo, a suburban housewife and a Roman Catholic priest. There were many efforts to help the stricken city after the riot but none managed to carve out a more endearing legacy of altruism the way Focus:HOPE did.

In 1968, Focus:HOPE began paving a road of humanitarianism through the riot torn neighborhoods of Detroit, which for years after the riot were saturated with fear and hate. They began with a massive food distribution program and now feed some 50,000 mothers, children and seniors a month. To create opportunity, they started a machinist training program that has placed thousands of young Detroiters into good-paying jobs.

Josaitis and Cunningham were both greatly affected by the Selma march of 1965. Josaitis, by chance, happened to be watching "Judgment at Nuremberg" when the movie was interrupted by footage of Alabama state troopers pummeling peaceful civil rights marchers. For her it was an awakening, "I kept thinking, what would I have done if I had lived in Nazi Germany? Would I have pretended that I didn't see anything? Then what am I doing about what's going on in this country?" Cunningham and Josaitis were a conscience looking for a cause. Fate would provide that for them in July of 1967.

Josaitis moved from the suburbs to Detroit shortly after the riot to establish Focus:HOPE, despite the fact that her family thought she was losing her grip on reality. She has lived in Detroit ever since. As a constant reminder that her work is never finished she frequently takes a different way home, making mental notes of the city's social conditions as she drives.

In the months after the riot, Cunningham once brought the Black Panthers and the KKK together and proceeded to lecture them at length about racial intolerance. Apparently his points were well-taken, for the two groups in turn began preaching an anti-hate campaign across the city.

After the tragic deaths of King and Kennedy in 1968, Focus:HOPE petitioned the city to cordon off Woodward Avenue downtown during the Labor Day weekend, challenging all creeds and colors to come down and unite for the betterment of the city. The city council thought it was a superb idea but not Mayor Cavanagh, who issued a warning to Focus:HOPE, "If this city riots again I'm holding you personally responsible." Needless to say it went off without a hitch. It may have been an obscure start, but it was a beginning of a much-needed healing. Even the greatest journey begins with a single step.

Courtesy Carl Bidleman

The fearless Father Cunningham took on all of life's challenges, including a charity boxing match against heavyweight champ Muhammad Ali in 1971. His specialty, however, was fighting poverty and prejudice in post riot Detroit. Cunningham's bout with cancer in 1997 was one battle he would not win but his legacy of salvaged souls throughout the city is testament to a man who was the embodiment of hope. Former Detroit mayor and close ally Coleman Young said of Cunningham: "He combined a compassion with vision, with energy and integrity. That's a rare combination. I have never seen the likes of someone like him."

The Wailing Wall

Photos courtesy Library of Congress

In the early 1940s, blacks seeking to escape the confines of Black Bottom moved out into the then vacant 8 Mile/Wyoming area. With jobs scarce and banks unwilling to loan them money, their dwellings left something to be desired. When a white developer sought FHA loans to build on the adjacent site, the federal government told him no because of the black housing next to it. In response to this, he built this six foot high wall as a racial divider and the federal loans were approved. It was regarded as a long- standing symbol of hatred by the black community, who dubbed it the Wailing Wall.

No longer a symbol of hatred, the Wailing Wall has undergone a transformation of sorts over the years. Local kids now use it to send adults their message of what society should be like.

The path to understanding - Children are by nature obsessed with physical growth. They stand erect next to a door and put a pencil mark above their head. Months later they return and repeat the process, comparing the two marks to see how much they've grown. So too must we compare our past with our present to realize how much we have grown as a society. In the final analysis it often takes the color blindness of a child to teach adults that character, not skin color, is the yardstick we should judge each other by.

Bibliography

Andrew, John A. III. *Lyndon Johnson and the Great Society.* Ivan R. Dee: Chicago, 1998.

Boesel, David & Peter H. Rossi. *Cities under Siege.* Basic Books, Inc., Publishers, New York: 1971.

Bullock, Paul. *WATTS: THE AFTERMATH BY THE PEOPLE OF WATTS.* Grove Press, Inc. New York: 1969.

Carmichael, Stokely & Charles Hamilton. *Black Power: The Politics of Liberation in America.* Vintage Books: New York, 1967.

Cleage, Albert B. Jr. *The Black Messiah*. Sheed and Ward, Inc: New York, 1968.

Cohen, Jerry and William S. Murphy: *BURN, BABY, BURN! The Watts Riot.* Avon Books: New York, 1966.

Dallek, Robert. *Flawed Giant: Lyndon Johnson and his times 1961-1973.* Oxford University Press: New York, 1998.

Fine, Sidney. *Violence in the Model City*. The University of Michigan Press: Ann Arbor, 1989.

Fogelson, Robert. *The Los Angeles Riots*. Arno Press: New York, 1969.

Goodspeed, Robert. *Urban Renewal in Postwar Detroit*. Unpublished Thesis, 2004.

Hersey, John. *The Algiers Motel Incident*. Alfred A. Knopf, New York: 1968.

Horne, Gerald. *FIRE THIS TIME: The Watts Uprising and the 1960's, DA CAPL Press:* New York, 1997.

Jacobs, Jane. *The Death and Life of Great American Cities.* Random House: New York, 1961.

Jones, E. Michael. *The Slaughter of Cities: Urban Renewal as Ethnic Cleansing*. St. Augustine Press: South Bend, 2004.

King, Martin Luther Jr. *The Autobiography of Martin Luther King Jr.* Warner Books: New York, 1998.

Lackritz, Mark E. *The Hough Riots of 1966.* Unpublished thesis.

Lardner, James & Thomas Reppetto. *NYPD: A City and its Police.* Henry Holt and Company: New York, 2000.

Lee, Alfred McClung & Norman D. Humphrey. *Race Riot: Detroit 1943.* Octagon Books Inc: New York, 1968.

Lewis, David L. *KING: A Critical Biography*. Praeger Publishers Inc: New York, 1970.

Litwack, Leon F. *TROUBLE IN MIND: Black Southerners in the age of Jim Crow*. Alfred A. Knopf: New York, 1998.

Moore, William Jr. *The Vertical Ghetto: Everyday Life in an Urban Project*. Random House: New York, 1969.

Niederhoffer, Arthur. *BEHIND THE SHIELD: The Police in Urban Society.* Doubleday & Co: Garden City, New York, 1967.

Oates, Stephen B. *Let the Trumpet Sound: The Life of Martin Luther King, Jr.* Harper & Row Publisher: New York, 1982.

Porambo, Ron. *No Cause For Indictment: An Autopsy of Newark*. Holt, Rinehart & Winston, New York: 1971.

Report of the National Advisory Commission on Civil Disorders (*The Kerner Report*). E.P. Dutton & Co., Inc: New York, 1968.

Schulman, Bruce J. *Lyndon B. Johnson and American Liberalism: A Brief Biograpy with Documents*. Bedford Books of St. Martin's Press: Boston, 1995.

Scott, William Walter III. *Hurt, Baby, Hurt*. New Ghetto Press Inc: Ann Arbor, 1970.

Shogan, Robert and Tom Craig. *The Detroit Race Riot: A Study in Violence*. Chilton Books: Philadelphia and New York, 1964

Stolberg, Mary M. *Bridging the River of Hatred*. Wayne State University Press: Detroit, 1998.

Strickland, William. *Malcolm X: Make it Plain.* Viking Press: New York, 1994.

Sugrue, Thomas J. *The Origins of the Urban Crisis.* Princeton University Press: Princeton, 1996.
Young, Coleman A. and Lonnie Wheeler. *Hard Stuff: The Autobiography of Coleman Young.* Viking Press: New York, 1994.
Wormser, Richard. *The Rise and Fall of Jim Crow.* St. Martin's Press: New York, 2003.

Newspapers

Cleveland Plain Dealer (CPD)
Detroit News (DN)
Detroit Free Press (DFP)
Los Angeles Times (LAT)
Metro Times (MT)
Michigan Chronicle (MC)
National Observer (NO)
New York Times (NYT)
State Journal (SJ)

Periodicals

Ebony Magazine (EB)
Detroit Blues (DB)
Life Magazine (LM)
LOOK Magazine (LOOK)
Newsweek Magazine (NW)
Readers Digest (RD)
Saturday Evening Post (SEP)
Time Magazine (TM)
U.S. News & World Report (USNWR)

Miscellaneous

Sidney Fine - *Detroit Riot Oral History Transcripts* (FOH): Bentley Library.
Public Broadcasting System (PBS)

Articles

Detroit fights Back - Julia Vitullo Martin.

Notes

Chapter 1: Along Comes A Man

"I remember that engine" Nevans, pg 54.

Chapter 2: Eatless Days in Black Bottom

"very dark days here" The Rise and Fall of Jim Crow, PBS.
"I'm gonna get me a job" Metro Times Blues, 7-25-00.
"lots of darkies" Levine, pg 54.
"Negroes can't work" Levine, pg 93.
"I was twelve years old" NYT 11-5-48.
"The street was known" DB, Spring 1997, pg 14.
"I was happy in Detroit" DN 6-23-01 pg 1D.

Chapter 3: 1943: A Race Riot There Will Be

"Few people doubt" Life 8-17-42 pg 17.
"I'd rather see Hitler and Hirohito" Shogan pg 32.
"We saw what happened to you" ibid pg 39.
"There's a riot at Belle Isle" ibid pg 41.
"We'll even this up later" ibid pg 50.
"I appeal to the good citizens of Detroit" ibid pg 77.
"Fix your bayonets" DN 6-22-43.
"Many times the good doctor" DFP 6-26-43.
"In the democracy of the dead" John James Ingalls.
"We were greenhorns" DFP 6-30-43.

Chapter 4: The 1950's: A Most Damning Time

"Sure, there have been inconveniences" Sugrue, pg 48.
Corktown poem: Detroit Public Library, Burton Historical Collection D/Neighborhoods/Corktown.
"Together, the united forces" Eisenhower 2-22-55.

Chapter 5: The Old Guard

"No policeman" Niederhoffer, pg 12.
"From within the system" Niederhoffer, pg 4.
"A black eye now and then" DN 5-9-58.
"If Detroit did blow up" Stolberg, pg 35.
"The police feel that they deserve" Niederhoffer, pg 8.
"Boss, we can't do that" Stolberg, pg 158.
"I look back over" Niederhoffer, pg 94.
"When you work in a precinct" FOH (John Nichols).
"The commandos were formed" DFP 5-28-72.
"We stopped this business" ibid.

Chapter 6: Jerome Cavanagh: A Last Flicker of Hope.

"Your imagination, your initiative" Dallek, pg 82.

Chapter 7: MLK Pays a Visit

"The same basic, underlying causes" MT 6-18-03.
"I told my child" LOOK 5-7-63.
"I've faced so many mobs" DN 6-24-63.
"The shape of the world" MC 6-29-63.
"You'll see no dogs" DN 6-24-63.
"I have a dream" MC 6-29-63.
"The rebellions will continue" NO 7-31-67.
"If you give me a gun" TM 8-4-67.
"strange kind of dream" Lewis, pg 125.
"I knew segregation" DN 7-26-77.
"There was an old man" Franklin: "Asking God for big things."
"We have become a Black Nation" Cleage, pg 13.
"Motown, if you don't come around" Fine, pg 30.
"There has been only" Carmichael, pg 50.
"The saddest day of the week" LOOK 4-9-63.
"There is no adjective" Schulman, pg 2.
"I could never forget" Schulman, pg 10.

Chapter 8: The Road to Detroit

Birmingham

"In the name of" Oates, pg 209.
"You don't win against" Oates, pg 207.
"I wasn't saved to run" Oates, pg 205.
"freedom is never voluntarily" Oates, pg 219.
"We proved to them" King, pg 178.

Harlem

"When I came here" LOOK 5-7-63.
"Law and order" TM 7-31-64 pg 11.

Watts

"You've got some Gestapo tactics" History Matters website: *'and this happened in L.A.'*
"I fought the best that I knew how." Strickland, pg 1.
"It was his mother" Watts Riots 40 years later - www.latimes.com.
"My black brother" Bullock, pg 44.
"How have you won?" Fogelson, pg 150.
"Everywhere I looked" Bullock, pg 39.
"We gonna have the biggest" Conot, pg 233.

Hough

"If I come back after death" Lackritz, pg 40.
"With conditions the way" CPD 7-22-66.
"you've got a riot out there" CPD 7-23-66.

Newark

"The Negro has lived" TM 8-4-67
"A project home" Moore, pg 37.
"There's no money" Porambo, pg 61.
"Picketing and marching" NYT 7-14-67.
"you uncle toms" NYT 7-14-67.

"There is still no organization" Porambo, pg 116.
"The line between the jungle" NYT 7-15-67.
"It's all gone" Porambo, pg 117.
"kill the bastards" NYT 7-15-67.
"We've scalped the white man" ibid.
"The thing that repels me" USNWR 7-24-67.
"The veneer that used to" NO 7/21/67.
"They are not oppressed" USN&WR 7-31-67.
"Yes, it was agitation" NYT 7-16-67.
"There is only one man" TM 7-28-67.

Chapter 9: Kercheval

"They don't believe in" USN&WR 8-15-66.
"Him and that urban renewal" MC 8-20-66.
"This is our neighborhood" Fine pg 96
"We could sense something" DN 5-17-87.
"Wait till tomorrow night" DFP 8-10-66.
"Hell, they did a much better job" MC 8-20-66.
"Please stay off the streets" DFP 8-10-66.
"Men are both inner" Richard N. Goodwin - *The Hard Path to Peace*: DFP 9-3-67.
"Being against violence" ibid.
"We know some things" ibid.
"Men truly without" ibid.
"Violence, although intolerable" ibid.

Chapter 10: The Nether World of 12th Street

"You take good care" NYT Magazine 8-27-67.
"It's a place where" ibid.
"A lot of politicians" DFP 8-6-67.
"We weren't ready then" DN 7-30-67.
"We'd been trying" DN 5-18-87.
"I had trouble getting in" DFP 7-19-87.
"don't let them take our people" Fine, pg 160.
"Let's get the hell" DN 7-23-67.
"What did you do?" FOH (Howison, pg 48).
"Detroit's second day of violence" SJ 7-25-67
"You try to talk to" NYT 7-25-67.
"They won't shoot" TM 8-4-67.
"It was at that point" DN 5-18-87
"usually the city isn't burning" FP 7-19-87.
"Clear, unmistakable and undisputed" DFP 7-19-87.
"charge that we cannot kill" Dallek, pg 414.
"Mr. President, we will only shoot" Fine, pg 214.
"We are to use as much force" LAT 8-26-67.
"unload all weapons" Fine, pg 220.
"Yes, I burned the damn" DN 8-7-67.
"We have 12th Street in flames" DN 8-7-67.
"Everybody off the streets" DN 7-24-67.
"I'll get that old man" DFP 8-17-67.
"Someone stop him" DFP 8-1-67.
"He came to this country" DFP 8-1-67.
"They're shooting at us" DFP 7-25-67.
"I hollered at the firemen" DFP 7-25-67.
"I live here" DN 5-18-87.
"They brought us food" ibid
"Now I know nobody" NYT Magazine 8-27-67.
"a Negro man standing" Hersey, pg 255.
"This latest phase" Young, pg 178.
"The mid day sun" DFP 9-3-67.

Chapter 11: Lesson Learned: The Kerner Report

"Detroit has opened the door" NYT magazine, 8-27-67.
"Let your search be free" Kerner Report pg v.
"Our nation is moving" ibid.
"We are being asked to probe" DFP 8-2-67.
"Segregation and poverty" Kerner Report pg 1.
"The principal measure of progress" Kerner Report pg 252.
"Does the public expect" SEP 9-23-67.
"It damaged a great many officers" DN 5-19-87.
"They cleaned me out" DFP 7-23-72.
"I'm wiped out" DFP 7-28-67.
"Cavanagh, he couldn't run" DFP 7-28-67.
"Who's this?" DN 7-30-67.
"One group that always" NYT 7-28-67.
"Too many Negroes who have" TM 8-27-65.
"The Lord is my Shepard" DFP 7-30-67.
"Tonya is the symbol" DN 8-2-67.
"I wouldn't go back to" DFP 7-23-72.
"I was surprised" DN 5-18-87.
"There is a huge section" DN 7-30-67.
"I got this scar" NYT 7-24-67.
"Look upon these ruins" FP 7-19-87.

Chapter 12: Hope is the last to Die

"With so many black people" FP 7-19-87.
"The poor have become" NW 8-7-67.
"When the family collapses" LBJ Howard University Speech 6-4-65.
"The gap between" Moynihan report.
"You can't believe" Ebony, Feb 1980.
"People used to" Black Enterprise, June 2003.
"Thousands of tourists" *Spirit of Harlem: A Portrait of America's most exciting neighborhoods.*
"I got things to write about" Playboy, 9-67.
"Stories aren't fancy things" ibid.
"Never know a begin" ibid.
"I have been asked" ibid.
"I can't read" LAT 10-18-05.
"Our lives begin to end" MLK
"Who live in bright and cheeried" *Broken Homes* - Helen Strummer.
"The riot put Detroit" Young, pg 179.
"I remember Henry Ford II" Vitullo-Martin.
"militant and venomous" Sugrue pg 138.
"The rage was there." FP 7-19-87.
"I issue a forward warning" Young, pg 200.
"Look any man" DFP 12-5-97.
"That son of a bitch Waldmeir" Young, pg 281.
"Beware of any benighted" DFP 12-5-97.
"I put tubs in front" NW 5-1-72 pg 123.
"You can't give people pride" RD Oct 72.
"We're trying to show" NW 5-1-72
"I read the bible" NW 5-1-72.
"Replacing despair with hope." DFP 9-3-67
"I kept thinking" interview Josaitis.
"If this city riots again" ibid.
"He combined a compassion" DFP 5-27-07.

Photographs courtesy of...

Associated Press/Wide World Photos: 43B,131,141,151,181,189,204, 205,232B,248,268-269,317,328B
Bentley Library, University of Michigan: 3,36B,39, 76-78,81,87,88,108T,109T,109M,110,111,241,244,255,291
Bancroft Library, University of California-Berkeley: 172,183
Birmingham Public Library Archives: 19TL,142,144,145,148,149,152,312
Bob Sherman: 187
Bryce Johnson: 221
Burk Uzzle: 310
Carl Bidleman: 345
Cleveland Public Library: 191T
Cleveland State University Archives: 12,130,175,188,190,191B,193,194, 196-198,200-203,225
Corbis-Bettman: ix,184,207
Detroit Institute of Arts: xiv
Detroit Public Library:

A) **Burton Historical Collection:** 2,10,11,22,25,40,41,44,49,51,59,63,83,89L,93,95M,97,109B 125,128,239T,240,254,261,283,284,295,297,298T,299,301,342

B) **National Automotive Historical Collection:** 5TL,5BL,5TR,5BR, 6-8,9TL,9TR,23,54,70

Getty: 219,235
Grosse Pointe Historical Society: 133
Igor Beginin: 280
Implosion World: 329,330
Jack Miller - Ypsilanti Historical Museum: 75M
Johnson Space Center: 157
Joye Opoku Ofei: 27,195
Library of Congress: 13-18,19TR,19BR,24,26,33T,34L,102T,114,115, 143,146,147T,159,160,161B,346

A) **LOOK Magazine:** 105(Paul Fusco),117(James Karales), 129(James Hansen)

B) **New York World-Telegram & Sun:** 155,164-169,178

C) **U.S. News & World Report:** 122,127,132,147B,150,161T,192,199, 217,326

Los Angeles Public Library: 174,176,177,182,186,309B,320,321,322
Los Angeles Times: 185 (copyright 2008, reprinted with permission)
Magnum: (Burt Glinn) 139, **(Danny Lyon)** 153
Massachusetts Dept of Corrections: 163
Newark Public Library: 208,210,211,214,218
Ohio Historical Society: 90
State of Michigan Archives: 43T,45,298B,305
The Henry Ford: 1,5M
U.S. National Archives: 140,206,220,286,288,289,307,313,319,323,324
Walter Reuther Library, Wayne State University: 9B,32,33B,34R,35,36T,47,60,61,64,65,67,68,69,75T,79,85,89R,92,94,95T,98 99,100,101,102M,104,106,107,108B,118,120,121,124,126,233,270,296B,298T, 311,332,337,338,339,340B,341BL,343

A) **Tony Spina Collection:** 230,231,232T,260,266

Wikipedia Commons: 179,312,328T
Windsor Star: v,223,228,247,249,258,259,262,264,267,270,294,298B,302

T-Top B-Bottom L-Left R-Right M-Middle

INDEX

F

G

H

I

J

K

L

HAVE A
C.YOUNG